The **Leader & Recorder's** History of the Life

THE LEADER AND RECORDER'S

History of the Junction

Edited by Diana Fancher

West Toronto Junction Historical Society ~ Toronto ~ 2004

Published by the West Toronto Junction Historical Society

145 Annette Street, Toronto, Ontario M6P 1P3
EMAIL: junction@web.ca
WEBSITE: www.junctionhistory.ca
TELEPHONE: (416) 763-3161

Designed and produced by Mark Fram, Polymath, Toronto.
Printed and bound by Coach House Printing, Toronto.

TITLE PAGE
Masthead of the
"original" *Leader and
Recorder*, 1896–1908

LIBRARY AND ARCHIVES CANADA CATALOGUING IN PUBLICATION

The Leader & Recorder's history of the Junction / edited by Diana Fancher.

ISBN 0-9686636-1-3

1. West Toronto (Toronto, Ont.)—History—Anecdotes. 2. Toronto
(Ont.)—History—Anecdotes. I. Fancher, Diana II. West Toronto Junction Historical Society.
III. Title: Leader and Recorder's history of the Junction. IV. Title: History of the Junction.

FC3097.52.L42 2004   971.3'541   C2004-903118-X

COVER
James Blomfield, *Dundas and Keele Streets,
Toronto* [June 1948].
Watercolour, w 5" (12.7 cm), h 6.8" (17.2 cm).
Archives of Ontario

The West Toronto Junction Historical Society would like to acknowledge the generous support of the people and organizations who made the research and publication of this book possible.

The Bank of Montreal
Celebrating 100 years of service to the Junction in 2003.

Originally the Bank of British North America opened a branch in a leased building on Dundas Street in February of 1903. In 1907 the bank purchased the building at 2859 Dundas St. W. and commissioned architects Ellis & Connery to refront and refurbish it. The Bank of Montreal bought the company in 1918 and continued to use the elegant building, which is listed on the city's Inventory of Heritage Properties.

Nexxt Development Corporation

Frances H. Bain
John Buchanan
Terence Corcoran
Ronald & Shirley Cornfield
Corinne Flitton
Gib Goodfellow
R. Donald Harlock, Principal,
  Annette Street Public School
  1979–90
Jane Ryding Kay
Claude McGilvray
Lorraine Rafferty
Anthony Rubin
George Rust-D'Eye
John H. Skogstad
R. J. Stewart, President,
  Andrew Merrilees Ltd.
Rona Stewart, Treasurer,
  Andrew Merrilees Ltd.
Dean Tudor
John R. Wilson

Donations in memory of:

Wilfred Thomas Bennett
George Theodore Heintzman
John Milton Evans and Emma Jane
  Megill
William Wilson (1860-1925),
  first principal of Annette Street
  Public School

Contents

Taking Care of Business
> Dundas Street W., looking east from St. John's Rd., 1923. *TTC Archives*

The Business of Government
> The whole town turned out to see the cornerstone laying for the new post office in 1903. Officiating with the silver trowel is Archibald Campbell MP. *Courtesy of Anna (Campbell) Darling*

Leisure Pursuits
> Advertisement for the Beaver Theatre in *West Toronto Weekly*, September 26, 1926.

Industrial Relations

"Union Stock Yards, Toronto, Canada's Leading Live Stock Market",
ca. 1920. *Bishop-Barker Aeroplanes Ltd.*

Rails from the Junction

Part of Plate 16 of the *Insurance Plan of Toronto Junction*. Toronto:
Charles E. Goad Co, 1903, revised 1912. *WTJHS collection*

Educational Experiences

The Grade 2 class of 1932. *Indian Road Crescent Public School*

Life on the Streets

Looking north along Keele St. from the street railway junction at
Dundas St. W., November 9, 1940. *TTC Archives*

Acknowledgments

THE *LEADER AND RECORDER* became the newsletter of the West Toronto Junction Historical Society in September of 1985, originally as a way of getting the news out to members about society activities. However, even the first issue contained a few historical anecdotes. In those early days of production by typewriter and photocopier, both editorial and production duties were shared by myself, Joan Miles and occasionally Doug Lister, with production and mailing assistance from Kay Karbownik, the secretary at the city's Planning and Development Department site office.

In March of the following year brief articles on Junction history became a standard feature of our four to six page publication, beginning with Tom Vella's two part exposition on 1930s entertainments. Lee Thirwall increased our range of illustrations and brought a more professional range of headlines to a few issues. Then in 1987 John Paulov took over design and layout, with Frances Labelle responsible for word processing and editorial advice on our much more professional looking eight-page bi-monthly publication. John Paulov and Joan Miles continued to be involved for five years, and Joan assumed editorial command for several issues.

At last in 1991 with Peter Mérey in charge of computerised design and layout, we were able to go to offset printing on a quarterly basis, and to begin using photographs from our extensive archival collection. Peter and I continued to produce the newsletter out of his basement on Gilmour Avenue for the next 10 years. Dolphin Printing Services supplied the high quality printing until John Sutton sold the business. More recently Mark Fram and Pat Trusty have provided the design and layout, with occasional editorial and photographic contributions from Mark. Our printing is now in the capable hands of Coach House Printing.

Without the continuing interest and active involvement of our members, who supplied the articles, photographs and information, none of this would have been possible. Mike Filey in particular was extremely helpful, forwarding copies of articles about our area which he discovered during the course of his own research. Paul S. Moore's dissertation research has made it possible to document the movie theatres on Dundas Street. Ted Wickson patiently answered queries about the history of street railways. Gordon MacKinnon provided last minute research, and Larry Burak made himself available to photograph difficult subjects at the last possible moment.

Almost all of the articles in this collection appeared in some form in the *Leader and Recorder*. Some of them appeared first in other publications. "Summer at the Doll Factory" was written for the *Bloor West Villager*. Carleton Wilson's "from Junction Sonnets" is reprinted from his chapbook, *Junction Sonnets*, published by Junction Books, 1999. Ray Correlli's "Show Biz Boom in a Stock Yards Breeze", as well as other material credited to the *Toronto Star*, is reprinted with permission from the *Toronto Star*. "Partial Imperfect and Prejudiced" is reprinted with permission from the *Globe & Mail*. Barbara Forsyth's "The Most Attractive Resort in the Town" is used with the permission of the Toronto Public Library.

Photos from archival or library sources are used with the permission of the various institutions. Goad's Fire Insurance plates are reproduced with the permission of CGI Information Systems and Management Consultants. The archival number for the National Library photo of the Beaver Theatre which appears on page 51 is PA119565. The number for the aerial photo from the Archives of Ontario, which appears on page 57 is S.6007. For other photographs from archival sources, we will be happy to supply the relevant archival numbers on request.

The staff at the City of Toronto Archives, the Archives of Ontario and the Canadian History section of the Toronto Reference Library have been most helpful with research and photo requests.

The authors of the articles have been patient and thoughtful in the reconsideration of their material, submitting to requests for updates and changes with good humour and useful suggestions of their own. Some have even gone so far as to make donations toward the cost of publishing the book, at the same time accepting without question what must have seemed at times to be arbitrary additions or deletions.

However, neither the editor nor the authors make any pretense of having the final word on the topics covered. For the moment we have put together the most accurate and interesting stories that we could, with whatever material was available at the time. The exclusion of footnotes was lamented by some authors, but it was my decision that footnotes did not fit with the informal nature of the collection. This should in no way detract from the excellent quality of the research by all concerned.

Another challenge to the assembly of this collection was to make sense of a myriad of sometimes conflicting spelling and stylistic conventions. In the *Leader and Recorder* the preferences of the authors were generally honoured. For this book I have attempted some standardization, but made no attempt to improve the grammar or spelling, (other than obvious typos, a very occasional comma, and providing correct locations for named places) of material reprinted from other sources. In the case of oral histories, I have reproduced, as much as possible, the speech patterns of the person interviewed, which adds an additional dimension to the story.

There is also a certain amount of humour in the common or uncommon misspelling of names which is picked up on by A. B. Rice in "Let There Be Light". In another article Rice takes an invented word, then spells it two different ways in the same article. And Carlton/Carleton really can be correctly spelled two different ways in the same paragraph, depending on time and place. Stock yards is two separate words in the Junction, thanks to the Union Stock Yards and the Ontario Stock Yards Board.

I am grateful to the following volunteer proofreaders who helped me to make some sense out of the general stylistic anarchy: Geana Demone, Corinne Flitton, Doris Nerden Fraser, Ed Freeman, Scott Howarth, Olga Klement, Pam Lindfield, Vandra and Volker Masemann, Peter Mérey, Ann Perry, Bob Roden and Martin Sneath. I am also grateful to Mark Fram for his always useful editorial comments. In no way are any errors attributable to any of them, however, that responsibility is mine alone.

Diana Fancher
junction@web.ca

Introduction

WE WERE IN THE GARDEN on a hot afternoon in the neighbourhood, and a visitor from the suburbs was admiring the great old oak tree next door and how it shades our garden so pleasantly. The tree must be, what, maybe eighty years old, we agreed, and we fell to speculating about just who planted these oaks that now rise from every third or fourth backyard all along our street, to our great pleasure and benefit. Those oak trees came from someone. They carry a hint of history. They remind us that people we barely know of contributed to this neighbourhood, even to the foliage above it, long before we dreamed of living here.

The day after that afternoon under the oak tree, I picked up the manuscript of this book, and I read with a shock of recognition about Mayor Clendenan. In 1896 Mayor Clendenan bullied the town council of West Toronto into spending $2000 for the planting of shade trees all over the neighbourhood. He foresaw how property values would benefit from the way the trees would shelter and beautify the community for generations.

This book is like that. It makes few claims to earthshaking consequence; it's just some local stories and the pictures that go with them. But for anyone who knows the Junction, High Park, Bloor West, and the other neighbourhoods of West Toronto, it is full of small explosions of understanding. It is a set of pointers to how this place got to be the place we know. These short histories of local people and businesses and locations over the last century or so are an index to what has endured here in West Toronto — and to much that has vanished like an oak tree chopped down, or like the farms along Runnymede Road in our grandparents' childhood years.

We send our children to the local schools, and it occurs to us dimly that generations of students and teachers and ratepayers have contributed to those institutions. We enjoy the park or the rink, and remember something about a rink that used to be in Ravina Park, and a pool down by Bloor and Clendenan, and dance pavilions down by the lake. Reading the real estate notices with proprietorial satisfaction or renters' dread, we realize how someone long ago made decisions that filled one street with row houses on narrow lots, another with detached homes on broad lawns. When we run our errands among the restored storefronts along Dundas Street, we have intimations of the business people who have thrived or struggled here during a century and more. Savouring the cultural diversity that has come to the neighbourhood in recent years, we might speculate about hardships and discriminations that other immigrant minorities must have confronted.

We pass by Mavety Street or St. John's Road, and maybe spare an idle thought about who gave names to all the streets. We watch the burgeoning development of retail stores and housing in the Stock Yards district, where there actually used to be stock yards, and we have just a sense of the economic forces, entrepreneurial efforts, and political decisions that have brought in great industries and taken them away again generations later. When we grab a bus down to the subway, do we ever consider how the buses came to follow the routes they do, or how the subway must have changed things?

No one absolutely needs to know how these things came to be or where they went. Perhaps we could get alone without knowing about how things were done around here before, or how they evolved into the civic fabric of which we are the custodians. But since you are reading this book, you have probably already sensed how we are enriched by those small bursts of understanding about where our community came from, by that expanded dimension of time-depth that is available to us.

For some years now, members of the West Toronto Junction Historical Society have been enjoying those small discoveries through the society newsletter, *The Leader and Recorder*. We have encountered Miss Cherry and what her teaching meant to students and teachers on Indian Road in the 1920s. We have discovered Harry Lee's very different experience in the school system and the story behind the plaque to his memory at Annette Street Public School. We have explored how generations of Martins ran a local florist shop long before anyone imagined cut flowers might one day be air freighted from Venezuela. We have read about the leagues that played at the local rink, and what a big deal artificial ice was to future NHL stars like Busher Jackson.

The Leader and Recorder has often returned to the steam trains that thundered down our rail lines, and the maintenance yards that sustained them, and the mills and the heavy industries they in turn sustained, and even to the local doll factory, the one that got by on child labour. It remembers the bootleggers of the neighbourhood after that rowdy night when all the bars were closed down, the pool halls and movie theatres of the Junction, and the dancehalls where you had to buy a membership to get around the law. It honours the family business that sold milk and coal for generations, the woman who attended all the home births, and the law firm that's been here more than a century. It evokes the assertive young Chinese Canadian girl who insisted on sitting downstairs, not in the balcony seats — and smashed a tradition of prejudice. Even Jenny Brown and the cow she herded through an ever less appreciative neighbourhood have not been forgotten.

This book is a sampling from *The Leader and Recorder*. Some of the stories here are first-person reminiscences of neighbourhood builders and pioneers. Some testify to the research and imagination of members and friends of the West Toronto Junction Historical Society. Some are drawn from the *West Toronto Weekly* and the other lively newspapers that served our community and the city a century ago.

"I never realized," said Stephen Leacock, "that there was history close at hand, beside my very own home. I did not realize that the old grave that stood among the brambles at the foot of our farm was history." In West Toronto, history can be the trees in our back yards, and the name on your street sign, and the new business in the old building down at the end of the street, and the rail tracks buried in concrete by the underpass. History is also the effort we make to see all that, and to document it, and to protect it, and bring it to the attention of those who might not yet have had an opportunity to notice.

This collection of stories and memories honours people and institutions of this community's past, and also the people and institutions who have maintained the record of those things. It is my experience that they ground me. They orient me to where I live and to how it all got here before I did. I think you will have the same experience.

Christopher Moore
www.christophermoore.ca

Christopher Moore is a Governor-General's Award winning historian who has written about many aspects of Canadian history. He and his family have lived in the neighbourhood for about twenty years. Though he has never actually written about West Toronto history, he has been a longtime member and supporter of the West Toronto Junction Historical Society.

Taking Care of Business

Adventures on Dundas Street 1912-1937

by Claude McGilvray

I WAS BORN IN THE JUNCTION on April 1, 1912, in the apartment above the store at 3095 Dundas St. W., that's on the south side of Dundas between Clendenan and Quebec Avenues. My father's name was Watson McGilvray and my mother's name was Sarah Rebecca Ford. My father was a tinsmith by trade and he first opened a tinsmithing business at a store across the road which was rented. Later he was able to build the building at 3095 in 1907. The basement was a tinshop and then upstairs he added hardware so it became McGilvray Hardware.

My father's background was in the country. His parents had a grist mill and also a farm. When he left the farm he went to Hamilton, where he drove an electric streetcar on Barton Street. It's not generally known that Hamilton had electric streetcars before Toronto. Then he went back to Orangeville, where he learned the tinsmithing trade, and came on down to Toronto, where he worked for a large sheet metal company before he started out on his own.

My mother's parents came from England and settled in Parkdale. My mother learned to be a tailor and she worked for one of the better tailor shops down at King Street. She used to tell me about travelling on the horse-drawn streetcar back and forth to work, and how in the winter it could be very cold. She used to also tell me that on the weekends there used to be a lot of bicycle clubs and she belonged to a girls' bicycle club which she evidently enjoyed very much.

World War I at Ravina Rink

When I was quite young we moved to a house on Roland Avenue, which runs west off Clendenan Avenue near Humberside Collegiate. We only lived in this house for a short time during the First World War. At the end of the street there was an open-air ice skating rink known as Ravina. During the war this was all changed into a barracks for the soldiers and their horses. As a little gaffer, why I found this quite interesting. In front of the barracks was the sentry box, and a soldier used to always stand guard there. We made a practice of begging cigarette cards from the troopers as they went back and forth. We kids used to watch the soldiers train. In the open fields at the end of Rowland Street, that was bayonet practice and mortar practice. We particularly liked it when the artillery unit travelled up to Scarlett Plains with their horses, and guns and wagons to practice gunnery.

After the war Mr. Norman Smith, who lived on the street, built a swimming pool where the barracks were, which was known in those days as a "tank". And if you could afford it, that's where you might go for your swim.

One thing about the war I always remember was that on Armistice Day, November 11, 1918, I would just be six years old, they hoisted an effigy of the Kaiser and they burnt the effigy right at the corner of Quebec Avenue and Annette Street. I thought that was an interesting sight. I also remember that when the troops were coming home from overseas they would disembark from the train at the CN or the CPR stations. My father had a 1910 Overland touring car, and my older brother had it all decked out with flags, and there was quite a parade when they would pick up their friends coming home and drive along Dundas Street. It was quite a sight.

When I was about four years old we moved back to the flat over the store. It was small and crowded and there was my mother and father, my older brother Harold, my older sister Hazel, my next older brother Bruce and myself. When I was young, the two things I always wanted most was a dog and to be able to live in a house. My mother finally bought me a mongrel collie when I was 10 years old. I remember the price very well, it was $6. He was my best friend for 13 years. My dog Ponto was named after my father's dog. And I believe that his father, my grandfather, also had a dog named Ponto. He was so intelligent, he was just a wonderful loving and intelligent dog.

First Job at Martin's Florist

Also when I was 10 years old, I borrowed $18 from my father and I bought a bicycle. On the bicycle I put a big metal basket on the front and another carrier on the back with a big box on it. I used to deliver flowers and plants for Martin's Florist. This took me out all over winter and summer. When I was quite young I spent quite a lot of time at Martin's. I used to help clean out the stables where they had the horses, Nell and Jess. I used to feed the horses too. The lane of course wasn't paved, and Sunday was a great day to get on the old horse Nell and ride bareback down the lane. That was great fun. Gord Martin eventually got a western saddle for his horse so that was

The McGilvray family ca. 1909. L-R front row: Harold, Bruce and Hazel with their parents Sarah Rebecca Ford and Archer Watson McGilvray.
Courtesy of Claude McGilvray

even better. Mrs. Martin lived in the old farmhouse (493 Clendenan Avenue) and was a great cook and a wonderful person. I used to like to be in the kitchen because she used to bake the most wonderful butter tarts.

One time, I was nine years old, Nell and Jess hadn't been out of the stables all winter, they were kind of frisky. Gord Martin's father, he had a stake wagon, it was just four wheels with boards across, then a seat up here, anyway he had this big load of lumber, mostly 2x4s and 2x6s. He had a ten-acre farm out in Cooksville, just north of Dundas. So I was delegated to drive the team out with this load of lumber. He tied it all down, snug and everything else. I got started and I came along Dundas Street, and I got to the Humber River, where you had to go down this hill. Going down there, this load of lumber kept shifting forward, hitting the horses in the rear end. They didn't like that. So I got stopped in front of the Lambton Hotel and there was some men sitting on the balcony there, on the porch, and, gee, they came out and they saw what the problem was, and they untied the lumber and retied it down, which I

thought was pretty good of them. I finally got out to the farm and I helped around a little bit, while Mr. Martin was doing some things, because he had a T-model Ford and I was getting a ride home with him. I was there all day and got the large sum of 50 cents. This Mr. Martin, he didn't overpay anybody. He had a reputation that way. That was quite an experience, to drive the team out there, but I was kind of used to horses.

Another time this other kid and I, we had our bicycles and we went out to the Humber River, we spent a lot of time on the Humber, where the railroad bridge goes across there. That Dundas Street bridge wasn't there then, you had to go away down the hill across a little bridge at the bottom (on Old Dundas Street). The railroad bridge is north of the Dundas Street bridge. But anyway, we decided to take our bicycles and walk them across the [railroad] bridge. And of course we made sure they wasn't any trains coming, but when we got about halfway or so across the bridge, sure as you live, there's a train coming after us. And, you see, these trains can't really stop on the bridge. They can slow down

and that. And, gee, there was this train, we see it coming and we're trying to hurry like crazy, but the timbers on those bridges were so far apart you had to be careful you didn't get your foot caught down there. We were going as fast as we could, and we just got across the bridge. And there was a bank there and the river's a way down there. We just got across to the bank and we threw our bicycles into the bank and jumped in there. And I'll tell you, what those firemen and the engineer said, boy, they really called us the stupidest brats in Toronto. You know we could have got killed. But anyway we survived it.

The Depression and Bootleggers
My father was an excellent furnace man and at one time he had as many as twenty-five men working for him. He installed many many furnaces in the Junction and the surrounding area. Later when the Depression hit, two large builders who owed him a great deal of money for work he had done for them, couldn't pay — and I think this was one of the causes of his later ill health. Gravity feed hot air furnaces died out, which meant that

Claude and "Watt" McGilvray in front of the family home and business at 3095 Dundas St. W. ca.1920. *Courtesy of Claude McGilvray*

the business then had to depend on maintenance, cleaning and repairs. As young lads my brother Bruce and I used to do quite a bit of this kind of work after school and on Saturdays. Sad to say the business became very unprofitable and times were very difficult.

During this period the Junction was a dry area, and it was fairly common knowledge that the area north of Dundas Street and west of Clendenan Avenue had a number of bootleggers. These bootleggers had stills that were made of copper and my father, when business was slow, would be happy to have the business of making these stills. The shop was checked periodically, but someway or another no stills were ever found in the making.

The policemen, they were usually in pairs, came in the store and they would clump around there with their heavy boots and talk to whoever was there for a few minutes, and then you could of course hear all this down in the shop. So that if a still was in the process of being made, there was ample time to hide it before the officers came down and took a look around, and they of course found nothing. It was always safely hidden away by the time the police checked the shop.

My father was delivering a still one day to a house on Maria Street. And they invited him in. He went into the kitchen and there were three policeman sitting down drinking, and they asked him to join them. We also had a policeman that lived not too far away,

and we could always tell when it was his day off, because he had trouble walking home. But that was the dry time.

I worked for Martin's Florist until I was 14. I usually worked at noon and after school, Saturdays and sometimes Sundays. But I found that when I was going to the Central High School of Commerce down on Shaw Street, and with all the homework that was required, that I couldn't continue to work those hours. And so I got a job with the Lucibellos, who had a very good fruit and vegetable store a few doors from Martin's, and I worked there on Saturdays from eight o'clock in the morning until eleven o'clock at night. The Lucibellos were wonderful people, it was a family business, and while we worked hard, I enjoyed it. Before this I worked for Graham Robinson's Drug Store, which was a few doors east of our store, at the corner of Quebec Avenue. I used to deliver there and also helped to clean the store, and then when he opened the Smiles and Chuckles candy store next door, I helped in there for some time.

My brother Bruce went to Humberside Collegiate for a couple of years. I went to the High School of Commerce for two years and then I started the first year at the new Western High School of Commerce, but after I had to leave to get a job because we needed the money. My uncle George Ford was a supervisor of the grand piano division of the Heintzman Piano Co., and he invited me down

there to look over the plant and to give me a real tour. A job was offered to me, but I just couldn't stand the smell of all the shellacs and glues and varnishes. It bothered me so much I couldn't get out of there fast enough.

Guns on Bloor Street

My first full time job was when I was 16, with the Dominion Bank at Bloor and Runnymede. That paid $500 a year. There were no breaks for lunch or coffee breaks or anything. One of the things that struck me as a foolish practice was that everyone in the bank, except the junior, had a gun. I had a gun on my desk. Everyone had a gun. We had no practice, we had no training whatsoever in the use of these guns. The only thing that we used to do was, some nights after work, three or four of us would go down in the basement and have some target practice. And I often think how dangerous it was, because the bullets could ricochet off the ceiling and it's a wonder one of us didn't get hurt. I always remember one teller, her name was Miss Gardner, she was a tiny woman. She had the biggest gun in the bank, it was a big 45 caliber.

Ruby and the Diamonds

My wife's name was Ruby Mason and her family lived on Annette Street. I knew Ruby slightly at the Western Commerce when I went there. I only went for a month. And then one day I was coming home on the Dundas streetcar, I would be 18, and by golly, who should be on the Dundas streetcar but Ruby. So we got talking and I asked her if I could phone her. And that's when it all started, on the Dundas streetcar. We went together from around 1931-37. I was making very little money and we paid board at home, you know. We used to have to put food on the table at home. But I bought her an engagement ring. I got this special deal on a diamond ring. It cost me $125 wholesale, and boy, that was a lot of money. But I bought that ring, it had three stones in it, and that was our engagement ring. Then afterwards, when she died, I had that ring cut and mounted onto my Scottish Rite ring. Oh, we were very fortunate, Ruby and I had a love affair of a lifetime, you know, not many of them around.

LEFT
Claude begged his mother for 50 cents to have this picture taken on a street photographer's horse ca.1920
Courtesy of Claude McGilvray

RIGHT
Claude and his future wife Ruby at a regatta in Port Dalhousie ca.1934. He is wearing his Argonaut Rowing Club sweater as a participant.
Courtesy of Claude McGilvray

Martin's The Flower People

by Diana Fancher

ALFRED WILLIAM MARTIN came to West Toronto Junction in 1890 at the age of 28 to begin his business career, fresh from a farm in the Brampton area where his family had settled after leaving England. He began working as a baker at George Robinson's bakery and confectionery located at 21 Dundas St. W. (now 2871). A year later he and a partner established Betts & Martin bakers on the north side of Dundas, east of Pacific. In 1894 the *West York Tribune* reported an employee injured at his bakery, although the address was not given. During this period his address changed frequently until he bought his own building on the north side of Dundas, east of Clendenan, in 1899.

Sometime before 1898 Alfred married Mary, possibly at Annette Street Methodist Church. Taking advantage of cheap land repossessed by the town for tax arrears, they acquired property at Clendenan and Dundas to build the three bedroom two-storey stucco house where they would live for the rest of their lives. The house still stands at 493 Clendenan Avenue, although the present owners have encased it in multi-coloured brick and added a second storey. The Martins owned a cow, not uncommon along Dundas Street, a horse for use with the delivery wagon, and a dog. In 1899 their son Gordon was born in the new home.

The Martins continued to buy property on the south side of Dundas across the lane from their home until 1907, often registered in Mary's name. Most of the parcels cost less than $300 for a 20–30 foot frontage by 130 feet deep. However, the final 32-foot frontage on Dundas, purchased from Alfred's first employer, George Robinson, set them back $1,000, a large sum in those days.

The small mortgages taken out on these purchases were mainly from Alex Hain, dairy owner and former town councillor. A large one in 1915 was borrowed from former mayor Peter Laughton, indicating that Alfred probably had a good credit rating in the town.

English-style Greenhouses

After the last purchase Alfred changed his career to that of florist, building greenhouses on this land in 1906-7. In 1906 he was listed as a florist for the first time in the Junction's assessment rolls. In 1908 he built a store beside the greenhouses. During these early years he also operated a confectionery business at the store. His grandson Bill found a building used as a bakery behind the house on Clendenan. Bill's Aunt Ethel, who worked in the store, told him that it was a combination of soda fountain and variety store with fruit and vegetables as well.

Bill describes the florist business in those days as "English-style greenhouses where you grew everything under the sun and made no money on anything. But that was the way you did it. You had a little patch of this kind of flower and another patch of another kind that required a different set of

Spring in the Martin's greenhouse. An unnamed employee prepares bedding plants for eventual sale in late May. The tomato plants at right would have been started before Christmas to supply fruit for sale in the family store. *Courtesy of Bill Martin*

growing conditions so obviously they got a poor crop on both. It was a real hodge podge, they had no idea of modern methods at all, everything was what they had inherited from the old English growers. The only time they made any money was at bedding plant season."

Alfred and Mary, their son Gordon and daughter Ethel, continued to operate the family greenhouses into the 1920s. Besides the flowers for cutting and the bedding plants, they grew tomato plants, started before Christmas, which produced early tomatoes to sell in the store.

During the 1920s, Bill has been told by many customers, there was a wooden sidewalk, a boardwalk in front of the greenhouses, "... you had to bend down quite low and step down a couple of steps to get into the greenhouses from the sidewalk. They built them quite low into the ground to conserve energy.

"People love to come into a greenhouse and walk around, in some ways you'd like to have that now because it's an attractive thing for people to buy in; they love the look of a greenhouse, the feel of it, the smell of it, especially when you get into ten below weather in the wintertime." The greenhouses were shut down around 1925 when the boiler ceased to function.

Mary died of cancer in 1925, and when Gordon married Jemima

Gordon & Mame (Gray) Martin, June 1925. Their wedding at Victoria Presbyterian Church was, of course, beautifully decorated with fresh flowers. Mame has fresh flowers in her hair and carries a "shower bouquet".
Courtesy of Bill Martin

"Mame" Gray that same year they moved in with Alfred for a few years to look after him until he married his second wife Jean.

"I was born in the old house in 1929, upstairs in the same room Dad was born in," Bill recalls. His sister Margaret was born in 1932, and Mary Jean arrived in 1933.

In 1928 two building permits were issued for the property, one for the present store at 3107 Dundas St. W. and one for the commercial residential building next door. Ever one for good timing, Alfred sold his land at peak market value.

Gordon W. Martin, Your Florist

The new store opened in 1929, inaugurating the era of Gordon W. Martin, Your Florist, as the business was called. Gordon, who had a flair for promotion, hired a brass band to play in the window for opening day. But "Alfie", as Bill affectionately calls his grandfather, was still active in the family's assorted business enterprises throughout the 1930s and 1940s.

"He looked stern, but he had a good sense of humour," Bill recalls. "He had an accident while he was still on the farm and in later years he walked with a tilt, slinging his leg to one side, but it didn't slow him down much."

Alfred kept a market garden on the Jane Flats west of Eglinton at the time when both streets stopped there. "Dad took the horse and wagon to sell vegetables to stores as far east as Ossington Avenue," Bill recalls. "He was a kind of grower-wholesaler." Alfred also had two beeyards, one in the Kipling-Rathburn area and one in Cooksville, where he would collect honey, render it and then sell it around the Junction area.

Like Alfie, Gordon was also known for his sense of humour. Bill describes him as "a real people

person, he understood how to bring people into the store and how to get their attention. He would write on the window with chalky stuff, probably lime, it would wash off. He used the window like a sign to advertise 'Roses 49¢ a dozen' or whatever flower he had got that day.

"He loved animals and he would think nothing of putting a bunch of animals in the window, rabbits or ducks, depending on the season. People would be attracted to them. He raised rabbits in hutches at the back, every kind you could think of, including Flemish giants. We also had guinea pigs later on; I liked them better because you could play with them."

After Alfie remarried, Gordon and family moved into the apartment above the store. "Dad always had candy for the neighbourhood kids, he always made sure I had money for an ice cream or to go to the movies, because he had never had that when he was a boy," Bill remembers. "He was known as the 'Lord of the Lane' because he was always organizing barbeques in back of the store."

By this time the growers were going store to store to sell their flowers. Bill remembers one grower in particular, Charlie Tizzard, who had leased land along the Hydro right of way near Royal York Road, where he had root cellars, long low tar paper shacks for starting bulbs, corms and rhubarb early. "He grew rhubarb in the winter when there was very little fruit; they would send up these beautiful yellow shoots, we used to use them in flower arrangements. He was also a master gladiola grower. He would start the corms in the root cellars and bring the flowers in just ahead of everyone else, he always beat the market and got the best price."

Bill Joins the Firm

But in 1950, just as Bill, a Humberside Collegiate graduate, was getting ready to study landscape architecture at the University of Guelph, both his parents became ill and there was nobody to look after the family business. Alfred had died a year or two before. His father died that year, leaving Mame alone to run the family business, so Bill joined her immediately. "We started in the hole, there was a funeral to pay for," he recalls, "gradually we turned it around. Mother did most of the worrying, the bookkeeping and planning, I just grew into the business. I enjoyed getting into the creative end of it."

Bill describes his mother as being at the forefront of changing times, of women in business and in getting away from the old routines and stereotypes. "We worked well together. She was also a very religious person, first at Victoria Presbyterian and then later, when I was 21, she joined a spiritual group." Mame's family had also grown up in the Junction area. Her father John Gray, was a stone mason who worked on the Old Mill Bridge as well as supplying stone fronts for several houses on Durie Street.

Soon after becoming a full-time member of the family business, Bill married Marion Cook. They lived in the old house briefly, then over the store, before moving to Etobicoke.

Flower arranging classes were popular at that time and Martin's held classes for up to 40 people in their store, often from church groups. Bill started his creative floral arrangements at age five, he was told, making an artificial wreath that was actually sold in the shop. He enjoyed giving demonstrations. Afterwards there was tea and cookies, the floral arrangements were given away and the participants could shop in the plant section in the back of the store. "We did that

for 10 or 15 years. It was a lot of work, but it made the business go."

International Flower Market

Technological change in growing and delivery has greatly changed the nature of the flower business since the 1950s, he went on to explain. "Computers control air, water, fertilizer, all the conditions in the greenhouse, and so many more flowers can be grown per square foot." South American growers have taken over segments of the cut flower market. "100% of my carnations are now coming in by air freight and truck from Colombia, 30% of my roses are from Ecuador. There is tremendous pressure from offshore growers." The increasingly popular pot plant market is one area where local growers are top competitors, however.

Buyers from the Toronto area now go to a "dutch clock" auction in Mississauga, where they can see all the flowers available that day, make their purchases electronically and arrange for delivery at the same time. In two hours, half a week's buying is completed. Flowers move from grower to retailer in 24 hours.

Increasingly, variety is the key to customer satisfaction, Bill went on to say, partly because of the increased availability of tropical flowers, as well as advances in growing techniques that make all varieties available year round. "There may be 30 different kinds of flowers available at the auction on any given day," Bill continues. Obviously he enjoys explaining the business, as well as conducting it.

Flowers Canada

Bill has also been involved in the organizational life of the flower industry, crediting his early interest in organizations to involvement in the Red Cross at Humberside Collegiate. Later, when he was invited to join the

FTD — the florist's wire association — he learned about the florist trade associations. When Flowers Canada was formed, he was the first secretary. Later he was elected president. In 1994 had been to all 26 of the association's annual retail conventions.

"The conventions are all across Canada, I really enjoyed getting to see Canada that way," he said, "I learned so much from my contemporaries in that association. I t really helped with the business, kept us from making serious mistakes. I've been putting it back over the years too, I still serve as secretary of the Toronto chapter."

Awards hang all over the walls of his tiny office behind the sales area; several are for "Retailer of the Year" and there is one for his contribution to the industry as a whole.

Bill is a tall, thin, energetic though modest person with a quiet sense of humour, who never sits still for any length of time. As he approaches 65, the age at which both is grandfather and his mother retired from the family business, he has become more active in the Etobicoke Rotary Club, taking over as president in July 1994.

"My wife Marion is only in two days a week now, and I'm pretty well down to three days," he explains. "My daughter Lynn (Freeman) has been working with us for 12 or 15 years now, she'll be taking over. She's more attuned to the finances, she does that now. She doesn't do much designing, she's not a bad buyer, she'll do a good job."

Epilogue

Lynn Freeman took over from Bill in 1995. Her oldest son Ryan started working at the store in his teens, calling customers to ask if they would like to be a part of a Reminder Service for birthdays and anniversaries. He joined the business full time in 1996, specializing in internet and telephone sales, as well as looking after the accounting. Ryan has also developed a consulting service to advise florists on the effective use of computers.

While the last two years were hard on florists generally, the Martins' broad customer base has helped them continue into their second hundred years of Junction business history with well over half a million dollars of flower sales annually from the small storefront at 3107 Dundas St. W.

Alfred Martin in his backyard at 493 Clendenan Ave. ca. 1930s or 1940s
Courtesy of Bill Martin

Gerry Linton: 43 Years at the Corner Store

by John D. Thompson

GERRY LINTON'S Dundas Street real estate/insurance office has given him a lifelong window on the changing scene in West Toronto Junction. His roots in the Junction area go deep; he was born in a house at 489 Clendenan Avenue, a few doors from his grandfather, Alfred Martin, at 493 Clendenan, and less than a block south of his office.

"I've been in business for 43 years," says Gerry. "My dad, Wilson Linton, started in 1923, in the same building, today's 3108 Dundas St. W., on the northwest corner at Clendenan, which he'd built in 1907 as a grocery store." In the last 30 years, Gerry has branched into insurance. "Dad later ran a grocery store on the south side of Dundas, renting out this store, but he sold that business to Loblaws in 1923, and went into real estate. It was a good move, as there wasn't much competition in the west end at that time." The elder Linton's business partner from the start, and for many years afterward, was a man named George Baker; his name is still on the office wall.

"This was a real railway town for years. The CPR (Lambton) roundhouse was at the southwest corner of Runnymede and St. Clair, and the yards and repair shops to the south and east. We had many railroaders as customers for a long time, but that gradually changed as they moved out of the area. The roundhouse was demolished in 1960. Often, after they retired, the railroad people sold their houses to their children and moved out of town."

In the old days, Gerry recalls, his dad opened the office at 9:00 a.m., but often didn't get home until midnight. "Most people didn't have cars, so we'd drive back and forth across Toronto, picking up and dropping off customers besides showing them houses."

For a long time, many houses in the Junction were rented, and Linton acted as agent for the owners. "During the Depression many sat vacant for years. I can remember seeing 400 house keys hanging on our office wall."

An essential link in the office for over 57 years was secretary Helen Dawson. "She started with Dad in 1930, and stayed with me here until 1987. She was a remarkable lady; never missed a day's work, and absolutely held this office together."

Gerry remembers the 1930s as "an unbelievably tough time. My dad worked day and night to support his family and build up a successful business."

The younger Linton showed entrepreneurial spirit at an early age by holding down two drugstore delivery jobs simultaneously. After graduating from Western Technical School he tried surveying for the Department of Highways, then running a service station, but the pull of the family business was too strong.

"The postwar years were incredibly busy for real estate brokers. Servicemen were getting married and looking for houses and there weren't nearly enough on the market. Building materials and skilled labour were scarce for a while. Whenever we advertised a house for sale in the *Star*, people would line up outside our office. Once we offered a house on Runnymede Road as a workingman's special — it sure was — for $9,500. But a fellow bought it, fixed it up nicely and lived there for many years."

The Junction prospered in the postwar boom. "The area of Dundas from Keele to Runnymede Road was considered the best half mile of retail shopping in Toronto." Gerry nostalgically recalls some of the old businesses: "Woolworth's, Kresge's, Tamblyn's, Dalton Furs, Simmon's Jewellers, Robinson's Jewellery, Murray's Pharmacy, Bassell's Restaurant, the Amo Café, the Prosperity Lunch, and the Coney Island Restaurant that

boasted of 'Canada's best hot dogs'." Martin's Florist was established by Gerry Linton's grandfather and was later operated by his cousin Bill Martin.

There was no shortage of entertainment in the area, either. "We saw movies at the Beaver, Apollo (formerly Crystal), West End and Crescent theatres. The Beaver was the classiest by far, a very ornate building. And there was bowling at the Roseland Alleys. It was a very close knit community."

Gerry recalls three smells from the Junction of old: the sharp tang of coal smoke from the CPR's steam locomotives; the less than fragrant stock yard odours; and the appetizing aroma of chili sauce in the autumn "when housewives did up their preserves for the winter".

He got into the insurance brokerage business, almost as an afterthought, to service customers buying houses. It has since "become his bread and butter". He offers property, automotive and travel coverage.

"People's attitudes towards insurance have changed. They used to just insure their houses for the amount of the mortgage. Now they get full replacement and contents coverage." Gerry says he could not have imagined in his wildest dreams 40 years ago the goods people would have in their houses today: "VCRs, stereos, expensive clothes, cameras and jewellery". The two-car family and the summer cottage are also common nowadays.

Today Gerry has customers from all across Toronto and as far away as Sudbury and Elliot Lake, "former local residents who've retired and moved away. After 90 years of the Lintons being in this area, we're not exactly strangers. People drop into the office and, after we've settled their business, they'll often stay just to chat. I sometimes think I should be called 'the Ann Landers of insurance'".

The family philosophy, Gerry sums up, has been to always remember "that customers are people, not objects. You have to take the time to understand them and their needs".

Postscript

Shortly after this interview was done Gerry Linton retired, closing the door on the family firm.

A Business Family in Pictures

MURRAY F. BIRKETT was born above the family store at McMurray Avenue and Dundas St. W. in 1913, although the family moved to a house in Lambton soon after. Her father Reginald had a grocery store at 1916 Dundas St. W. (now 3050). Her sister Margaret married Albert Bull, who managed the Joseph Cooper Meat Store at 2932 Dundas St. W. Murray herself started with Taylor Shoes in 1937 and worked in the store for 50 years.

In 1917 the *Commercial Industrial & Progressive Edition of West Toronto, Ontario* had this to say about her father's store:

Every branch of business in West Toronto has its worthy representative. We want to call particular attention of our readers to the establishment conducted successfully by Mr. Reg. Birkett. This store carries a fine line of staple and groceries and fruits, butter, eggs, cooked meats, hay and feed. All goods are bought on a quality basis and are sold at fair and reasonable prices. Competent and experienced clerks are employed and orders delivered with promptness and despatch. The premises occupied at 1916 Dundas St. W., phone Jct. 1 and 3, comprise a store of large dimensions. This well known business was established by its present proprietor seven years ago. He is an able and experienced businessman of unquestioned integrity and enjoys the confidence and esteem of friends and patrons and the farming community generally . . . all the surrounding country. He is at all times interested in all matters pertaining to the general advancement and welfare of the community.

BOTTOM LEFT
The Family Store: Birkett Bros. Grocers, northwest corner of Dundas and McMurray Ave. in 1913, showing an interesting variety of merchandise and advertisements. The building still stands. Left to right: Michael Birkett, his son Reginald Birkett, Reg's daughter Margaret, Alf Francis and Roy Kitchen.

BOTTOM RIGHT
Bill from Birkett Bros.
Courtesy of Tom Wogden

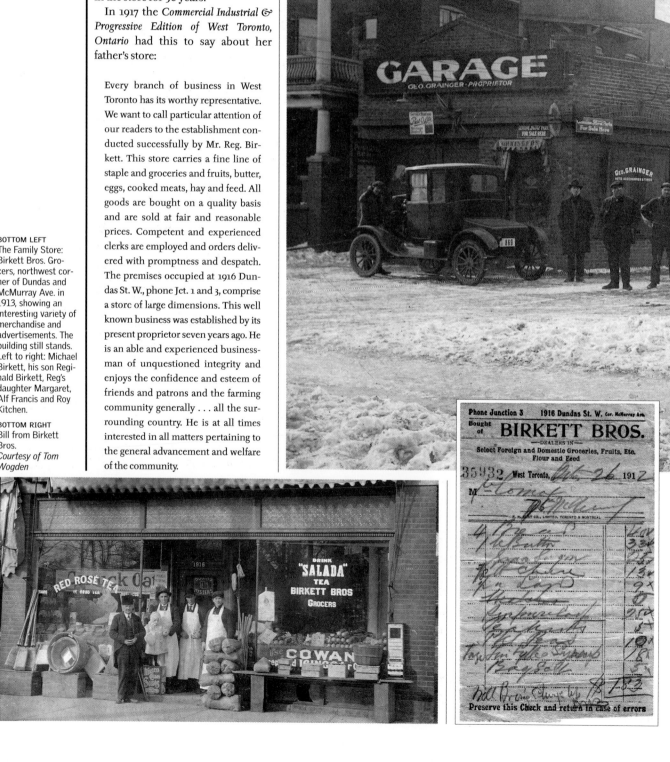

Photographs from the collection of Miss Murray Birkett

LEFT
Grainger's Garage and Supply Station stood on the west side of High Park Ave. and Dundas St. W., immediately south of the corner building. The garage building is still there. George Grainger is second from the left in the centre group. Frank Birkett, fifth from the left in the centre group, was a junior auto mechanic when this picture was taken, ca. 1918.

BOTTOM LEFT
Margaret "Peggy" Birkett in the window of The Carlton Press, where she worked, ca. 1925. The building, later demolished, was on the east side of Keele Street a few doors north of Dundas.

BOTTOM RIGHT
Heading for the horses' garage in a back lane near McMurray Ave., north of Dundas, ca. 1910. Top of the wagon centre, Roy Kitchen; top left Fred Webb; top right Frank Birkett; middle centre Casey Jones; on the wagon, lower left, Alf Francis; still on the wagon, lower right, Reg Birkett.

Delivering the Junction

by Marion Gardner Holroyd

ON SEPTEMBER 14, 1906, Edith Shore boarded a ship bound for Canada. It was her birthday, she was 22, leaving a large and loving family. She carried a letter to certify that Banns of Marriage between herself and James Arthur Holroyd had been declared and duly signed by the vicar of St. Augustine's Anglican Church, Halifax, Yorkshire, England.

Edith came directly to the home of a family friend, Mrs. Charles E. King, on Cawthra Avenue, above Dundas near Keele. Rev. L. Cowen officiated at the wedding one week later. James had built a small frame house at 651 Willard Avenue, north of Annette Street in York Township, where they lived for 10 years. She moved several times later, but never far from this first home.

Her son Arthur was born in 1907. Dr. Kayler attended at the birth. He lived on Annette between High Park Avenue and Pacific Avenue. When Arthur was seven months old, Dr. Kayler came to the door one day and asked if she would take in a lady who was about to have a baby. Edith and her husband thought it would be impossible, because their home was very small. But Dr. Kayler said, "Well, you must make room for she cannot have her baby in a hayloft, which is exactly where she is living with her husband at the present time."

They gave up their bed and the doctor was on hand the next morning when the baby girl was born. The mother stayed for two weeks. The neighbours knew of the case and brought food and clothing for mother and child. This was how Edith began helping Dr. Kayler — he trained her to assist at births and to care for mother and baby during confinement. Some of these "babies" kept in touch with Edith for the rest of her life.

Edith also worked for Dr. Hugh Norman on St. John's Road, who would call her at any time of the day or night. She recalls receiving a message at three o'clock in the morning asking her to set off as soon as she was ready, as they were needed right away at a home on Clendenan Avenue, so off she went with her bag of "essentials". As she hurried along, a policeman called to her and wanted to know what was in the bag. Edith told him that it was not his business what was in the bag, that she was out on a call and was about to be met by a doctor.

About this time Dr. Norman arrived on the scene and assured the policeman that this was indeed a respectable lady and that the contents of her bag were not for public show. When I asked what was in the bag, Edith laughed and said, "Oh just the necessities — a bed pan and a syringe and such. I wasn't going to show those things to a policeman!"

Dr. Norman loved children and didn't mind taking youngsters with him for a ride in his car. One day as he was making a call on Gilmour Avenue, the boys put the car in gear and off it went down the hill with Dr. Norman in hot pursuit.

Dr. Minerva Reid, a true pioneer, wore a panniered skirt on her calls. It was gathered at the waist and pleated over a frame down to a large hoop at the hem. Edit says Dr. Reid seemed to take up the whole street as she walked to make her calls, and when she sat down on the settee, one had to give her a lot of room. She lived on Annette, at the southwest corner of Mavety Street.

Edith also remembered Dr. Perfect on the southeast corner of High Park Avenue and Annette Street, where the beautiful gladioli grew, and Dr. Puffer on the opposite corner of High Park Avenue, as well as Dr. Hopkins, Dr. Butt, Dr. Dow, Dr. Clendenan and Dr. Mavety. Dr. Pratt took over Dr. Kayler's practice when he retired.

Grocery shopping was a far cry from what it is today. On Marinosa Avenue (Winfield Avenue), the third north of Annette off Willard in the township, was the home of Frederick John Ward, a CPR engineer. Mr. Ward had a few acres of land here and grazed enough cows on a small pasture to supply the neighbourhood with fresh milk. A strip of tickets cost a dollar and allowed you to purchase 34 pints of milk. Edith had a quart container and walked over to the farm each morning for a refill. Mr. Ward's daughter Mabel married Robert Hofland, a son of John Hofland, who operated a general store at 368 St. John's Road, between Willard and Windermere Avenue. The store was later converted to a house.

Edith Shore and Arthur Holroyd on their wedding day, September 29, 1906
Courtesy of Arthur Holroyd

Eaton's delivered groceries in those days and one day Edith asked the Eaton delivery driver if she could order meat from Eaton's as well. He told her that she had a good butcher here in the west end at the [southeast] corner of Mavety and Dundas. As she was longing for the taste of some liver, off she set with Arthur in the carriage, and arrived at Wm. Rowntree & Sons. (today's 2881-87 Dundas Street)

She asked for 2 cents worth of liver and Mr. Rowntree said, "Oh, lady, where are you from! We use that for fertilizer here." The result was that a large bundle of the beast's parts were handed to Edith. All eleven pounds for 2 cents! There was heart, tongue, kidney, entrails, and liver in the parcel. Without refrigeration it had to be used immediately, so on the homeward walk Edith called on all the households she knew and gave it all away, with the exception of what she could use that night. It had been a wonderful day for her and she recalled it with great pleasure.

LEFT
(L-R) Mrs. Shore, Edith Shore Holroyd and Arthur Holroyd, age 4, in England, 1911.
Courtesy of Arthur Holroyd

BELOW
Interior of Wm. Rowntree & Sons store ca. 1900.
Courtesy of W. K. Rowntree

A Century of Change at the Heydon House Hotel

by Alexander Heydon III

14

THE NORTHWEST CORNER of Old Weston Road and St. Clair Avenue has been an important part of the social life of Carleton village and West Toronto Junction since the 1860s, when Brian and Hanna Irvine operated the Durham Heifer Hotel there. Little is known of the original building except that, according to A. B. Rice, it was a "roughcast structure, a storey and a half high and glazed with panes 7 x 9 inches in size".

In 1867 the Durham Heifer was purchased by a newcomer to the village, Francis Heydon, who had previously owned a successful saloon in Peel County. He did such a brisk business over the next 15 years that he was able to buy the hotel in 1883. Three years later, however, he sold the hotel to his son, moved into Heydon Villa on Davenport Road, and began to take an active interest in local politics. He served on the town council of 1890, shortly after the amalgamation of Carleton, Davenport and West Toronto Junction, and again on the 1893 town council. He was also active in fundraising for St. Cecilia's Catholic Church.

His son, Alexander Heydon, was an ambitious businessman who quickly became dissatisfied with the limitations of this modest hostelry. The rapid growth of the nearby Canadian Pacific railyards led him to envision a much larger and more permanent building for the site. He set up a public subscription in the late 1880s to help him pay for the construction which, it was hoped, would attract more business to the area. For the price of $33,000 the old Durham Heifer was torn down and a handsome new three-storey brick structure put up. It towered over all the other buildings nearby. The corner turret and high vaulted entrances were the height of style. On top of the south and east facing walls stood large signs announcing the name "Heydon House".

Open for Business

In the spring of 1891 when Alexander and his new bride Mary opened the Heydon House for business, it was widely regarded as the finest hostelry outside Toronto's city limits. It contained 25 guest rooms, a tavern, a dining room, and also a ballroom called the Alexandra Hall.

In the first years of the hotel's operation, many of the rooms were occupied by travellers making the long journey on horseback or by wagon from the outlying towns into Toronto. However, the largest part of the hotel's patronage was CP engineers and conductors who ran the daily trains out of the Junction yards. These men worked up ravenous appetites by the end of the day, and Mary soon learned to keep the hotel kitchen locked overnight so as to be sure of having

enough for breakfast in the morning. A bartender, porter, horse groomer and two servant girls were employed to help cater to the needs of the guests.

In the early 1890s Heydon House hosted musicals and a wide variety of entertainments. Safety bicycles made their first appearance during this period and it became popular for groups of cyclists to spend the day riding in the countryside. On such occasions the hotel dining room was reserved for the returning parties to

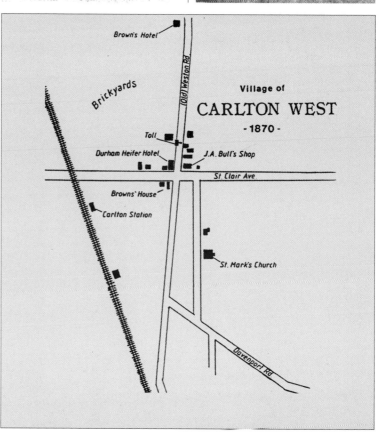

ABOVE, LEFT & RIGHT
Francis and Isabella Heydon came to Carlton in 1867 to operate the Durham Heifer, which they later renamed the Carlton Hotel. Francis also served as alderman on the first town council.
Courtesy of A. J. Heydon III

BOTTOM
Map, 1870.
Heydon, A. J., The Heydons and Their Hotels, p. 37

dine and refresh themselves. The local bicycle club, The Rangers, held many of its social activities at Heydon House. The hotel made a specialty of catering to bicycling and sleighing parties and seemed to have been headquarters for the sporting life of the community in this area.

The second floor ballroom was used by the local chapter of the Canadian Order of Foresters, and on occasion by the local Orange Lodge, even though the Heydons were well-known Catholics. This same ballroom was also regularly used for illegal cock fights. Fifty or more people would assemble, often including contestants from as far away as Cleveland or Detroit. Around 10 o'clock, when sufficient alcohol had been consumed to put everyone in a gaming spirit, the fight began. The price of admission was two dollars and the wagers ranged from $25-35. Although cock fights continued to be popular, several police raids resulted in a move to the privacy of the hotel loft.

Hard Times for Hoteliers

By the mid-1890s the boom had collapsed. Most of the hotel's shareholders lost all their investment and many of them moved into the hotel as residents at no cost. The Heydon family moved out, taking up residence further south in the Subway Hotel at the corner of Keele Street and Vine Avenue.

At this point the hotel was rented to the charismatic and eccentric Baron Earnst von Heimrod, formerly the German consul to Toronto. He was believed to be a "black sheep" of an aristocratic German family who came to Canada looking for investment opportunities. The von Heimrods decorated the hotel with German colours and celebrated all the German holidays with elaborate banquets. They operated the hotel at a loss for three or four years before their money ran out and they moved to a small house on Osler Street.

The Toronto Brewing and Malting Company leased Heydon House in 1897, doing a moderate business during the next few years, catering to railway men and factory workers. On the weekend of September 12, 1903, a raucous brawl occurred at the hotel, causing considerable property damage and resulting in three men being charged with assault. This bar fight may have been the one that has since become something of a legend in the Junction. It was said to have been fought between some cattlemen from the Union Stock Yards and a group of CP railway workers — the subject of disagreement having been the favour of one of the neighbourhood prostitutes. It began as a minor skirmish which took place at the hotel on a previous night, sparking bad feelings between the two already antagonistic groups. Later the tension broke into a weekend-long battle of words, and this climaxed in the memorable fight — reported to be the catalyst for a successful prohibition campaign in the town.

When the town voted to ban the sale of alcohol in January of 1904, it proved to be a fatal blow for Heydon House, as well as most of the other local hotels. However, the new proprietor was known to do a thriving business as a bootlegger. Alex Heydon owned two other hotels in the town and "repossessed" Heydon House in

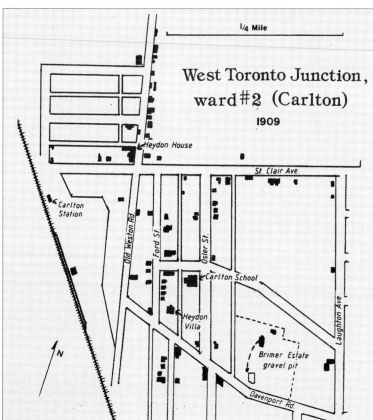

West Toronto Junction, ward #2 (Carlton) 1909

ABOVE, LEFT & RIGHT
Alexander and Mary Heydon operated the hotel in early 1890s, before moving on to a lucrative business in gravel extraction and real estate investments.
Courtesy of A. J. Heydon III

BOTTOM
Map, 1909.
Heydon, A. J., The Heydons and Their Hotels, p. 86

1906, although by this time his interest was purely financial. The West Toronto Junction Hotel, for example, was torn down in 1903 to make way for the new Post Office and Customs House building. Also on the eve of the temperance vote, the Subway Hotel, where Alex and his family had been living, was leased to a new proprietor. The Heydons moved to increasingly substantial homes as their real estate ventures continued to prosper. They were also generous parishioners of St. Cecilia's Catholic Church.

Flying Corps Barracks

By 1911 Heydon House had become a boarding house, continuing in that capacity until sometime during the First World War, when it was briefly rejuvenated as a headquarters and barracks for the Royal Flying Corps,

Heydon House in 1927.
City of Toronto Archives

along with the adjacent property on Old Weston Road. There was a supplies store, and a training and maintenance shop where sections of aeroplanes were disassembled. Hundreds of airmen were stationed there during the last years of the war.

When the war ended the hotel was quickly abandoned, and the stores and equipment were left behind unguarded. Children in the area wasted no time breaking in and pilfering whatever they liked, until every kid in town owned a pith helmet, according to several residents. One bold thief was seen walking away with the wing of an aircraft. Supplies of calcium carbide, used to make acetylene, were also raided and used by the same culprits to make crude incendiary devices. The military did eventually return to clean up what was left of the supplies, resulting in a giant rummage sale of clothing, boots, and helmets.

Before the building was reoccupied by civilians, some of the upper brickwork was removed, possibly for safety reasons. And it was about this time that Alex Heydon, by now a wealthy real estate investor, sold his interest in the building. A major renovation took place between 1948 and 1951, when the corner turret was knocked down and the interior rearranged to make it into apartments. In this capacity Heydon House has quietly endured the last 50 years, with Casa del Baby Beef housed in the hotel's former garage.

Passing its hundred and tenth year in 2001, Heydon House is one of the last reminders of the 1890s in the Carlton portion of West Toronto Junction. In 1983 it was designated as an historic building under Part IV of the Ontario Heritage Act.

TOP
Advertisement,
*Charlton's West
Toronto Junction
Directory 1890*

BOTTOM
Advertisement,
*West York Herald,
September 28, 1911*

The Hain Family: Scottish Business Pioneers

by Doug Hain

Dr. Cecil Hain, the last of the Hain family to earn his living in the Junction, passed away on August 6th, 2000, after a life that spanned the 20th century. He was born on March 6th, 1902 at 136 Osler Street, the youngest of six children. His parents, Alex Hain and Mary, née Malloch, emigrated from Auchtermuchty, Scotland in the 1880s and resided on Pelham Avenue before moving to Osler Street.

Cecil's birth certificate records his father's occupation as "dairyman", as he owned and operated St. Mark's Dairy in the early 1900s. This involved gathering milk from nearby farms, then doling it out (unpasteurized) from the large cans to smaller containers used by householders. Eventually, milk bottles with the etched name "A. Hain" and the phrase "Please wash and return" were used. New rules regarding pasteurization were probably responsible for changing the business to that of coal distribution.

The Osler address was immediately north of the railway lines level crossing, allowing coal, mainly from Pennsylvania, to be dumped in bulk on the property beside the house. It was then delivered by horse-drawn wagon to houses and businesses in the area. The coal business lasted until the mid-1950s, when oil became the main household heating fuel.

A. B. Rice profiled Alex Hain in the 1901 *Tribune Souvenir Edition*, noting that already at that time he enjoyed, "the distinction of having been continuously in business in Toronto Junction longer than any other man.... His business has grown to large proportions and he has been very successful. He has a large stake in the town, owning valuable property on Edmund (Osler) Street, besides a lately acquired coal and wood yard property just across the city boundary".

In 1918 the *Commercial, Industrial and Progressive Edition of West Toronto, Ontario* was even more enthusiastic:

Mr. Hain has been engaged in business in this section for 32 years. The office and yards are located at 112-134 Osler St., phone Jct. 165. He is a dealer in coal and coke. The facilities at hand enable him to deal with customers most advantageously and his prices are always found to be the lowest. By energy and perseverance, the display of executive ability and fair and honourable dealings, this house has built up a trade and acquired a connection which places it in the front in its line in West Toronto. The business is conducted under the sole management of Mr. Hain. He possesses comprehensive knowledge of all its details, is fair and generous in his dealings and enjoys the confidence of all who come in contact with him.

In the family photo taken in 1907, Cecil is the youngest child. The boy with the bicycle, John, was to run the coal business after his father Alex retired in the 1920s. Alex was in his 100th year when he died in 1956, while his son John was in his mid-nineties when he died in 1989. Both were active in the Masonic Temple (Kilwinning Lodge), Alex as a founder and John as treasurer for over two decades. Cecil was also a member for over fifty years.

The two older boys, Alister and Norman, were killed in action during World War I. The other boy, Gordon, served with the Royal Navy as a doctor in that same war (even though he was only in his third year of medical school at the time!) and resumed his education afterwards. He was aboard a destroyer at Rosyth when the German fleet appeared on its way to surrender at Scapa Flow. He later practiced in a small town in Mennonite country near Elmira. The girl, Irene, cared for her aging parents; she died in 1964.

All the Hain children attended Carleton School and Humberside Collegiate — Cecil graduated in 1920. He attended, then graduated from, the University of Toronto's medical school

The family of Alex and Mary Hain at 136 Osler St. in 1907. (L-R) John, Cecil, Mary, Gordon, Alister, Norman, Alex and Irene.
Courtesy of Doug Hain

in 1926. He then worked with various doctors in the High Park Avenue area — Dr. Butt, Dr. Perfect and Dr. Clendenan — before establishing his own practice at 321 High Park Avenue.

Much of Dr. Cecil's work was with the CPR, examining the workers from the yards at St. Clair Avenue, and attending to the accidents that occurred there. These yards were among the busiest in Canada, and the constant, round-the-clock shunting activity resulted in many injuries. His medical activities included work at Toronto Western Hospital and the US Consulate. He made house calls, often at night, and recalled being paid 50¢ per visit during the Depression. He delivered hundreds of babies, often at home, many of whom reminded him of their entry into the world by his hands at the Humberside Collegiate reunion in 1992.

Cecil's father Alex was a founder of Victoria Presbyterian Church in 1885, when it held its first services in the waiting room of the first CPR West Toronto Station (north of what is now Heintzman Street). Cecil's children and grandchildren were baptized in the church — five generations of Hains have worshipped there, including his grandfather, who had emigrated from Scotland after the death of his wife. Cecil served as an elder at the church for sixty years, and recalled the events of 1925, when the United Church was formed from Presbyterian and Methodist congregations. High Park United Church was a result of that event in West Toronto.

Alex Hain served as town councillor 1903-9. He was on the council when the City of West Toronto was annexed to the City of Toronto in 1909, and a leading crusader for the "local option" by-law, which was retained to keep the area "dry" as a condition of the merger. He was a part of the old Scots Presbyterian tradition from the early days of the Junction's history. A look at area war memorials confirms this tradition. Over four hundred members of the Victoria congregation joined the army in World War I, most with the Toronto Scottish Regiment. Fifty-five were killed from that congregation.

Dr. Cecil Hain retired from medical practice in 1963 when he moved to Swansea, but continued to work in his own medical examining business until his mid-eighties!

After the Carleton Village School reunion (he was Class of 1915) in 1989, he visited the old family home at 136 Osler Street, meeting the present owners and explaining where the milk sheds had been and where the horses were kept. The coal yard is now part of Brothers Plumbing and the garden south of the house is gone. The basement has an apartment in it and the attic is now heated. A small vineyard occupies the area where milk, then coal, was prepared for delivery. Cecil was happy about this!

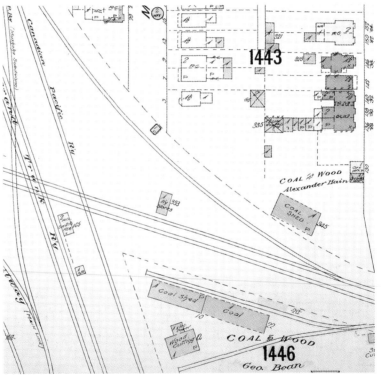

ABOVE
Alexander Hain's coal and wood business, shown on part of Plate 24 of the *Insurance Plan of Toronto Junction.* Toronto: Charles E. Goad Co, 1903, revised 1912. *WTJHS collection*

BOTTOM

LEFT
Alex Hain. *Tribune Souvenir Edition 1901*

MIDDLE
Gordon Hain, 1918. *F. A. Swaink, London, England*

RIGHT
Dr. Cecil W. Hain on the occasion of his 90th birthday. *Felix Russo*

Starting Life at the Stock Yards

by Claire Hodgson Binnie

I SUPPOSE THERE WEREN'T MANY babies born at the stock yards, but my father, Clare Hodgson, was born there in 1904. His grandfather, W. W. Hodgson, was general manager at the time and was living in the large brick house right on the property. As was often the case in those days, Dad's parents were at the grandparents' home for his birth. Dad's first connection with the Union Stock Yards was with his first breath.

By the time Dad was a teenager, his father, C. Bell Hodgson, had built the family home at 52 Kenneth Avenue, and Dad was working after school delivering orders by bicycle for the local butcher around the corner on Dundas Street. Here he gradually learned the butcher trade from Mr. Bridgen. In 1932, recently married and expecting their first child, my parents Clare and Sylvia Hodgson rented a store at 2832 Dundas St. W. near Keele Street, and opened their own business.

The apartment above the store had not been lived in for a while, but they cleaned and improved it to a habitable state and we lived there for ten years with police and fire sirens turning the corner and streetcars rumbling inces-santly under our living room window. One of the improvements during those years was the addition of a homemade, soldered, galvanized iron bathtub. My father, like all the Hodgson men, found or manufactured a way to do whatever had to be done. Anyway, that tin tub was a heck of a lot better than the tub on the kitchen floor. During the ten years of his occupancy, Dad believed that he had paid to the landlord, Mr. King, the equivalent of the building's value.

Reading the news about the imminent demise of the Ontario Stock Yards at the end of 1993 made me think of trips with my Dad to the abattoir to personally choose the beef for his shop. Our friend, Jim Blaney, also operated a butcher shop on Bloor St. W. near Indian Grove.

In the early years, sales were meagre and Dad would keep the shop open until midnight on Saturday evenings to catch any last straggler going home from the Beaver Theatre.

He must have been a good butcher because Dad developed a clientele who followed him to 291 Pacific Avenue when he was able to buy the business previously run by the Benn family. The customer who most encouraged this move was Agnes Quinn, who then became a close neighbour. She and Harriet Spurling across the street circulated a petition among the neighbours so that a business license could be issued to the new owners for a butcher/grocery shop in the residential area. I can still remember the first night on Pacific Avenue. It was so quiet I couldn't sleep.

The Benn family had operated this shop for many years and their stable and hayloft remain a reminder of home delivery by horse and wagon. "The customer was always right" in those days, and received home delivery from our store also, but by bicycle only. Two of the delivery boys who continued to live in the area were Bill Purdy and Jack Deeton.

The corner store really sees the neighbours and there wasn't a better group than the Pacific/Aziel/Humberside block. Customers could also approach through the garden via the back gate. One of the neighbours well known at the Stock Yards was "Doc" Melhuish.

When Loblaws built the large, modern supermarket on Pacific Avenue one block away, Dad feared that his business would fail. The neighbours, however, made sure that did not happen, and Hodgson's Meat Market remained until his retirement in 1960.

FACING PAGE
The neighbourhood. Plate 3, *Insurance Plan of Toronto Junction.* Toronto: Charles E. Goad Co, 1912, revised 1930. *National Map Collection*

LEFT
2832 Dundas St. W. in 1938, showing Claire, age 6, and her mother's sister, Hazel Smith. *Courtesy of Claire Hodgson Binnie*

MIDDLE
291 Pacific Ave. in 1946. *Courtesy of Claire Hodgson Binnie*

RIGHT
Clare and Sylvia Hodgson in 1946. *Courtesy of Claire Hodgson Binnie*

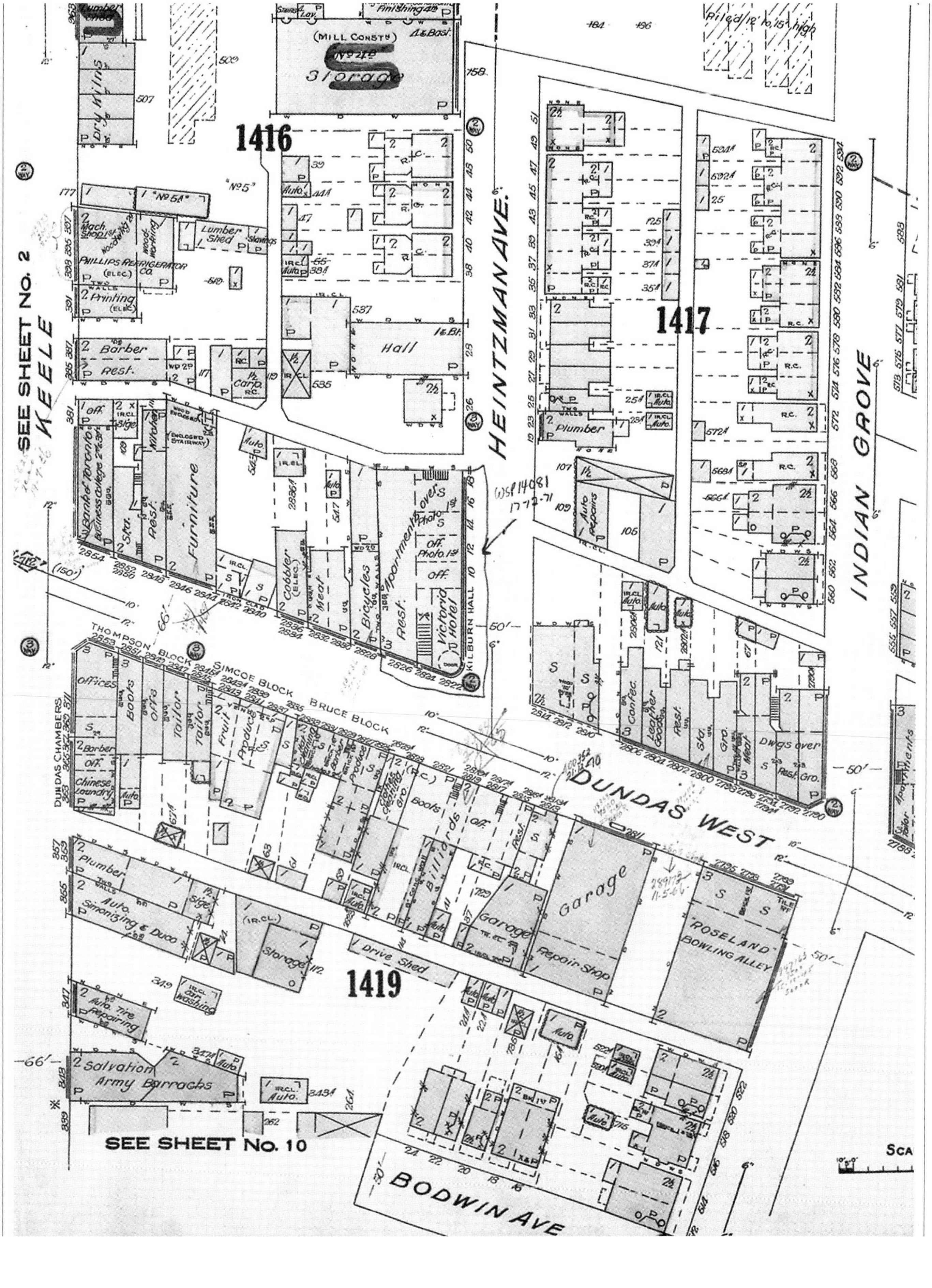

Lumber Shed

Dry Kilns
507

(MILL CONST'N) Nº 2½ Storage
Finishing &c.
L & Bast
Stairs Lav.

1416

"Nº 5"
"Nº 5½"
Auto
R.C.

Lumber Shed
Slaving

Mach Shop
Wood Working
Wood Working

Phillips Refrigerator Co. (ELEC.)
TWO WALLS

2 Printing (ELEC.)

SEE SHEET NO. 2

KEELE

Barber
Rest.
Carp. R.C.

Hall
1 & 2 St.

Off.
Kitchen
Stge.

Bank of Toronto Business College
Rest.
Furniture

ENCLOSED STAIRWAY

Auto
IR.EL.

Cobbler (ELEC.)
Meat
Bicycles
Rest.
Apartments over
Photo
Off. Photo 1st
Off.
Victoria Hotel
Kilburn Hall

HEINTZMAN AVE.

Plumber
Auto Repairs

1417

INDIAN GROVE

R.C.
R.C.

Thompson Block
Books
Offices
Barber
Off.
Chinese Laundry

Simcoe Block
Tailor
Tailor
Fruit
Produce

Bruce Block
Boots
Rest.
Off.

Leather Goods
Rest.
Confec.
Gro.
Meat
Gro.
Rest.

Dwg's over

DUNDAS WEST

Apartments

Plumber
Auto Simonizing & Duco
Stge.
Storage
Washing

Billiards

Garage
Repair Shop
Garage

"ROSELAND" BOWLING ALLEY

Auto
Drive Shed

1419

Auto Tire Repairing

2 Salvation Army Barracks
Auto

SEE SHEET NO. 10

Auto

BODWIN AVE.

SCA

The Business of Government

A Glance at the Past

Front page editorial from the First Edition of West Toronto Weekly, *May 4, 1922*

There are still quite a number of West Toronto people who have vivid recollections of the time when what is now Ward Seven was a separate municipality with a Mayor and Council of its own. We gather from the remarks of these old timers that in what they recall as the good old days, public utilities and civic politics generally were much more discussed in the homes, on the streets and wherever people foregathered than they are today. People recall things that happened when Dr. Clendenan or Peter Laughton or the late James Bond was Mayor and it is said that a comparatively trivial incident seemed to arouse more public interest than the most important question affecting the Ward today.

Sometimes the old days were scrappy days. The town had two lively local papers and the municipal elections were keenly contested. There were differences of opinion on many matters of civic policy and the older citizens delight in recalling many a battle royal between the *Tribune* which was conducted by Mr. Rice, the present chief of the local customs staff, and the *Leader and Recorder* whose editor was the late Mr. Fawcett.

It is said that the two papers sometimes caused faction feuds that stopped at little short of actual bloodshed, but it is agreed that the result was public interest in civic matters such has never been known since the old town merged with the city. It is also recalled that the community spirit was such that whenever the town's interests were menaced from without all local differences were forgotten, the hatchet was temporarily buried, the citizens closed up their ranks and went in solemn formation against the foe.

Postscript: Ward 7 is now split into four, in spite of a 1999 Ontario Municipal Board decision that the Willoughby Estate area, east of Keele in Ward 13, should be reunited with Ward 14. The other two wards, both north of the CPR mainline tracks, are 11 and 17.

Assembled in solemn formation ready to confront the foe, are Mayor G. W. Clendenan, the councillors and municipal staff of Toronto Junction, including the horses that pulled the fire engine, in front of the firehouse doors circa 1896. The building also served as city hall and police station. The mayor is front and centre, Aldermen Sam Ryding and Reuben Armstrong to his left and right in the back row. Chief of Police Josiah Royce is to his right, and Dr. J. T. Gilmour MPP is at the far right.
Courtesy of George Windsor Clendenan

My Father the Mayor

The following colourful description of life in the Daniel Webster Clendenan household at the turn of the century is excerpted from letters written by Charlie Clendenan in 1954. Copies were supplied by Mimi Hayward, daughter of Charlie's sister Mary. Charlie was the eldest child, born in 1879. He attributes his father's name, "Daniel Webster", to Grandfather George Clendenan, a United States citizen, being a "Whig" (Liberal).

MY FIRST MEMORY is of living in a summer cottage on the lake side of Hanlan Island, but no details recur. My next memory is of moving to the house built on High Park Avenue, No. 191. There was a big stump in the middle of the vacant corner lots. That summer my father was gone some days to the summer encampment of the Queen's Own Rifles. He was a lieutenant for some years, but dropped out after that summer, when he also had a vicious case of sunburn.

I have many memories of the house, but not in any chronological order. Our house was almost an hotel, for so many people came and went. The big table in the dining room nearly always had its full complement of extra leaves. One I shall always remember and admire was Miss Lelean. The true stories she told me so well are the foundation of all the history I know.

At this minute I can see in front of me Columbus on his deck with his half mutinous crew. Also the story of Cartier, of Champlain, of LaSalle, of Frontenac, of Iroquois raids and of less admirable characters such as Laval and Denonville. Not to mention those two very fine soldiers and gentlemen, Wolfe and Montcalm, who were both years ahead of their age in military strategy.

Another frequent visitor and close friend was a Mr. Wallace, MP for west York and Grand Master of the Orange Order. He was a lame man and not much of a speaker, but influential because he worked hard at the routine chores that make up most of any task. He lived in the small village of Woodbridge. Two brothers named Munro were frequent visitors; one was a chemistry student at the University of Toronto, who later became pastor of the Disciples church. Preachers of assorted vintages were so many at table as to be a dime a dozen. All preached temperance and all were terrific eaters.

There was also Dr. George Clendenan, who was second cousin of father if my memory is correct. He was fat, a hale and hearty hustler. He settled in the Junction as soon as he was out of medical school and built up a good practice. A great joiner, he belonged to thirteen lodges. He also became local doctor for the CPR and later married Miss Gilmour, sister of the MPP. I liked Dr. George. He liked to see people eat. When we visited him he kept my plate heaped up. What small boy ever objected to that?

When we first lived in the Junction we went to the Methodist church, as being the only one handy. It was one block north and half a block west [Quebec Avenue at Annette Street]. Church with us meant twice on Sunday, plus Sunday school, plus Wednesday evening prayer meeting. Soon the Disciples organized, first in a room over a store on Dundas, then they built a church at Keele and Annette Streets. Father was a liberal contributor to all the churches. Sometimes he took May and I to St. John's Anglican, which was some blocks away.

We always had at least one horse, a Jersey cow and bantam chickens. The horses were a happy memory. We had a buggy, a surrey, and a sleigh. And we had an Irish setter good enough for a show dog. The garden was large in the back, best rhubarb ever grown. The stable, painted red, was a good size. It had a hay loft and a half cellar. The house had a large lawn with a big flower bed. Back of the lawn was a high lattice fence, and behind that the stable. Three lots fenced in made up the place [southeast corner of Humberside Avenue, now third from the corner at No. 191].

The house was on the northwest portion of the lot. It was two and one-half stories tall and of red brick [with yellow brick trim]. The porch was small and on the south side, with the door at the east end of the porch. The entrance hall had the stairway in front and to the left hand the door to the large parlour which covered the whole front of the house and had large bay windows. It was almost impossible to heat the parlour in the winter. To the right hand of the front door was the door to the library, really the living room most of the time. Behind that was the dining room, connected with the library by big sliding doors.

The entrance hall extended across the width of the house. To the right was a narrow hall leading to the kitchen and beyond the hall the door

LEFT
Mayor D. W. Clendenan.
York Tribune, 1889

RIGHT
191 High Park Ave. soon after it was built.
Saturday Globe, July 25, 1891, p. 2

to the cellar where the furnace was located. The kitchen was also entered from the north end of the dining room. It was a fine, big kitchen, and had need to be. It was a busy place for we ate well and a meal without visitors was news. During canning season it was one of the busiest places in the universe.

There were no cards or alcoholic drinks in our house. However we spent hours on a card game with authors' names and titles. Later, in some mysterious manner, euchre was permitted. There was a very fine grand piano. Mother played well, while Aunt Via [McMillan], one of my real favourites, was an exceptionally talented musician.

There were three servants, a cook, a maid, and a stable man who was also gardener. For a long time the man and maid were a married couple, members of the Salvation Army, fine people. He taught me to ride and drive. The cook was a squat, stout, red-faced person, perhaps illiterate in books, but proficient in her sphere. She could look the other way when a small boy purloined a between-the-meals snack.

The second floor had a large front bedroom with the proportions of the parlour. The hallway was large and well lit; it was used as a sewing room. A seamstress [came] in every year for numerous days. Of course, in anything connected with sewing or needle work mother was the expert of experts. Aunt Via was also highly proficient in fancy needle work. She did a stork on brown velvet background that hung in the parlour. There were three other bedrooms and a bathroom. The upper half storey was two rooms, which the servants used.

Father was really the town. All that was done he began and kept going. He was a very busy man with many irons in the fire. He was gregarious, made friends easily and was a natural born salesman. He not only laid out the town, but did his own selling of lots, and counselled the lot purchasers on their home building. He was a genuine "Poo Bah" in the neighbourhood, consulted on many things. He organized the local government and became its head. The celebration [of incorporation] was the biggest open house we ever had; it was standing room only.

That was the evening father was presented with the silver water pitcher which is still around. I remember the size and shape of it well. There were nautical figures on it, which do not come to mind so readily, however. Father was quite a water man, a strong swimmer and a fair sailor. He could not get to the beaches as often as he would have liked, but I can still see him in the choppy water at a beach somewhat west of High Park.

On a normal evening when father was at home, there were business visitors. But town business and politics kept him out at least half the evenings. In politics, father was a staunch Conservative, he was that in general. I distinctly remember him saying more than once that the Stuarts were the legitimate monarchs and the Hanovers usurpers. Father did not belong to the Orange Order on account of mother's strong objections to joining in general.

Father had quite a law library, but I never saw him open a law book. He was too much the extrovert to be studious. There were plenty of other

books in the library. We were a pretty straightlaced house, but nobody ever censored any of my reading; I read whatever was around. The *Globe* came every day and I think also the *Mail and Empire*. There was a journal published by the Disciples (of Christ) in Cincinnati, and the *Christian Standard* as well. We got the *London Illustrated News* often and the Christmas number of the *Youth's Companion*. I almost forgot *Saturday Night*, a clever journal almost too cerebral to be popular. It had a remarkable cartoonist, Bengough. He gave public exhibitions, and I saw more than one. We had a fair library, all of Dickens and Thackeray. *Pickwick Papers* was a book I really enjoyed, however *Vanity Fair* and *Martin Chuzzlewit* were my favourite novels. There were also a number of religious books. From the time I learned to read I was required to memorize a certain number of verses of the *Bible* every day.

After two years at a private school in Toronto . . . in 1889 I went to the public school at the Junction and had Mrs. Rice for a teacher. About that time father developed an interest in phrenology. My head was read by a quack away out Yonge Street. Fortunately I do not remember any of the things he predicted. Also around this time Aunt Via lived with us most of two years, doing advanced work at the Toronto Conservatory of Music. Dr. Gilmour, the Liberal MPP, paid her marked attention. That made tongues move, as it was already known that father would be his next opponent. As it all turned out, that election was a very bad thing for us. The campaign was long, bitter and expensive. When father's own affairs needed close

LEFT
Family Portrait: Christina (Clara) Clendenan surrounded by her children, ca. 1900. Clockwise from bottom left: Ann (Annie), Ernest, Charles, May, George and Mary.
Courtesy of Mimi Hayward

RIGHT
Miss Via McMillan & Toronto Junction College of Music.
Tribune Souvenir Edition, 1901, p. 5

attention and he needed to build up cash resources, politics made constant demand on time and money. Father lost by 120 votes, mainly because he had a prohibition plank in his platform, while shortly before he had sponsored a petition to get a liquor license for the man who opened a needed hotel at the Junction and could not make it pay without a liquor license.

Grandfather McMillan retired from the farm in Erin and built a house not far from us at 319 High Park Avenue in 1888. In 1890 he was injured in a fall on the cellar steps and lived only a few days. He was 75. Grandmother's maiden name was McDougall and she lived to be 80. They both came from Scotland to Canada. The acquaintance of the Clendenan and McMillan families came about when grandfather Clendenan, a Disciples of Christ minister, conducted revival services in Erin.

Postscript

Soon after this, around 1892-3, the Clendenans were financially ruined. D. W. went to the United States and the family lost track of him about 1900. In another letter Charlie mentions a land purchase in the Don Valley, which may have also contributed to the financial collapse. His wife Christina (Clara) moved to Guelph with Charlie and the rest of the children, where she made her living as a seamstress. Grandmother McMillan continued to live at 319 High Park Avenue until her death. Via McMillan opened the popular Toronto Junction College of Music in the house in 1897. By 1901 it had outgrown the house and removed to spacious quarters in the Campbell Block at Dundas and Keele Streets, where it occupied nine rooms and a concert hall. However, on the death of her sister Annie, Via married the widowed Dr. McKinnon, and left town around 1905, undoubtedly to look after his four children. The Keele Street Christian Church is still a Disciples church and recently enlarged its building. Miss Lelean may well be Mrs. Edith Lelean Groves, a long-time public school trustee who took as a "pet project" the establishment of Western Technical and Commercial School. The fate of the Munro brothers remains unknown.

Then There Was Light

by A. B. Rice, **Toronto Star Weekly,** *October 18, 1930*

THERE MAY BE here and there a pupil who has been taught "civics" in Toronto schools and who can repeat the names of all the mayors from William Lyon Mackenzie to Bert Wemp. Such a student would be surprised were he to pass over the overhead bridge spanning the railway tracks where they cross [Old] Weston Road, and, looking westward, see a legend carved in stone which gives the impression that in 1891 the city had a mayor named D. W. Clendennin.

Of course, Toronto never had such a mayor and some citizens have suggested that the inscription on the tablet be removed or revised, since it preserves information which, while originally correct, is now misleading, and which, being chiselled deep in stone may outlive contemporary printed and written documents to the confusion of civic historians of the future.

The inscription itself recalls to old-timers the stormy meetings of the Toronto Junction council which preceded the advent of electric light on the streets and in the homes of a section of the city which is now populated by 50,000, but was then a town of 4,000 inhabitants and a high-vaulting ambition . . .

Clendenan was the town's chief magistrate when the citizens tired of coal oil lamps and started a movement to obtain the most modern means of lighting their homes and their streets. Toronto, the town's big neighbour, was mostly electric-lighted, and there was a popular demand for the same sort of a service for the Junction.

There was, however, a minority headed by the mayor who thought the new-fangled light an extravagance. Public ownership was abhorrent to this minority, even for street lighting. Indeed, even the "ginger group" who finally put the street lighting scheme across had not the temerity to suggest a publicly-owned plant to provide interior lighting. The mayor advocated a long-term contract with Consumers Gas Co. to light the streets and backed by a few councillors, put up a stiff fight against Councillor Thomas Gillies and his followers who were the proponents of electricity. By the way, Mr. Gillies is still a resident of Toronto, and as far as the writer knows, is the sole

survivor of those whose names adorn the tablet.

The fight was long continued and grew bitter as the weeks passed. Recriminations and charges and counter charges of "graft" were features of the meetings, but finally the principle of a publicly-owned electric system won the day.

Hydro power was undreamed of in those days and the committee set to work to erect the building in which a steam-driven electric lighting plant was installed. The mayor's name was omitted from the tablet as first erected — a circumstance which led to another storm in council. The committee disclaimed any desire to belittle the mayor and assured him that the omission of his name was due to the belief that he would not desire posterity to learn that he had any part in the erection of a building that he so much despised.

Finally the committee undertook to send a man up a ladder to chisel his worship's name in the stone. It would appear that he was provided with incorrect copy, either by accident or design. Hence Mayor Clendenan's name was spelled "Clendennin".

Erected 1891
Ball Electric Light Co. of Toronto
T. Gillies, ch'man, W. H. Millichamp,
J. W. Campbell, J. B. Bruce, committee;
J. Marr, cont'r, J. H. Venables, engin'r,
D. W. Clendennin, Mayor

Note:
The building was located under the Old Weston Road Bridge and, like the bridge, has been demolished.

While no photos exist of the original street lights, by the early 1900s at least, Toronto's familiar "beer stein" lamps, in evidence throughout this book, were the norm. They were replaced over the years by other equally unremarkable fixtures. In 2004 the Junction business district opted for a new standard and fixture, referencing turn-of-the-century ironwork in a thoroughly post-modern adaptation.
Larry Burak

My Grandfather the Doctor

by George Windsor Clendenan

George Clendenan recently discovered a box which contained the contents of his grandfather's desk, which was cleared out after his death in 1939. Some of the artifacts found in the box are the basis for this article.

GEORGE WASHINGTON CLENDENAN graduated in medicine from Victoria College at the University of Toronto in 1882 at the age of 21. His early graduation makes it obvious that the medical profession in those days was a simpler one.

He began the practice of medicine in Norwich in the New Durham area just to the southwest of Brantford, Ontario, staying there for about four years. Two clippings from the area newspapers mention his move to West Toronto Junction, his loss to the Literary Society of which he was president at the time and the fact that he was going into practice with Dr. John T. Gilmour:

> Along with some humorous remarks made by the Rev. C. S. Pedley, he was presented with a gold ring as a memento of the esteem with which he was held by the members of the society. The Dr. replied in a neat speech and bid them all fare-well.

It was in Norwich that he also began his lifetime association with the Masons. In 1939, the year of his death, the *In Memoriam* notice in the *Masonic News* points out that he was initiated into St. John's Lodge, No. 104, Norwich, July 1st, 1885. Later of course he was a Charter Member, as well as Master, of Stanley Lodge in the Junction and Deacon of the Grand Lodge of Canada.

When he came to West Toronto Junction in 1886 at the urging of his cousin Daniel Webster Clendenan, he first of all secured a house on May Street (now Mavety) which is one block west of Keele Street running south from Dundas Street. His mother, Margaret Jane Claus Clendenan, came as his housekeeper. His father Daniel had passed away in Jordan in September of the previous year, 1885. The obituary mentions the two sons:

> His elder son, Dr. Geo. Clendenan, of New Durham, Ont., a man of excellent ability and great moral worth, and Charles Clendenan, the youngest, an amiable young man, teacher in the public school in Wainfleet. Both sons left their profession and came to their father's bedside and did all they could, but in vain.

Very shortly after his arrival in the Junction, he fell in love with his new partner's sister. Annie Maria Gilmour had come with her brother from Port Hope to act as his hostess in his new home on Davenport Road. Dr. Gilmour's first wife had died. In anticipation of his marriage to Annie Gilmour in 1889, grandfather built a very fine home on the northeast corner of Pacific Avenue and Dundas Street. This would be the site of his medical office and dispensary until encroaching commercial development made it more comfortable to move to a new home and office designed for him by architect Ewart G. Wilson and built on the northwest corner of Annette Street and High Park Avenue in 1924. The Pacific Avenue house was eventually demolished. The house at 268 High Park Ave. has changed very little in appearance over the years.

Coroner of York Township

In 1887, the year after his arrival in West Toronto Junction, he was appointed Coroner of the Township of York, a position later changed to assistant coroner for the City of Toronto, which he held for the rest of his life, a long service record for city coroners at that time. He was also Medical Officer of Health for West Toronto Junction for many years. Among his papers are two interesting pages which acknowledge remuneration due to him for services rendered as coroner and the names of the people whose deaths had been subject to review. He must have kept scrapbooks of articles written in the newspaper concerning his investigations and inquests, although only a couple of pages have survived.

LEFT
Dr. G. W. Clendenan in tuxedo and full masonic regalia, undoubtedly taken in 1893 when he was Master of Stanley Lodge. He was also Mayor of Toronto Junction 1896-8, as well as the town's Medical Officer of Health for many years. His mayor's chair was donated to the WTJHS by Stanley Lodge.
Herbert E. Simpson, photographer

RIGHT
Dr. and Mrs. Clendenan with their children Douglas Gilmour and Jane Marguerite on the front steps of the family home on the northeast corner of Dundas St. and Pacific Ave. during the bicycle craze of the 1890s.
Courtesy of George Clendenan

One article describes the death of Stanley Boyd as the result of anthrax. He developed a boil on his neck and died within a very few days. Mr. Boyd worked in a local tannery and it was the conclusion of the inquest that he had contracted the fatal disease from the handling of South American hides. Another tragic story cites the death of a five-year-old boy who was playing on the roof of the chicken coop in his parents' backyard when it caught fire. Everyone thought he had jumped down and run away, probably because he had been playing with matches. When he did not show up by suppertime the ruins were checked more carefully and the little charred body was sadly discovered where the roof had caved in.

One of grandfather's great crusades was to warn parents and drivers about the ever-increasing threat of the automobile to children. In 1927, after the death of Freddie Osbourne, aged 5, on Dundas Street, the third such death in the area that year, he was quoted in the local paper:

From the evidence submitted to you to-night," said Coroner Dr. Clendenan, "you must recognize that we are again face to face with the modern juggernaut, the automobile, in relation to the safety of young children and pedestrians on the street." Dr. Clendenan thanked the press for its campaign of publicity against the automobile menace, and expressed belief that the new government regulations requiring all drivers to be licensed would prove to be a factor of safety for pedestrians.

There were many doctors in the family, including his partner and brother-in-law, Dr. John Gilmour, the MPP for York West, and his son Dr. Charles Gilmour, grandfather's nephew, who practiced at 866 Keele Street. Charles wrote a letter in 1912, thanking grandfather for a set of books, *The Makers of Canada*.

You are indeed too good to me and I hope at any and all times you will feel that I am at your service in as far as I may be of assistance. In this small way I may hope to show you that I appreciate your very many kindnesses to me.
Very sincerely yours
Charles H. Gilmour

Grandfather's younger brother (by three years), Dr. Charles Wellington Clendenan, after his school-teaching days in Wainfleet, went to medical school. The two brothers were close confidants and great friends throughout their lives and the surviving letters from Charles to George are an illuminating source of information about their activities.

A prescription pad provided by Robinson's Drug Store, which was located near Pacific Avenue at 3083 Dundas Street, indicates that, for a period of time in the 1890s, Charles joined the practice at 417 Pacific Avenue. He also was married to Elgan Johnston in September of 1889, the same year that Annie and George were married in April. Subsequently he and Elgan went to the United States. He practiced right up until his death in 1934 in North Tonawanda, New York.

Grandfather's son, my father, Dr. Douglas Gilmour Clendenan, graduated with a B.A. from McMaster University when it was still located in Toronto in 1915, went overseas in the First World War immediately after graduation, and then after the war returned to medical school at the University of Western Ontario in London. He graduated in 1923. In the years before the establishment of his own practice in Winona, Ontario, father helped out grandfather in his office at 268 High Park Avenue in the late 1920's. Grandfather was beginning to slow down a bit as indicated by a letter written by his wife, Annie, from the cottage at Pointe Au Baril.

My Dearest –
I am hoping that you are all right by this time and I am anxious to know that you are quite yourself again. I am so glad Douglas is with you and he can do your work if you are not feeling up to the mark.
I see your name in the paper about the blind woman. I think you should have an inquest as there should be some guard on a blind person and gas stoves.
The moonlight is lovely. We had a wonderful bass dinner from Harold's catch.
With fondest thoughts
Your own
Annie

Around Christmas time in 1930, grandfather was a bit under the weather and had been feeling a bit dizzy with a few chest pains. A letter from his friend and doctor, Dr. Norman Gwyn, indicates he probably was suffering some stress and needed to slow down and take a holiday. The stock market crash in 1929 and the subsequent Depression probably did not help. Shortly after this episode his wife passed away early in 1931.

CPR Doctor
Another major facet of grandfather's medical career was his position as Surgeon to the Canadian Pacific Railway. This turned out to be a major part of his practice and medical income. His papers include one such invoice to the railway for services performed, indicating a wide variety of injuries. A grit in the eye was a very common occurrence and treatment usually was billed at one dollar. A lot of the other problems dealt with sprains and back problems brought on from lifting and

Jane Marguerite, Douglas Gilmour, Annie May Gilmour and Dr. George Washington Clendenan pose for a family portrait circa 1904. *Courtesy of George Clendenan*

loading heavy objects. A few burns from steam were also noted.

Most of the claims were routinely accepted by the CPR Claims Adjuster, but one for $5.00 for treatment to Norman Pate, a Shop Laborer, for a twisted arm was turned back because "compensation for medical aid could not be allowed as the disability did not appear to be the result of an accident." It was suggested that grandfather forward the bill directly to Norman Pate for payment.

A nice perk of this job was free transport on the railway for the family. It was very convenient to be able to hop on the train at the Junction, travel up through Gravenhurst, Bala and Parry Sound and then get off at the Pointe Au Baril station. A twenty-minute water taxi ride would then get George and Annie out to the island cottage on Georgian Bay which grandfather built in 1911.

Cottage Doctor

With all his experience in the city as coroner, medical officer of health, and general practitioner, and because of his tremendous energy, it was natural for him to slip into the role of cottage doctor in the Pointe Au Baril area while he was at the cottage during the summer. It was his custom to spend the month of August there with other members of the family using it in July as well. A number of doctors with cottages would be on call when they were in residence. In 1927 he seems to be the co-ordinator of the various doctors' responsibilities.

A letter from Dr. C. W. Carr from Ojibway Island, written on August 30 of that year, indicates that he was responsible for these duties during July and August of that year and is reporting on his work to grandfather. He mentions quite a list of items including:

- two cases of accidental drowning
- one case of measles
- three cases of smallpox
- water-sampling for the Provincial Board of Health
- the need for more chloride of lime to be used in the privies
- warning of offending parties for throwing refuse in the water
- investigation of a near drowning of a man hitting his head on a diving board

He concluded with the statement that, all in all, the health of the Pointe Au Baril district had been very good over the summer.

A few other items of interest have been found among grandfather's papers. Cancelled cheques that had been written to the various drug com-

TOP
The elegant high-style home built by Dr. Clendenan for his bride Annie May Gilmour at the northeast corner of Pacific and Dundas in 1889 (demolished). *Harold McCormack Collection*

MIDDLE
A view of the Pacific Avenue house with storefronts on Dundas, not long before the family and the practice moved to the new house on High Park Avenue. *TTC Collection, City of Toronto Archives*

BOTTOM
The Clendenan home and office at 268 High Park Ave., designed by architect Ewart G. Wilson, soon after it was built in 1924. *Courtesy of George Clendenan*

panies showed that he had ordered a lot of medicine and supplies from the N. Powell Chemical Co., the J.F. Hartz Co., Ingram Bell Company and the E.B. Shuttleworth Co.

A Schedule of Fees approved by the Council and Special Committee of the Toronto Academy of Medicine for the year 1921 covered just about every possible condition. The amputation of a finger or toe was $25, but each additional toe or finger was only $10. A real bargain! A haemorrhoidectomy was quite expensive at $50 and up. Doctors probably did not get too excited about doing one of these. You could have a baby for only $25. The statement at the bottom of the page is interesting:

> Nothing in the above schedule should interfere with giving assistance to the needy poor, as has been the custom in our profession.

A letter, written in 1935 by Edna Burkholder, the daughter of one of his patients who lived on Humberside Avenue, indicates that grandfather was still active in his practice when well into his 70's. It also shows the high esteem in which he was held by those whom he helped in the Junction area:

> *All through these last few years while dear mother was in such frail health, I have been strengthened in the knowledge that in you I had a friend upon whom I could rely in any emergency. The times I have had to call upon you during the night have been many and each time I have felt so keenly your utter sympathy and desire to help. Especially have I felt this since last March, when you worked so hard that we might have our Mother a little longer. I have realized that she could not remain with us much longer, but how thankful I am that she was spared to me during these last difficult months. I do thank you with all my heart for your great kindness to us.*

At his own death on March 18, 1939, the funeral was held at his home, officiated by Rev. W. H. Hincks, retired minister of High Park United Church. Pallbearers included Dr. H. A. Beatty, Dr. J. H. Dow, Dr. A. T. McNamara, Dr. J. S. Hart, F. C. Colbeck and D. G. M. Galbraith. Masonic rites were part of the ceremony. He was buried with his wife at Prospect Cemetery.

Reflections for a Centennial Summer

by A. B. Rice, West Toronto Weekly, [Midsummer] 1934

NATURE'S MIDSUMMER SMILE on West Toronto is brighter than ever before. On the business streets the shops look cleaner and smarter and all the residential sections have become more inviting. It would appear that the Mayor's clarion call to "renovize" has been so effective that one can almost forget the atrocity of the word. At any rate one sees the effect of renovation on every hand.

There is another reason for the enhanced beauty of the residential streets however. The trees have had another year of growth and are therefore a little more beautiful than ever. This reminds one that West Toronto's claim to midsummer beauty is based on the fact that it is so well treed. For that West Toronto owes a debt of gratitude to a mayor who served it well when it was a town.

In the middle eighteen nineties Dr. G. W. Clendenan was elected Mayor on a platform of economy and it was under his guidance that the town emerged from a deplorable financial condition into a period of such remarkable prosperity that ten years later Toronto began the wooing which resulted in this community becoming part of Greater Toronto. The town was only about one lap ahead of the sheriff and the citizens were all so poor that they were ashamed to meet one another on the street when the popular doctor was installed as Mayor.

Along came a nursery firm with a bargain day offer to plant vigorous young shade trees all over town for about two thousand dollars. The council was aghast. Two thousand dollars looked bigger to the councillors of the harassed town than two million would to the city aldermen even in this year of retrenchment. The mayor was an economist all right but he was also a man with a vision. He foresaw the great population of the future and realized how kindly nature would covert the two thousand dollars worth of trees into an asset of incalculable value a few years later. Finally he won a majority of his colleagues to his viewpoint. The trees were planted in that hard times year.

Many taxpayers murmured but they all took a pride in the trees, watched them grow with increasing cheerfulness and I never heard of one of them being wantonly destroyed. It is gratifying to know that the far seeing mayor of 1896 shares the credit with the "renovising" mayor of 1934 for West Toronto's prettiness in its centennial summer dress.

Pacific Avenue trees in summer, ca. 1915. *Postcard view courtesy of Ken Heaman*

It Was "Fierce" at the Junction: Ten Thousand People Celebrated Local Option

Toronto Daily News,
Monday, May 2, 1904

ALAS FOR TORONTO THE GOOD! "Going up to the Junction to get a wet?" Every man seemed to be asking his neighbour the same question, and getting the same answer, as the groaning cars, packed to their utmost capacity, pitched and swayed on their way up Dundas Street. All the curious spirits of Toronto with a strong leaven of the rougher characters seemed bound the same way and the atmosphere on some of the cars was a study in breaths. "It'll be fierce up there," was the general prophecy.

Of course, in the strictly literal sense of words, there was no need at all to go to the Junction on Saturday afternoon "to get a wet". All one had to do was to stand out in the rain in the middle of the road until one felt wet enough. But the particular kind of inward and spirituous moisture which the speakers referred to could only be obtained that day at Toronto Junction owing to the fact of the bye-election taking place in the city. The fact that Saturday was the last day

before the local option by-law came into force at the town of Toronto Junction gave an added zest to the process of "getting a wet" that evening.

And they got wet, externally and internally, as wet as men could well get. The first view, as the car drew up in the middle of the stream of mud which represented Dundas Street that evening, was of a swaying mob of some 200 men trying to get into the "Peacock" bar. The situation appeared to be complicated by the frantic struggles of a number of others to get out. Through the steam-covered windows was a blurred vision of a swaying crowd of heads within. Four policemen were more or less lost among the crowd outside.

A band of newspaper men who had come up to see the sights, consulted how they might accomplish their purpose and then, forming a phalanx, shouldered their way gradually through into the bar.

Inside there was barely room to line, and as the shouting mob surged to and fro in their struggles to get at the bar, it seemed as though someone must be trampled on. Many of them were mad drunk already — it was

about half past five o'clock — and some were dead drunk. But in the dense press a man might be dead drunk comfortably, for there was no room for him to fall down. Behind the bar, the bar-tenders, with the sweat pouring down their faces, were handing out liquor as fast as they could. "Here's your change!" they would shout as a man thrust a dollar or a half-dollar on the counter. But the buyer would snatch feverishly at his glass of beer, consigning the change to perdition. Or perhaps the fighting crowd would sweep him aside before he could take it. "I've had three drinks!" one man declared in steaming triumph to a group of envious friends. To succeed in getting three drinks was evidently an achievement in the crowd.

The phalanx of journalists was broken up before it got a yard inside the door, and the individual members fought their way through to the door on the other side as best they might.

The closing of the Peacock was one of the events of the evening. The situation there was getting desperate. The mud-bespattered crowd outside had its attention temporarily diverted by a

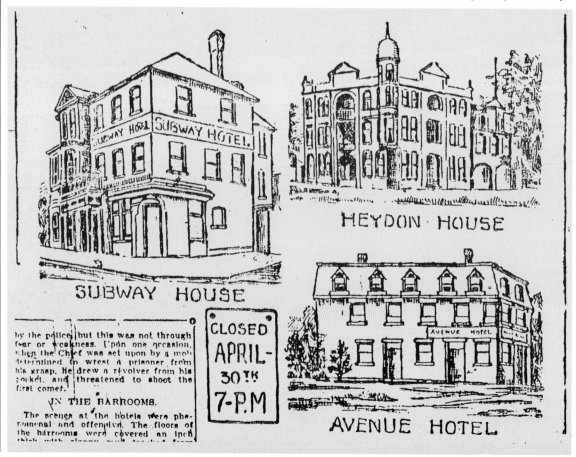

by the police, but this was not through fear or weakness. Upon one occasion, when the Chief was set upon by a mob determined to wrest a prisoner from his grasp, he drew a revolver from his pocket, and threatened to shoot the first comer.

IN THE BARROOMS.

The scenes at the hotels were phenomenal and offensive. The floors of the barrooms were covered an inch thick with slime . . .

SUBWAY HOTEL · SUBWAY HOTEL

HEYDON · HOUSE

SUBWAY HOUSE

CLOSED APRIL 30TH 7·P.M

AVENUE HOTEL

AVENUE HOTEL

Drawings of hotels.
Toronto Star, May 2, 1904

contest in the middle of the road between a man said to be "Professor" Brown and a pony which was frightened by a passing train, and which the crowd with yells and hooting, tried to make worse. The pony, jerking on the cord which held it, pulled the man over in the slime, and the crowd roared with delight. But the "Professor" held on manfully, and though drenched with mud, kept his hold of the cord, and he and the pony tugging in opposite directions, splashed off on their contentious way.

Meanwhile the police and the saloon-keeper, Mr. Francis Watt, had taken counsel together, and the landlord had come to the wise decision to forestall disaster. The supply of drink was cut off, and the four policemen under County Constable Brown, took their courage in both hands and went in to clear the place. This was an operation which took the better part of three-quarters of an hour and it speaks well for the diplomacy of the constables that notwithstanding the wild excitement and drunkenness of the mob, there was no actual fighting, there was a lot of "passive resistance", and the language employed would have filled a book. The ejected crowd drifted up the muddy street and helped to swell the ranks of the roistering crew who filled all the town.

One of the liveliest incidents of the evening took place at the Avenue Hotel. The scene there was similar to that at the Peacock, and there also the landlord closed before the statutory hour of seven. But at the Avenue there were no police — at least not at the particular time when a big Englishman was telling an acquaintance he got out of the bar. He was a very big Englishman — so big that one would have thought that even a drunken man would have remarked upon his fighting weight. But unfortunately for him, he was standing right in the path of a gang of wild young drunks who had just come out. One of these, for no apparent reason whatever, hit the unsuspecting Briton a tremendous blow on the jaw. So violent was the blow, that John Smith, big as he was, went down like a ninepin, and before he could recover, the gang set on him and began to kick him. Some cried, "Shame!" and the momentary diversion was John Smith's salvation. With a roar like a wounded bull, he was on

his feet, and in another minute he was knocking chips off those venturesome youths in all directions. He was sober, except for his fury, which helped him the more, and in a very sort time indeed his assailants were fleeing before him like the Philistines before Samson. John Smith, his face and mouth dripping blood, was after them, and pursued and pursuer disappeared in the muddy distance.

Earlier in the afternoon Herbert's liquor store had been closed, and there was no trouble there.

The Subway Hotel was cleared by the police under Chief Royce, shortly before seven. During the process, there was a brief fight, in the course of which a one-armed man received a knock in the eye, about which he raised a vigorous complaint, drawing the attention of the public to his affliction by holding up his empty sleeve. "Look at me — I'm a poor one-armed man," he said. A callous bystander suggested that the man who hit him probably thought he had two, owing to a temporary optical delusion. This did not mollify the one-armed man, though it pleased the crowd greatly.

The crowd, as the police pushed them from the doors, held out their hands in maudlin friendliness. "Good-bye, policeman, I'll meet you in heaven," said one man.

The last of the four Junction hotels to be closed was the Occidental. The crowds ejected from the others had assembled outside Mr. Kelly's house, and the leaders in drunken hilarity were booing the police, and raising a roar at everything which passed. For some time before the police came up the hotel front door had been locked, and an attempt had been make to keep the mob out of the back. But there some of them actually effected an entrance through a small window that was left open and though they could not get near the bar, helped to render yet denser the crush within. Chief Royce got the front door unlocked to him about a quarter to seven, and tried to enter with several of his men. Then the waiting rowdies saw their chance. They charged up the step behind the police, and though the latter forced their way in after a fierce struggle, a number of the mob got in, too, before the door could be thrust to again. Then those outside clung on to the door, shouting to

those within. It was twenty minutes after seven before the police could get the place cleared.

For some time hundreds of rowdy spirits lined both sides of the road outside the Occidental. Then a select party of them reeled along, shouting and bawling, till they came outside Mayor Chisholm's clothing store. The Mayor is well-known as a temperance advocate, so, with tipsy humour, the roisterers leaned in a ridiculous circle against the lamp-post outside, and favoured him with the ditty, "Glorious Beer", in the most awful series of discords that alcohol could produce. They followed this up with other lays of a more or less disreputable character, till, finally, getting tired and hoarse, they concluded with:

Good-bye, Chizzy, we must leave you,
To the City Hall well go;
There we'll get the by-law altered,
Good-bye, Chizzy, oh!"

Chief Royce, from photo on pp 22–3.

At least this was the closest approximation of their farewell which *The News* reporter could get.

The News reporter asked Mayor Chisholm his views on the disputed validity of the prohibition by-law.

"I don't think it will be upset," said the Mayor. "Our solicitor stakes his legal reputation on its validity."

Evidently, however, the license-holders have not lost heart altogether. They were not all available, as may well be supposed on Saturday night, but *The News* reporter got some interesting statements from one or two of them.

Mr John Harris, of the Subway Hotel, said he paid $15,000 for his license and the goodwill of his house last September, at the same time signing a ten years lease. "I paid spot cash, and it is all gone," he said.

"Shall you make any attempt to carry on a temperance hotel?"

Mr. Harris shook his head. "I have sent away all my boarders, and shall close up. I had 14 regular boarders, and from 50 to 75 to dinner every day, besides many to breakfast and tea. I don't harbour the least bit of hatred against anyone, but this I say, that I would not do what has been done to me, not to anyone. And I have every hope that me and my little bit of change will meet again."

Less hopeful was Mr. Lefler, of the Avenue Hotel. He owns the property

LEFT
Tribune, Souvenir Edition, 1901, p. 7

RIGHT
Leader & Recorder, March 26, 1903, p. 4

and said he reckoned his loss at $20,000. He could have got $25,000 for it last year, "and now I don't suppose it would bring $5,000". He also will close his house altogether, and says he has sent away eight boarders and four regular mealers and a number of occasional ones. He has been in the premises three and one-half years.

"They carried away $15 worth of glasses to-night," he said. "Some they broke, but others they kept for souvenirs, I suppose. At 6 o'clock we had not enough glasses to serve a dozen people. I could easily have taken another $50 if I had had the glasses. I never saw the like of it in my life."

They also took a number of glasses from the Peacock.

Mr. Chas. Kelly, proprietor of the Occidental Hotel, when seen by *The News* this morning, said he estimated his loss at about $25,000, the property being his own. There were eighteen boarders and six who got meals regularly, and all had been given notice to leave. He was bound to keep some of the boarders until the 17th of the month, and thought the chances good for winning the legal fight on May 9th.

Mr. Francis Watt, of the Peacock Hotel, will close his hotel and stables, his estimated loss being in the neighbourhood of $15,000.

All the saloon keepers intend to close altogether.

The police estimate of the number of the crowd who visited Toronto Junction during the day was between 8,000 and 9,000, but this was given before the later roisterers arrived, so that the number probably reached nearer 10,000. All day long the cars going to the Junction were full. According to Junction men, the rowdies mainly came from the city, though they were said to be considerably recruited from the CPR works. To cope with this unruly mob —

which was of course spread over the day — there was a force of only ten police, under Chief Royce, the local men being strengthened by several from the county. Had the crowd ever really got nasty, as a whole, the police would have been utterly helpless. As it fortunately turned out, the really dangerous disorder was confined to the few individuals from time to time, and the half dozen or so of arrests which were made during the evening were unattended by any organized attempts at rescue. It is stated however, that at one moment, while the police were on their way to the Subway Hotel, Chief Royce had to draw out his revolver and threaten the following crowd.

After the closing of all the bars the crowd relieved its feelings by walking up and down the muddy streets, roistering and bawling, for some time, but gradually melted away.

As if by a judgment on them, the streetcar service was tied up just as many of them were wanting to return to the city. . . .

A great amount of drinking from bottles was indulged in on the streets after the bars had been closed, no less than twenty-eight beer bottles and a large number of broken ones being picked up by the police around the corner of Dundas and Keele streets.

One man who was not in a condition to take care of himself had a gold watch and chain stolen at the corner of High Park Avenue and Annette Street.

MR. J. R. CHISHOLM'S STORE.

J. R. CHISHOLM,
Mayor of Toronto Junction.

One Hundred Years of Law in the Junction

by John Buchanan

O N OCTOBER 10, 2002, the law firm of McMaster, McIntyre and Smyth celebrated the centenary of W. A. McMaster's arrival in the Junction to begin the practice of law. The event was hosted by the current partners in the firm, W. A. (Sandy) McIntyre, W. A. McMaster's grandson and namesake, and James A. (Jim) Smyth, the husband of W. A. McMaster's granddaughter Mary. Except for overseas service during World War One, W. A. practiced law for almost 58 years, residing in the Junction from 1902 until his death in 1961. The law practice he founded continues to be a thriving general practice and a vital part of the present-day Junction business district.

William Alexander McMaster was born in Ekfrid Township, Middlesex County, Ontario, on February 7, 1879. He completed high school at Glencoe, southwest of London, going on the read law with Glencoe lawyer Alexander Stewart. He then completed his legal education at Osgoode Hall in Toronto, where one of his teachers was John King, the father of future Prime Minister William Lyon Mackenzie King. He graduated and was called to the Bar in 1902.

His first job was with a branch office of lawyer Donald L. Sinclair at 76 Dundas St., W., Toronto Junction, later at 26 Dundas St. W. One of these buildings was the Tribune Block, where A B. Rice edited *The Tribune*

newspaper until 1904. Sinclair's main office was in the prestigious Canada Life Assurance Building on King Street West in downtown Toronto. It's likely that he operated the office on his own for the most part and indeed, the city directory shows him practicing on his own at 26 Dundas St. W. within three years.

W. A. found lodgings a short distance away on Annette Street, west of Keele and, like many single men of the period, continued to live in boarding houses in a variety of locations close to the office until his marriage. Already active in local politics by 1904 as secretary of the town's Citizens' League, he told a Toronto *Daily News* reporter that, "there's plenty of board to be got here". He was referring to the closing of Junction hotels due to the local option by-law which came into effect on April 30 of that year. "Accommodation may be needed for the stock yard men," he said, "but that is about all the travelling public there is here. If the hotels keep open, we won't want to do anything [to provide additional room and board]".

Shortly afer the amalgamation of West Toronto with the City of Toronto in 1909, W. A. joined A. J. Anderson in a practice located at 936 Keele Street, "the fourth door north of Dundas" according to the firm's advertising. Anderson, who also came from Middlesex County, was sixteen years older than his new partner and had practiced law in various partnerships since 1894. He had served on the Toronto Junction Council 1899-1902 and was also the Solicitor for the town and the short-lived City of West Toronto.

Ten years into his legal career, in August of 1912, W. A. married Elsie Louise Whitmore, a native of Edgeley, Ontario, and the couple settled into the

handsome house at 144 High Park Avenue, which had been designed by architect H. G. Paull and built by Mather & Fogg in 1909. It remained home for the rest of their lives together. By 1912 Anderson & McMaster had moved to the Rowntree Building at the southwest corner of Dundas and Mavety. The offices were located on the second floor above Rowntree & Sons Grocers and Butchers. Although the official address was on Dundas Street, the main entrance to the office was probably at the side of the building at 225 Mavety Street.

War Hero

In April of 1916 W. A. McMaster was 37 years old. He had been married less than three years and had two very young children, sons Donald and William. However, at that time he enlisted with the 109th Regiment of the Militia and volunteered for overseas service with the 204th Infantry Battalion in the Canadian Expeditionary Force (CEF).

The 204th Battalion left Canada for England on March 26, 1917. McMaster was assigned to the 2nd Reserve Battalion on arrival. Although he held the rank of major in the militia, he reverted to the rank of lieutenant when he was assigned to the 3rd Battalion in the 1st Canadian Infantry Brigade (CIB) in early August of 1917. The 1st CIB had earlier been commanded by the Junction's own Malcolm S. Mercer.

A year later in August of 1918, McMaster's battalion was involved in the "Hundred Days" campaign that ended World War One and in which the Canadians were key participants, achieving some of their greatest victories of the war. However, the successes

W. A. McMASTER,
Vice-Pres. Y.M.L.C.A.

LEFT
Cameo picture, W. A. McMaster.
Leader & Recorder, March 26, 1903, p 4

RIGHT
Lieutenant W. A. McMaster (front row, right) with fellow officers from the 3rd Battalion, 1st Canadian Infantry Brigade in France during the summer of 1917.
Courtesy of Dorothy McMaster McIntyre

came at great cost. The Canadians suffered 45,835 casualties, almost 20% of the casualties suffered by the CEF during the entire war.

The Battle of Amiens was the Allied breakthrough that marked the beginning of the end for the Germans. As German General Erich Ludendorff would later write: "August 8 was the black day [*der Schwartze Tag*] of the German Army in this war".

It was on the first day of the Battle of Amiens, that Lt. W. A. McMaster earned the Military Cross. The citation for the decoration that appeared in despatches read as follows:

> For conspicuous gallantry and skill in handling his company. After the company commander was killed, he took charge, leading his men forward over 7,000 yards of machine-gun swept country, taking advantage of cover that he had but few casualties. He was thus able to support the attacking companies, and turned the tide in our favour. Later, after the capture of a village, he, with great initiative, formed an outpost line in front of it on high ground. His determination had great effect.

On September 8, W. A. was confirmed in his position as acting captain.

The 3rd Battalion was in the thick of the action on September 27, 1918, the first day of the operations at the Canal du Nord. The partly-finished canal was a key part of the German defenses to the west of the city of Cambrai in northeast France. Any attack on it would face furious resistance.

For his actions in leading his company across the Canal du Nord to a position north of Bourlon Wood, A/ Capt. McMaster was awarded a bar to his Military Cross, one of only 294 Canadian officers to achieve this double award. The citation for this decoration read:

> For marked gallantry and good work in command of a company during the Bourlon Wood operations on 27th Septem-

ber, 1918. Under point-blank fire from an enemy battery he pushed a platoon forward on either flank and captured the guns with their crews. Later, by good leadership, he silenced a machine-gun post. On reaching the final objective he ably consolidated. His company captured nine guns.

Ironically, he survived some of the fiercest fighting of the war only to nearly lose his life to influenza in Belgium at the beginning of March 1919. He was hospitalized in England for almost a month before returning to Canada for demobilization.

Returning to his law practice and family life, W. A. continued to prosper for a time. He and his wife had three more children: daughters Dorothy and Margaret, and another son, Angus. However, unforeseen complications in the partnership during his absence resulted in economic hardship for W. A. and the eventual dissolution of the firm by the mid-1920s. The breach with Anderson was a serious one, so much so that W. A. McMaster did not take another law partner for the remaining 35 years of his legal career, even though he practiced with his sons and a son-in-law for the most of that period.

Anderson won the Conservative nomination for York West riding in 1925 and was elected to the House of Commons with a 75% majority. He held the seat for 20 years, although with reduced majorities, until the age of 82.

Political activist

As a life-long temperance advocate, W. A. was opposed to Premier Howard Ferguson's proposal to replace the 1916 Ontario Temperance Act with the government-controlled sale of alcohol. The 1926 provincial election became a referendum on the

issue. The local Conservative candidate, former Junction mayor and Ward Seven alderman W. A. Baird, supported this move away from prohibition. He was unopposed by the Liberals, going so far as to call himself the Liberal Conservative Candidate. McMaster agreed to run as the Temperance Union candidate for High Park Riding, pulling in an impressive 6,809 votes to Baird's 10,653.

Later, in 1935, he was in charge of campaign publicity for Stevens Reconstruction Party candidate Dr. Minerva Reid in her bid to oust A. J. Anderson from his federal seat. At her nominating meeting, Dr. Reid, a popular school trustee, described the movement as "initiated primarily for the purpose of rescuing Canada's wasted youth from the desert of lost opportunity." The election, one of the most hotly contested in many years, featured a heated battle between Anderson and Liberal candidate J. C. McRuer, who later became Chief Justice of Ontario. There was also a CCF candidate, D. M. LeBourdais. Although Anderson won, no candidate received a majority of the vote, according to A. B. Rice.

The new firm

W. A. established his new office above the Bank of Montreal at 2958 Dundas

LEFT
W. A. and Elsie Louise McMaster with a very young Dorothy and her two brothers, Donald and William, circa 1922. *Courtesy of Dorothy McMaster McIntyre*

RIGHT
Campaign ad. *West Toronto Weekly, November 11, 1926*

St. W., corner of Keele. The practice would remain at this location for over fifty-five years. In 1928, W. A. was appointed King's Counsel. By the end of the 1930s, his two eldest sons, Donald and William, had followed him into law and joined him in the firm which was renamed McMaster and McMaster. In later years his third son, Angus McMaster, also joined the practice.

Donald McMaster joined the RCAF after the outbreak of World War Two. In 1943 the family received the terrible news that Donald had been killed in action over North Africa. His name is carved in stone at Soldiers' Tower, Hart House, with that of other men from the university who died in the world wars.

W. A.'s daughter Dorothy qualified as a teacher and took a position in Maple Grove, east of Oshawa. While there she met Roy McIntyre and they were married in 1942. Alexander Roy McIntyre hailed from Elora, Ontario. After graduating from Victoria College in 1939, he went to work for General Motors. Then in 1942 he joined the War Services department of the YMCA of Canada, serving with the "Y" in Canada, England and Europe. At the end of the war he took a position with the Dominion Life Insurance Company for a time, but found himself drawn toward a career in law. After graduating from the University of New Brunswick Law School, he joined his father-in-law and brothers-in-law in the family firm which was renamed McMaster, McMaster and McIntyre.

Return to Politics

On the retirement of A. J. Anderson, the Progressive Conservatives in High Park riding nominated W. A. McMaster. On June 11, 1945, he was elected to the House of Commons. High Park had been a safe Conservative seat for many years, but during the 1930s the political balance began to shift towards the Liberals, although W. A. increased the margin substantially for his party in that election. W. A. was 66 years old when he took his seat in the House. He stood for re-election in June of 1949 but was defeated by fewer than 500 votes. In July 1957, the *West Toronto Weekly* ran a profile of W. A. McMaster for its readers. "First in the office every morning, and last to leave at night" was the way the daily routine of the 78-year-old lawyer was described, a man of "keen mind, strong convictions, leadership and highest regard for the true ideals of life" highlighting his service to High Park United Church and to the High Park YMCA. W. A. McMaster died on March 4, 1961 at the age of 82. He continued to practice law until a few months before his death, more that 58 years after he arrived in the Junction as a young, newly-qualified lawyer.

McMaster McIntyre & Smyth

After W. A.'s death, the practice was continued by William McMaster and Roy McIntyre until the sudden death of William in 1968 left Roy McIntyre as the sole principal in the practice. Frances Bain, a founder of the West Toronto Junction Historical Society, was an employee of the firm from 1962 until 1978.

In the same way that Roy McIntyre's father-in-law led him to make a career change and go into the law, so too did he inspire his son-in-law, Jim Smyth, to make such a change. Jim had qualified as a Charted Accountant before he decided to make the change to the law. What motivated him, he said, was the example of how Roy McIntyre related to people and how he conducted himself in his professional life. Jim enrolled at the University of Toronto Law School a year before his brother-in-law, Sandy McIntyre, began his law studies at Queen's University. Before Jim and Sandy completed their studies, Roy McIntyre's health failed and he died in January of 1978. After their admission to the Bar, Sandy McIntyre and Jim Smyth became partners in the law firm of McMaster, McIntyre and Smyth.

Shortly after taking over the practice, Sandy and Jim were faced with the need to look for new premises as the Bank of Montreal had tripled their rent. The firm purchased a modest commercial building down the street at 2777 Dundas St. W. which had been used for a variety of purposes, including a kitchen-cabinet shop, a laundry, and a plumbing-supply shop. It was completely renovated before the firm took over in 1984. In the revitalization of the Junction Business District along Dundas Street, McMaster, McIntyre and Smyth were clearly "ahead of the curve". It is interesting to note the chambers over the Bank of Montreal have remained unoccupied for almost twenty years.

Sandy McIntyre also followed his father and grandfather in his involvement with the YMCA. In 2002, after over two decades of volunteer service in the Toronto YMCA, Sandy became Chair of YMCA Canada, the YMCA's national organization.

BOTTOM LEFT
W. A. McMaster Campaign Headquarters 1945. The candidate is at the back with the box and Gordon Cunningham's head is to his left. Let us know if you recognize any of the other campaign workers.
Courtesy of Dorothy McMaster McIntyre

ABOVE & BELOW
2777 Dundas St. W. then and now — above in May 1937, below in February 2003.
TTC Archives; John Buchanan 2003

Partial, Imperfect and Prejudiced: Profile of Alderman Wadsworth

Sideviews of the 1932 City Council As It Does Not See Itself
Globe & Mail, *December 22, 1932*

SINCE TORY TORONTO's Tory machine begins to need justification for its continued existence, here is William J. Wadsworth, President of the Central Conservative Association of this city and Alderman for Ward 7.

And the funny part of it is that William J. Wadsworth comes closer than you'd believe to filling the bill.

For Alderman Wadsworth is as likeable a man as you'd be likely to meet in a Masonic Grand Lodge, a County Orange Hall, a Synod meeting, a bowling tournament or a Conservative Party Convention. He is a sound citizen, a good fellow, a relic of national health, and the owner of one of the pleasantest dispositions in municipal politics.

Some day, unless something fetches loose in the Foundations of Civilization, W. J. Wadsworth will be a member of Parliament. He will, as sure as Provincial election days come around in Toronto and Central Conservative Association decides the results.

This is the second year Bill Wadsworth has been President of Central. You know what that means. But Alderman Wadsworth would rather not talk of that sort of thing now. Plenty of time, he says. He's young yet.

W. J. Wadsworth was born at Flesherton Station, Southeast Grey, forty-six years ago. They call the place Ceylon now. Miss Agnes Macphail, MP, lives there. Ceylon is the only thing that the President of Central Conservatives and Miss Macphail have ever had in common. And, at the age of one year, William Wadsworth's

prophetic soul made him hasten to sever that solitary bond.

The Wadsworth family came to Toronto in 1887, and moved to West Toronto Junction when the CPR shops went there in 1889. The next twenty-five years were ready written for the youthful Bill. 'The Junction', West Toronto, Ward 7, school, a job, marriage, lacrosse with the old Shamrocks, baseball with the Pianomakers' League; the Masons, the Orange Order, and an active hereditary interest in the West Toronto Conservative Association.

About the time West Toronto Conservatives became Ward 7 Conservatives, it grew clear that there wasn't much future in finishing piano actions. So Bill Wadsworth forsook music for city hall.

Naturally.

He was at the Hall for ten years. For the last six years he has been in business for himself, and as Alderman for Ward 7.

Throw in a dozen or so Masonic offices, the Mastership of an Orange Lodge, three chairmanships of three major committees of Council, and a campaign against parking in parks. And 'Central'. You'll get some idea of what has kept William J. Wadsworth busy all these years.

Out of mischief, too. For let it be known that golf is his only vice, and he hasn't got that badly yet.

His characteristic oddity is a quick little jerk of the shoulders. His characteristic expression is of unruffled calm. His eyes, round and blue, and his mouth — one of those rosebud ones — are set in quite a lot of face, either side and below quite a lot of nose. For the rest, his voice is soft, soothing and seldom raised in the Council Chamber.

LEFT
Controller William J. Wadsworth and his wife Ethel in his office at city hall, shortly after another successful election to the Toronto Board of Control, January 9, 1941.
Courtesy of Gordon Wadsworth

RIGHT
Ad for Wadsworth's coal company.
West Toronto Weekly, October 23, 1935

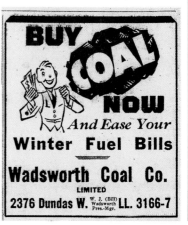

Motorist Captured at Keele and Annette

Another thirty or forty pounds and Alderman William J. Wadsworth of Ward 7 might almost be mistaken for Tom Bell, MPP for Bellwood. Not quite, though. The guile that lurks in Tom Bell's eyes is not in Bill Wadsworth's. Not to be seen.

Nevertheless, as President of Central, W. J. Wadsworth has established peace, or the semblance of it, among the warring tribes of Ward 4 Conservatism. He has done more. He has succeeded in pouring oil on the troubled Tory ladies of Wards 2 and 3.

How did he manage it? Diplomacy and fair dealing. It is the peacemaker's own recipe in his own words.

Ask Alderman Wadsworth whether he has ever cast a vote against his own party. He purses up his lips, shakes his head and a look of mild wonder clouds his blue eyes. Then he decides you're only joking, and unpuckers his lips and smiles a pleasant smile and says he's never seen any reason to.

Say 'socialism' to Alderman Wadsworth and he cocks an ear as though at the song of an approaching mosquito. Then, remembering Central's mosquito nettings, he uncocks his ear, smiles another pleasant smile and says nothing.

The present system of government we've got — this one with the Conservatives in power and the Liberals in Opposition — is the best that can be brought to light, Alderman William J. Wadsworth believes.

He realizes though that:
1. These are Strenuous Times
2. Big Problems must be Faced
3. Reactions are to be Expected

But he'd rather not talk about that either. He doesn't like talking; not very much. He got all the talking he wanted trying to pacify Ward 4 Tories. Speaking of talking; there's a lot of Council's time wasted at it, Alderman William Wadsworth thinks. Everybody knows when they come to the meeting exactly how they're going to vote, anyway.

Postscript

Politicians who don't talk too much have been remarkably successful in the Junction. W. J. Wadsworth was elected another year as alderman, followed by 11 years on Toronto's Board of Control. Wadsworth Park is named for him.

West Toronto Weekly,
August 1, 1935

Chased for miles at a speed up to 60 miles an hour through the west end of the city early Tuesday, a man driving an auto was arrested by Acting Patrol Sergeant Raymer and Constables Sandford and Humphrey, Claremont Street Station, charged with being drunk while driving.

In the chase which started at Queen and Bathurst Sts. and ended at Keele and Annette Sts. with the cars involved careening from one side of the road to the other, Constable Sandford had his eye cut, his head striking the car at one stage when he tried to jump on the side of the car.

Failing to understand why the man refused to stop when ordered and not wanting to shoot into the car or at the tires, P. C. Raymond threw his flashlight against the fleeing machine. Later he tossed his baton, but the driver kept on going.

"My officers said it was the most dangerous chase they have ever had in years," stated Inspector Charles Scott.

The car was sighted going west on Queen Street at Bathurst Street. The lights were out and the officers took up the chase. The man drove west and at Gladstone Avenue the police came alongside of him, ordering him to stop. As the police tried to force the machine to the curb the driver, police say, tried to crash their car. This kept up for some time. Near Humberside Avenue and Dundas Street when the pursued car slowed down, P. C. Sandford got on the running board of the car, but the man raced away at 60 miles per hour again, Sandford hanging on. At Keele and Annette Sts. the police forced him to stop. Instead of returning to their own division the police locked the man up in Keele Street station.

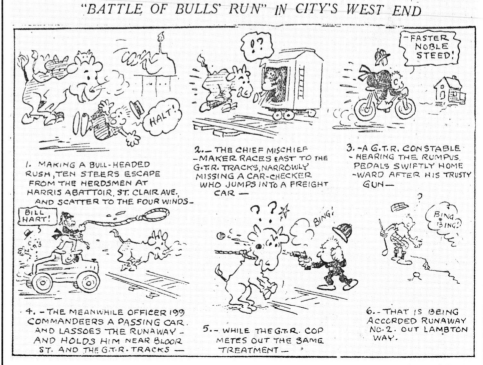

"BATTLE OF BULLS' RUN" IN CITY'S WEST END

Toronto Star, July 21, 1921

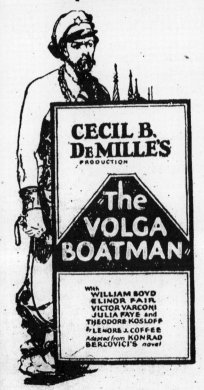

Showbiz Boom in a Stock Yards Breeze

by Rae Corelli, Toronto Star,
February 24, 1964

AROUND THE JUNCTION, they still talk about the time that Ernie Dalton rescued a US theatre group whose Toronto engagement was jeopardized by the second male lead who got drunk and went AWOL.

The Junction knew Ernie Dalton best as a furrier. But the stories that had come out of his shop near Keele and Dundas Streets had woven such a legend that people were more proud than surprised when Ernie got a frantic summons one Friday night in 1925 from McKenna, the costumer on King St. W.

The American road company had hit town the day before to do Henry Arthur Jones' "The Silver King", a turgid little item about a man who believed himself guilty of a murder he didn't commit. The posters plastered on the front of the Princess Theatre on King Street hailed it as "a sensational drama".

When the second male lead failed to show for the Friday night rehearsal, lead Hugh Buckler frantically sought out McKenna who hesitated only momentarily before turning to Ernie Dalton as "the only man in Canada" who could avert theatrical disaster.

Dalton read for the part all day Saturday and Sunday. On the opening night Monday, he gave a near-faultless performance.

By Tuesday morning, when the second male lead had been run to earth and sobered up, the incredible Ernie Dalton was back calmly selling furs in the Junction store so full of legends. The man responsible for them was a kind of latter-day Canadian Leonardo and the comparison is not really outrageous.

At various times, he had been the lead tenor of the Chicago Light Opera Company, a member of the Canadian Bisley rifle team, a member of the Canadian fencing team at the 1932 Olympics in Los Angeles and again at Berlin in 1936. He was a painter in oils whose work was exhibited by the Royal Canadian Academy in 1927. That same year he staged and directed the entire "Sixty Years of Confederation" pageant at the Canadian National Exhibition grandstand. And he became a member of the Canadian AAU Hall of Fame.

But it was always the Junction that Ernie Dalton came back to and it was symbolically fitting that he did. For most of his life, he seemed to be at a kind of crossroads and that is precisely what the Junction was.

Under the square clock tower in the old red-brick post office, the broad intersection of Keele and Dundas looked like Friday night all week long. For years, the four corners comprised the heart of the universe for tens of thousands of people who lived as far away as Swansea to the south, Lambton Mills to the west across the Humber, and Weston to the north.

The streetcars that ran to the Toronto city hall started at Keele and Dundas. So did the Davenport Road cars that went north on Keele and east on St. Clair Avenue. There were Lambton cars and Weston Road cars and, later in the 1920s, the Guelph radial car that brought the milk in big metal cans that clanged loudly in the frosty stillness of a cold winter morning.

For every streetcar line, there were a half-dozen roads radiating in all directions and down them came people in Model T Fords and horse-drawn wagons to shop shyly for tight-fitting, four-button suits at Gordon Sheppard's on Dundas near Mavety, or to

Wins Dominion Championship

ERNIE DALTON

West Toronto citizen and business man, who won the Dominion Championship recently at Winnipeg, and who was tendered a civic reception at the City Hall upon his return, and was presented with a medal by Mayor Simpson. Dalton is considered one of the most skilful handlers of the buttoned blades ever developed in Canada. He is planning to make a bid for the Olympic title.

LEFT
Portrait of Ernie Dalton by Archibald Barnes, from the cover of an exhibition catalogue of Dalton's paintings, March 1946.
Art Gallery of Ontario

RIGHT
West Toronto Weekly, June 6, 1935

42

search the shelves in Jim Rowntree's grocery, whose 20 delivery wagons were the sharpest things on wheels in the Junction.

Things were never the same for Jim Rowntree after that hectic carnival-like day on Dundas Street when Loblaw's opened their first self-serve store in Toronto. The crowds that lined up five deep reached the proportions of a Princess Theatre opening night.

The lineups were no less enthusiastic for the Saturday night hockey games at the Ravina rink where, from early October to late March, the Stock Yards, CCM, Goodyear's and the Imperials ripped each other apart in bloody pursuit of Junction approbation, and a young firebrand called Harvey (Busher) Jackson began attracting attention.

The game drew upwards of 4,000 fans — men freshly scrubbed from a day's work at the Heintzman piano factory, the CPR roundhouse or the vast stock yards and meat packing complex that stretched west from Keele Street to Runnymede Road on both sides of St. Clair.

When the breeze blew from the north in the heat of the summer, shoppers crowding the sidewalks at Keele and Dundas never had to be reminded of the Junction's most prosperous industry. Nothing that emerged from the two livery stables on Keele south of Dundas could assault the nostrils with the nauseating vigour of the stock yards.

It even penetrated the gloomy interior of Billy Duncan's ice cream parlour, next to the Sterling Bank, were kids gathered after skating at the Smith brothers' arena to sit on iron chairs around marble-topped tables and spoon up great gobs of ice cream at a dime a dish.

From the end of World War I to the mid-1920s, Hazel Corinne and Dan Malloy headed a stock company that played the old Beaver Theatre at Dundas and Medland. At least once a year, they did "Uncle Tom's Cabin" and little Eva went up to heaven a different way every time.

At the Wonderland Theatre down the street, an ancient mechanical organ wheezed an accompaniment to some of the most dreadful material ever put on celluloid, while at the Crystal Theatre across the street, Pearl White — pale but game — coped with evildoers whose serialized machinations could occupy most of a summer.

Summer brought the bands back to Baird Park, on Keele south of Annette, for rousing concerts atop a wheeled bandstand that was pulled into position on the grass by horses. Summer was also a time for remembering Mary Etta Cherry, principal of Western Avenue School, who fought long, hard and successfully to have the board of education open the playgrounds to children after school hours.

Western's pupils frequently went on nature hikes, and in the 1920s nature wasn't far from the Junction. They rode a Dundas car south to Bloor and transferred for the short trip west to High Park Avenue. At that point, where Bloor Street became a sandy trail and Dr. McCormick's mineral baths and two swimming pools did a roaring hot-weather business, the kids spilled forth into acres of wild flowers.

After Sunday school, townsfolk walked to the valley of the Humber where, for years, a steep hill posed a continual weekend challenge to motorcyclists, who would gun their engines furiously in rarely successful attempts to reach the top, while hundreds cheered them on.

But when it came to seasons, winter somehow seemed to suit the Junction best. The kids who skated on Saturdays at Town Park at Oakmount Road and Glenlake Avenue, tore home for lunch without even removing their skates. When they weren't skating at Town Park, they were playing hockey, and the Harvey Jackson fans at Ravina Rink had their counterparts at Town, who watched with admiration a young man by the name of Joe Primeau.

Unlike some neighbourhoods of that day, the Junction's social scale went all the way from nickel beer to vintage champagne. A few blocks from Fullerton's blacksmith shop on Keele south of Dundas, the Heintzmans and the McCormacks shared top drawer social leadership in huge red brick mansions that sat across from one another at Laws and Annette.

But it was also a district that encouraged close friendships and none was more enduring than that between Dr. McKerroll, the six-foot, 200-pound pastor of Victoria Presbyterian Church, and Father Tracey, the priest of St. Cecilia's Roman Catholic Church. McKerroll teetered around the Junction on an over-sized bicycle and when he died, no one mourned him more than Father Tracey.

Every April, attendance at Annette Street School fell off sharply, and Wes Fydell, the assistant principal, would know that the suckers were running again in the Humber River.

THE WEST TORONTO WEEKLY

THE "QUARTER MILLION DOLLAR" TRIO
(By Dave Kay)

"BUSHER" JACKSON   JOE PRIMEAU   "CHUCK" CONACHER

A value of $250,000 has been placed on these three players and in talking to Frank Selke this week it was made quite clear to the writer that they could not be bought for this amount but the "quarter of a million" was their actual value to the Leafs.

LEFT
West Toronto Weekly, November 21, 1935

RIGHT
West Toronto Weekly, January 10, 1935

Memories of the First Junction Movie House

A collaborative effort from the recollections of L. R. Bannon, George Cooke, Jack Dargavel, Edith Holroyd, Ted Langley, Greta A. Macdonald, R. M. McLean, Maynard Metcalf, Pat Mitchell, and Jim Turkington.

THE FIRST MOVING PICTURE theatre in town was the Wonderland in 1907, a nickelodeon on the north side of Dundas, just east of Speers undertakers. It was owned by Will Joy and not the least of its popularity came with the piano player who, between pictures, sang a popular song, illuminated on the screen by a reproduction of its cover on a coloured slide. The success of the Wonderland led to the opening of the Crystal Theatre on the opposite side of Dundas in 1910 by Robert Bruce. Not to be outdone, Mr. Joy followed in 1913 with the larger and more modern Beaver Theatre, later taken over by the Allan chain.

The Saturday matinee, originally three cents for kids, later raised to five cents, included one feature, usually a cowboy film, a serial, one newsreel and a comedy with piano accompaniment. Slabs of wood would be placed across each of the seats and children could sit on these slabs with their feet on the seats. Free popcorn was handed out to children leaving the theatre as a reward "to behave yourself", Joy told them. In fact, the Wonderland may have been the first movie theatre in Toronto to serve popcorn.

But R. M. McLean had a less pleasant memory:

"Saturday was a special day for me to go to the Wonderland Theatre to follow the serials that always ended with the heroine about to be killed by a fiend and the hero racing to save her. One Saturday I was late because I had delivered my *Pictorial Review* magazine and arrived at the Wonderland around four-thirty. I paid my five cents and since all the seats were occupied, I had to go down to the front. I was sitting there about two minutes when Mr. Joy tapped me on the shoulder and said, 'You have already seen the show,' and ordered me out. I protested to no avail, and he had me out of the show within minutes. That was the last time I ever went near the Wonderland Theatre."

Edith Shore Holroyd had one of the few "adult" memories of the Wonderland. She and her husband James, when they lived on Willard Avenue, took a coal oil lantern to light their way to an evening show in the days when the Wonderland was the only theatre in the area. They hung the lantern on a tree at St. John's Road and Dundas, where street lights began, and picked it up again when they returned after the show.

FOR A REFINED AND SELECT PROGRAM COME TO THE

WONDERLAND
AMUSEMENT HALL

1756 DUNDAS STREET.

We cater to the patronage of those who desire a highly interesting and educative entertainment drawn from the world's best motion pictures. High-class music from the Wurlitzer Electric Orchestra of seven instruments. Change of programme daily.

Open evenings from 7 to 10.30 p.m.   Sats. 2.30 to 11 p.m.

Ventilation a feature.   Attendants courteous and obliging.

W. L. JOY, Proprietor and Manager.

TOP
Toronto Sunday World, June 8, 1913

BOTTOM
The Wonderland Movie Theatre on Dundas St., ca. 1915. Ernie Cooke, the projectionist, is on the right; the number on the wall is 1756 (today's 2824). There are posters of actor Joe Ryan, and Hal Roach presents The Vanity Fair Girls in "Queens Up". *Courtesy of George Cooke*

The Beaver Theatre: In a Class by Itself

by John D. Thompson

FOR ALMOST HALF A CENTURY, from its opening in 1913 until its closure and subsequent demolition in 1962, the magnificent Beaver Theatre was the place to see movies in the Junction.

The design of the building was unusually elaborate for what was, in effect, a neighbourhood theatre, particularly as the showing of movies had only recently graduated from the basic storefront "nickelodeon" settings. The name presumably originated from Canada's national emblem, which was shared with another West Toronto landmark, the Canadian Pacific Railway.

The Beaver was situated at 1784 (now 2936-40) Dundas St. W., east of Pacific Avenue. As the picture illustrates, it was built in the Beaux Arts revival style popular at the time for major public buildings such as theatres, railway stations and post offices.

The main façade was designed in buff coloured terra cotta of a smooth glossy finish. The mirrored entrance doors were of quarter sawed oak. The entrance was located between two storefronts which had, for the time, unusual curved plate glass display windows.

The lobby and foyer had alternate mirror panels in terra cotta frames, as well as rouge-noir and Italian marble. The auditorium was decorated in old ivory and green, with a mural centre decoration of flying cupids. It seated eight hundred. Because the Beaver was built on a narrow 50' x 176' lot, the boxes extended along the sides, causing the main gallery to be placed 50' from the stage.

Four large dressing rooms were situated on the main floor. These were for use by participants in live performances, such as in plays, variety shows and musical performances, which often supplemented movies in the early days. Vaudeville shows were advertised from the beginning.

Earl McLean remembered an amateur theatrical group of men and women who gave performances at the Beaver after World War I. It was organized by the Eastern Star, the women's branch of the local Masonic Order. Their plays ran for a week. The director was Ernie Dalton, the furrier.

The basement featured a large tiled barber shop, presumably opened to the public. A mezzanine floor contained the manager's office and janitor's quarters. The second floor accommodated five offices, and a common waiting room with a stained glass window.

In the gallery (balcony) area the colour scheme was various subdued tints of bronze, while the proscenium arch and sounding board were heavily decorated in relief.

An early form of air conditioning gave Beaver patrons some measure of relief during Toronto's muggy summers. A large fan beneath the stage circulated air throughout the building.

Great emphasis was placed on making the building secure from fire. The curtain across the screen was made of fireproof material. The walls were brick, the roof of tile and gravel composition, the doors of fire-resistant material; an elaborate system of standpipes and firehose was provided.

The Beaver Theatre, 1784 (now 2936-40) Dundas St. W., as it appeared in 1915
Construction, 8 April 1915, p. 153

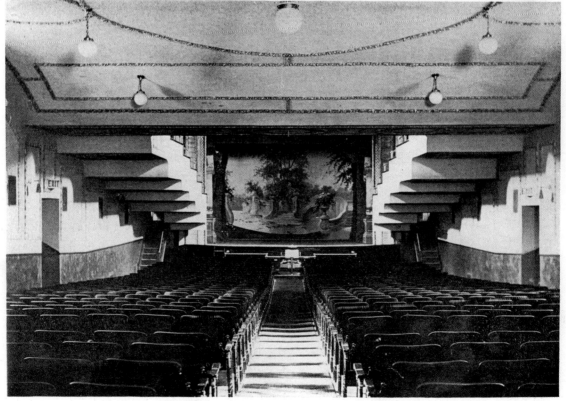

Two internal views of the Beaver. The first is from the stage, showing the pianist's box, the second floor balcony boxes and the balcony proper. The second view is from the back of the theatre, ground floor, toward the "fire-proof" curtain. *Construction, 8 April 1915, p. 152*

BEAVER THEATRE, TORONTO—TWO INTERIOR VIEWS.

NEIL G. BEGGS, ARCHITECT.

The entire cost of the building to W. L. Joy, owner, was approximately $60,000. The architect, Neil G. Beggs, attempted to use all-Canadian materials.

The following 1917 writeup from a local promotional pamphlet, *The Commercial, Industrial and Progressive Edition of West Toronto*, is indicative of the prominence the Beaver was designed to hold in the life of West Toronto — it's refreshing to see the strong belief held by the Beaver's owners in giving value for money:

In this age of hurry and business worry, no city or community is complete without some place of amusement and relaxation. This want has been well and amply supplied in West Toronto by the above named theatre conducted under the management of Mr. H. F. Brown. . . . Should you visit this theatre we are sure you will leave it feeling your time and money have been well spent. It has been the aim of the management of this house to supply the most refined and educational subjects to be had through the medium of moving pictures. Many subjects of the higher class have been shown. This showhouse is open every afternoon and evening, with change of pictures three times each week.

Tom Wogden recalls the Beaver:

It was a prestige theatre. People "treated to the show" for any reason had to go to the Beaver; nothing else would do. About 1930 my mother promised to take my brother Harry to the Beaver. She tried to get him to go to the local Major theatre, because of the long walk to the Beaver, but Harry insisted, and they went to the Beaver. Harry pointed out in his seven-year-old way that this would teach Mom a lesson — trying to substitute something for the Beaver!

In 1926 my father took me to see the Dempsey-Turner World Championship Fight on the Beaver's screen. It was silent, of course, but explanations were flashed on the screen between rounds. He also took me to see the rematch in 1927, with the famous long count. This special attraction would be shown with the regular feature, twice each evening. Double bills were the norm.

A normal program would be the Pathé News (or similar newsreel), a short comedy and the feature, twice each night. I believe there was only one show on Saturday afternoons. The Beaver admission was pricey, being 35 cents versus 25 cents for the lesser theatres.

The Major was owned by John Major who also owned the Mount Dennis, Royce and Rogers Road Theatres. He also owned the Texaco service station near the corner of Old Weston Road and St. Clair Avenue; it was operated by his son Jack.

During the Depression the Beaver, like other theatres, held china and/or silverware nights to boost business. This was the only thing that kept theatres open. In 1939 and 1940 the Dundas Business and Professional Association held "Prize Nights", donating lucky number prizes. Taylor's Shoe Store (next door to the Beaver at that time, still in business today at a newer location) donated two vouchers, one for a pair of men's shoes and one for a ladies' pair.

The three stores now at 2936, 2938 and 2940 Dundas St. W. Are on the site of the Beaver. No time was lost between the closure of the Beaver, its demolition, and construction of the three stores — apparently all pre-arranged.

George Cooke remembers the Beaver:

My dad, Ernie Cooke, was the projectionist at the Wonderland Theatre, until it closed. When talking pictures came in (late 1920s) the Beaver was the first theatre in West Toronto to offer them. Those theatres having a seating capacity above a certain number were required to have two projectionists. Dad became the number two projectionist at the Beaver.

When the Mayfair Theatre opened on Jane Street, Dad became the projectionist there. Just one man was required, due to its seating capacity. Dad finished his career at the Odeon Humber (Jane and Bloor).

The first picture I saw at the Beaver was the "Son of the Sheik", starring Rudolph Valentino. Dad took me up to the ticket taker and said, "This is my son", so I walked in free.

The Beaver was the high class theatre in the Junction. It featured all of the best films. The Mavety, behind the old Keele Street Firehall (Number 9), although the area's newest theatre, was not in the same class as the Beaver. The Crystal, on the south side of Dundas at Mavety, was the number two theatre in terms of status. The other West Toronto theatre was out at Dundas and Gilmour; it was called the Crescent, but nicknamed "the flea pit".

Epilogue

The Beaver, finally owned by Famous Players, was demolished in 1962. Frances Bain remembers seeing "Gone With the Wind" just before it closed, a fitting end for a movie house era. Presumably it was a victim of television competition, as have been most of Toronto's neighbourhood theatres. The demolition of such a fine building is tragic, equalled only by that of the local post office building and, more recently, West Toronto CP Station. Unfortunately, there were few voices speaking out for preservation in Hogtown in those days.

BEAVER THEATRE

DUNDAS STREET

TORONTO'S LEADING MOTION PICTURE AND VAUDEVILLE THEATRE.

Introducing several of the best and latest Films and the most up-to-date Vaudeville Acts procurable.

Complete change of program twice weekly. The Music is supplied by the most wonderful invention of modern times—a complete orchestra operated by a single player. Popular prices.

WATCH FOR THE PONY COMPETITION.

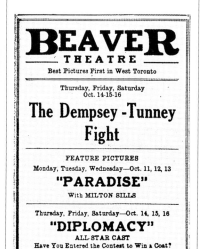

BEAVER
THEATRE
Best Pictures First in West Toronto

Thursday, Friday, Saturday
Oct. 14-15-16

The Dempsey -Tunney Fight

FEATURE PICTURES
Monday, Tuesday, Wednesday—Oct. 11, 12, 13

"PARADISE"
With MILTON SILLS

Thursday, Friday, Saturday—Oct. 14, 15, 16

"DIPLOMACY"
ALL-STAR CAST
Have You Entered the Contest to Win a Coat?

LEFT
Toronto Sunday World, June 29, 1913

RIGHT
West Toronto Weekly, October 7, 1926

Cutthroat Competition in the Junction's Theatre District

by Diana Fancher from research by Paul S. Moore

THE JUNCTION ONCE BOASTED five movie houses along Dundas St. W., if you count the Mavety, only one building removed from the main street. Four of them were in place by 1914, followed by the Mavety, with its grand opening November 24, 1919. And four of them were within a block of each other, the "outsider" being the Crescent Palace on the southeast corner of Gilmour Avenue.

The Mavety Theatre

However, in the highly competitive core of the Junction theatre district, the Mavety was the outsider, coming late to the scene and struggling constantly with its firmly entrenched competitors. It was also unique in that it followed the lead of Loew's Wintergarden downtown by having a second theatre upstairs (seating for 400), an elevator to reach it, and entirely unique to itself, the added feature that the chairs could be removed and the auditorium turned into a dance hall. Downstairs the more conventional theatre with a balcony could seat 900. Since the building had originally housed a transformer station, the large open shell was no doubt more amenable to this kind of innovative design. The less desirable frontage on a side street also influenced the design.

The Crystal Theatre

Robert J. Bruce's Crystal Theatre was the second of the five major theatres to begin operation. Bruce purchased the large three storey building on the southwest corner of Mavety in 1909, adding an extension onto Mavety to house the stage. The entrance was through a narrow storefront on Dundas, beside what was soon to become his hardware store on the corner. The theatre opened in December of that year. By 1912 it was doing so well that Bruce hired local architect Percy Wright to enlarge the addition. When complete, the theatre extended all the way to the lane behind the original building. The taller section at the rear, still in evidence today, was to allow for raising the curtain. There were dressing rooms to the east of the stage. Exits opened onto Mavety Street.

In 1927 Bruce rented the theatre to Ben Freedman, who gave this interesting evidence to the 1931 *Investigation into an Alleged Combine in the Motion Picture Industry in Canada*:

Mr. Bloom (of the Bloom and Fine, or B&F chain) told him, "what kind of a fool I was to take over the Crystal theatre under the circumstances. . . . Well, because the situation there of getting pictures was so hard." Later Bloom made him a proposition: "We will close up the Mavety and pay the rent out of the Crystal to keep the Mavety closed and then we would split the profits of the Crystal theatre between him and me and I would get a salary for managing the theatre . . . by coming in with him I would be able to obtain pictures . . . which I was not at that time able to get."

However, the deal did not go through until 1928, in spite of threats from B&F to make sure Freedman could not get any films — Freedman managing to subsist on RKO and Columbia pictures plus vaudeville until he could get a favourable price for the "merger".

Two years later Bruce took back his theatre, remodelled it and put in sound. Bloom approached Bruce and his son with a similar deal, but was rebuffed. A "price war" between the Beaver, the Mavety and the Crystal ensued, no doubt to the delight of their patrons. Adult prices were 20¢ at the Mavety, 25¢ at the Crystal and 22¢ at the Beaver in 1931, down from 30¢, 35¢ and 30¢. Bruce, however, continued to operate his own theatre during the early 1930s.

By 1935 only the Beaver and the Lyndhurst (on Bloor Street) were advertising their movies regularly in *West Toronto Weekly*, with modest ads that ceased abruptly toward the middle of the year, except for a minuscule blurb now and again for the Lyndhurst or the more distant Oakwood. The newer and larger Runnymede Theatre on Bloor Street sponsored a hockey team in the Mercantile League during the 1934-35 season and advertised special activities such as fashion shows and concerts. The Crystal was refurbished and renamed the Apollo in 1936, when it became an Associated Theatre. Famous Players had the lease in 1951.

The Crescent Palace

The Crescent Palace Theatre on the southeast corner of Gilmour and Dundas (demolished) took its name from the Crescent Line which turned onto Gilmour Avenue at that point, before continuing along Fairview and Evelyn Avenue to the end of the line at Evelyn Crescent. There was already a

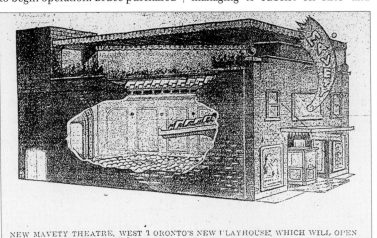

Drawings of the Mavety Theatre. *Weston Times & Guide, October 19, 1919*

NEW MAVETY THEATRE, WEST TORONTO'S NEW PLAYHOUSE, WHICH WILL OPEN THE LATTER PART OF OCTOBER—REFINED PHOTOPLAYS AND NOVELTY ATTRACTIONS

The New Mavety Theatre

Crescent Theatre on Roncesvalles Avenue at the time, making the "Palace" a necessary addition to the title. The theatre was likely open by the end of 1913 since a building permit had been granted earlier in the year to owners Abraham and Jennie Rappaport. It was uniformly referred to by all informants as "the flea pit" and occasionally as the "little garlic". No one who remembered the theatre had been inside more than once. Other than that, the only information available is the names of a succession of short term managers, including Mr. Rappaport himself during the First World War, before it was sold by Mrs. Rappaport in 1922 to Bernard Press for $37,000. In 1951 is was operated by Victor Boksew with 487 seats, up from 363 seats when it opened.

The B&F chain, better known as Famous Players, also purchased the Wonderland in the late 1920s, but only operated that theatre briefly before closing it up, as they had hoped to do with the Mavety. By 1931 the Wonderland had been converted to a store. And in 1932 or thereabouts the Mavety was also removed from the competition, until the surge in movie going during World War II led to its reopening in 1942 as the West End. In 1956 one last attempt was made to keep the West End competitive by refurbishing it and installing a wider screen. However, by 1958, all but the Beaver had closed for good. Four years later the Beaver was closed and demolished, leaving the Runnymede and Humber Odeon theatres on Bloor Street to finish the century, and to finish completely, neighbourhood movie-going in the west end.

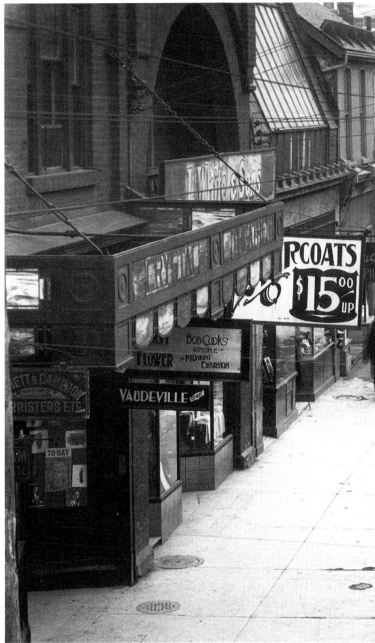

Crystal Theatre marquee, 2901 Dundas St. W., looking west from Mavety, 1923. *TTC Archives*

BOTTOM LEFT
The Apollo Theatre, 2901 Dundas St. W., late 1930s. *City of Toronto Archives*

BOTTOM RIGHT
The West End Theatre (formerly The Mavety), at 215 Mavety St. in 1954. *Toronto Reference Library*

Mavety Theatre
The Home of Supreme Photoplays
DUNDAS & MAVETY STS.   **PHONE JUNCTION 9222**

Thursday, Friday and Saturday, 2nd, 3rd and 4th
THE STAR WITHOUT A FAILURE
FRANK MAYO
In a Great French-Canadian Northwest Drama

The Canadian Northland—where trees and men grow straight! That's where Frank Mayo wins new screen laurels in "Out of the Silent North."

His love was so great he saved the other man for her. See Frank Mayo in "Out of the Silent North."

The majesty of a scenic masterpiece of Nature's pervades "Out of the Silent North." If you love scenic beauty, you'll see the picture.

AMATEURS EVERY THURSDAY NIGHT—PICK OF THE BEST.

Comedy and Weekly also, fourth episode of "Adventures of Tarzan."

Send the children Saturday afternoon. Ten 50c prizes given away. Only 6c.

FRANK MAYO
In "OUT OF THE SILENT NORTH"
A UNIVERSAL ATTRACTION

Monday, Tuesday, Wednesday, 6th, 7th and 8th
Big Special Holiday Attraction
Charles (Buck) Jones
The Daredevil Fox Star in
"The Fast Mail"
in a Thrilling Western Ranch Drama
ROUGH SHOD

ROUGH SHOD

IT'S A FOX PICTURE
Another Western play of distinction is coming to this theatre. It is a William Fox production, entitled "Rough Shod," and has the popular Charles Jones as its star. The story is from the pen of Charles Selzer, noted as a successful author of ranch life tales.

A GOOD FOX COMEDY AND WEEKLY
SPECIAL MATINEE THANKSGIVING DAY
AT 2.15—16 CENTS AND 6 CENTS

New Year's Eve
MIDNIGHT SHOW
BEAVER THEATRE

Best pictures first in West Toronto
Come and see the Old Year out and the New Year in

FUN   **MERRIMENT**   **LAUGHTER**   **BIG VAUDEVILLE BILL**

Twenty minutes of Jazz with the Big Jazz Band
YULE AND JEEVES   THE McAVOYS
BURGESS AND SILK   PARMENTER AND GALL
Favors, Souvenirs for everybody—Horns, Gazoos, Balloons, Noise Makers
Come and enjoy the fun.   Comedies galore.

PERFORMANCE AT 11.30 SHARP

THURSDAY, FRIDAY, SATURDAY, DECEMBER 31, JANUARY 1 & 2
"THE ANCIENT HIGHWAY"

MONDAY, TUESDAY, WEDNESDAY
"GO WEST"
With BUSTER KEATON

COMING—JANUARY 11th
"The Ten Commandments"
Return engagement by special request.

ASSOCIATED THEATRES
ALLENBY
Danforth at Greenwood—Free Parking
Gladys Swarthout 'Rose of the Rancho'
"2 Heads on a Pillow' Neil Hamilton
CARTOON—NEWS—ALWAYS COOL

APOLLO
JU. 5654
2901 DUNDAS ST. W.
DOORS OPEN 6 P.M.
2 SMASH HITS
OPENING TONIGHT
'LAW IN HER HANDS'
WITH WARREN HULL MARGARET LINDSAY
'PALM SPRINGS'
FRANCES LANGFORD SIR GUY STANDING

ARCADIAN
Queen at Yonge
Warren William
"TIMES SQUARE PLAYBOY"
'TOO MANY PARENTS' Frances Farmer
Midnite Show Sunday
COMPLETE CHANGE OF PROGRAM

BEVERLY
Adults 20c to 6.15
Mohawk 2121
SHIRLEY TEMPLE—Slim Summerville
CAPTAIN JANUARY
Reginald Denny—Gail Patrick

JOHN BARRYMORE IN
"The Sea Beast"
MAVETY THEATRE
215 MAVETY ST.

3 Days Only 3
Monday, Tues., Wed., Sept. 27, 28, 29

First Time Shown in This District

A PICTURE THAT WILL THRILL YOU FROM START TO FINISH!
NO ADVANCE IN PRICES   ADULTS 25c; CHILDREN 15c

Delores Costello and George O'Hara and other great Stars, headed by

2 Shows Each Night
7.30 and 9.30 p.m.

JOHN BARRYMORE in SEA BEAST

Another View of the Movies

by Henry Noyes

ON A SATURDAY, especially when it rained, we used to spend the afternoon in the balcony of the Beaver Theatre. The Pearl White serial was our favourite. One Saturday we would see her latest boyfriend about to be crushed between two walls slowly moving toward him. Of course, even in his dying hour, he wore his hair immaculately slicked back with bear's grease and looked like the kid brother of Rudolph Valentino. Our young hero was somewhere in the Far East because only orientals, we were led to believe, were capable of devising such terminal tortures — Fu Manchu and his like.

So we would stamp our feet when the bad guys appeared with slant eyes, and cheer when Pearl White's boyfriends with arm and leg muscles of a Tarzan came to rescue her from a fate worse than death. In the serial the following week, our about-to-be-crushed-to-death hero showed such body strength that his feet and hands burst holes in the bricks and he stepped unscathed through the offending wall to claim a kiss from Pearl's waiting lips. Orientals and American Indians were foils for cowboys and state troopers.

My early life in China — raised as I was on the back of a Chinese woman and treated with affection — made me question the truth of what I saw, so I had to develop a dual theory under cultural assault from Hollywood. There were orientals and orientals, Indians and Indians. Henry Roe Cloud dispelled a lot of illusions among my Beaver Theatre companions when he came to visit us in Toronto from Oklahoma. Great Aunt Anna on my mother's side of the family had adopted him as a child.

He was of Cree or Blackfoot origin in a community predominantly Cherokee. He became president of a mission college and eventually, during the New Deal in the United States, was one of Harold Ickes' appointees to the Bureau of Indian Affairs. We had a family and local people pow wow to hear what a living Indian had to say about cowboy and Indian films. My friends were impressed by the friendliness of a six-foot-four native American who wore a western-style sombrero and could handle the English language better than they could.

Another more lasting influence on the shaping of my ideas about nationalities was Anne Leung. My parents invited her to live with us long enough to complete her public school education and two years of high school to qualify for a nurse's certificate. So, for five years I had a Chinese sister who countered any possible racist thoughts among us four brothers and our friends. Anne had guts. She went back to grade school at the age of 19. Too large to sit in grade school seats, she was provided with a special desk and quartered in the aisle.

It was unbelievable to me, knowing Anne and her friend Jean, that Chinese were not permitted to sit downstairs in the picture houses in downtown Toronto, only in the balconies.

On one memorable occasion Anne and Jean were accidentally sold main floor tickets at the Palladium. When the usher refused to seat them, they began to scream until the whole audience turned heads to investigate the uproar. The manager rushed out of an inner office to enforce quiet. But Anne and Jean hollered all the louder. In a lower key, the manager apologized for the mistake at the ticket counter and tried to woo them back upstairs into the balcony with a few soothing words. But Jean and Anne went on shouting, and by this time some of the audience were giving them support.

"Aw, give the girls a break," a few youngsters cheered and clapped, just to get into the act. Oldsters growled, "Shut up, you fools."

The manager scuttled back to his office and immediately the confusion ended. Anne and Jean sat in seats of their choice and the show went on. That was the end of discrimination against orientals at the Palladium. It was also another powerful extra-curricular lesson I learned when Anne came home in triumph to tell her story, ending with the final punch line, "We fixed 'em but good!"

The Beaver Theatre as photographed by Pringle & Booth in October of 1930. *National Archives of Canada*

Bootleggers, Bookies and Billiards, but Mostly Dancing

by Tom Vella

IN ITS EARLY DAYS, the Palais Royale, the shrine for many dancers, was open six nights a week, winter and summer. The Seabreeze was open six nights a week in the summer months only, as it was open air. By the late 1940s or early 1950s dancing was only Friday and Saturday nights. Biggard's Milkshake was a very popular spot in the summertime as well, especially among zoot suiters in the 1940s. Biggard's was a refreshment stand located just west of the wire fence owned by the Boulevard Club. I might interject that the Palais, Seabreeze and Biggard's were on the south side of Lakeshore Boulevard in Sunnyside within two hundred yards of each other. Biggard's had a Wurlitzer in front where people would put in a nickel to hear a 78 record. They would take turns contributing to the Wurlitzer, so you could dance all day and evening at a very reasonable price.

One thing different between the Palais and the Seabreeze was that you paid one flat fee for the evening at the Palais, but you bought tickets for each dance at the Seabreeze. I believe these were called nickelodeon dances. Some people danced at both the Palais and the Seabreeze, in summer, while others would dance only at one or the other. Some of the girls would not be seen alive at the Palais, although many a bride and groom met there. One of its highlights was a jam session held at intermission. In the summer it would be held outside on the terrace, and in the cooler weather on a small bandstand in the corner of the dance floor near the fireplace.

Some of the bands that played at the Palais were Bert Niosi, who was a fixture for years, with Doug Hurley singing. There was also Boyd Valleau, with Shirley Harmer singing; Mark Kenney with Norma Locke and Art Halman; Boby Gimby, Ellis McClintock, Art Halman, and Maynard Ferguson. Maynard Ferguson was probably the best known, since he played with Charley Barnet and Stan Kenton [in the US] before returning to Canada to form his own band again.

There are pictures of the various bands and singers who performed at the Palais downstairs between the men's and women's cloakroom. They had a variety show on Sunday nights, circumventing the Blue Law by serving refreshments free. There was a boat company located in the basement under the dance floor. I guess that's about it for Palais memories, except to say men genuflected as they walked past the shrine, while others tipped their hats when they passed by automobile, bus or train.

Some other local dance spots were in Heintzman Hall, Ramona Gardens, the Silver Slipper (also known as the Dirty Boot), and Club Top Hat. Heintzman Hall and St. Paul the Apostle Roman Catholic Hall were open on Sunday evenings. The Toronto Blue Laws were circumvented by issuing membership cards, thus becoming private clubs. Heintzman Hall was on Heintzman Street (No. 28), just north of Dundas. Liberty Hall was on the south side of Dundas between Pacific and High Park Avenue.

St. Paul's Hall was located at about the same area as the present hall and church. I say about the same area, as the old hall and church were half underground and did not cover as large an area as the present buildings. Ramona Gardens was about two doors west of Beresford Avenue on the south side of Bloor Street. At the time I believe it was upstairs above either a Woolworth or Kresge store. The Silver Slipper became the old Club Kingsway, which was located near what is now Lackie Marina or a service station. When the old Club Kingsway burned down, a new one was built on the Queensway.

There's a story that Biggard's Milkshake was the scene of a brawl between men from the navy and zoot suiters during the Great Interruption. Zoot suiters usually had their hair grown a little longer and thicker than the average male and wore Sammy Taft wide-brimmed fedoras, suits consisting of wide-shouldered jackets, trousers with wide knees and tight cuffs, with pointed straight last shoes which were always well shined. Of course they had the proverbial gold chain which looped down to their knees. The girls had similar suits, but of course with skirts rather than trousers. The girls also wore wide-brimmed hats.

Some of pool rooms I remember were as follows: Freeman's, upstairs next to the bank on the northeast corner of Keele and Dundas, one between Quebec and Clendenan on the north side of Dundas, one on the southwest corner of Dundas and Fisken. There was one on the south side of Bloor, just east of Windermere, I think, named the Lakeview. There was one above Goody Rosen's Restaurant at Bloor and Dundas. Goody played baseball for the Brooklyn Dodgers. I believe there was also one just west of the Runnymede Theatre on Bloor, and one next to the Apollo Theatre on Dundas called Junction Billiards.

There were a few bootleggers or "blind pigs" in the area around the Dundas, Runnymede, Gilmour, Maria Street area. There were also a few gambling or bookie joints in the same area — one a few doors east of the Crescent Theatre at Dundas and Gilmour, another on the north side of Dundas, just west of Fisken Avenue.

The Most Attractive Resort in the Town

by Barbara Forsyth

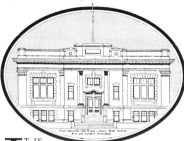

IT IS MOST GRATIFYING, viewing the situation over the great gulf of time, to discover that the Junction's library service has existed since 1888. The village was barely one year old when its founding fathers had the vision and wisdom to set aside money for the West Toronto Junction Mechanics' Institute. So uplifting was the place that the Women's Christian Temperance Union noted in an 1889 letter to the *Junction Comet* that they felt it was an appropriate antidote to the temptation of billiards:

> [Police] Inspector Archibald . . . tells us that in his experience in the City of Toronto, both pool and billiard rooms have a most demoralizing effect on the community. Could not the present Mechanics' Institute be made the most attractive resort in town, provided with first-class reading of all kinds, and various games of an innocent nature, so that young men would be encouraged to go there and improve themselves by so doing?

Mechanics' Institutes were begun in 1830 in Great Britain for the mutual improvement of its members in useful scientific knowledge. They attempted to educate all working men (mechanics) by setting up a library and offering classes ranging from philosophy to architecture and mathematics.

The quotation from the *Comet* shows that by the 1880s the original ennobling concept had been diluted. To reflect the change from an educational role to one which provided reading materials and recreational activities, the library had its name changed in 1895 by an Act of Parliament to Toronto Junction Public Library.

The location of the Junction's first library was listed in *Charlton's Directory of West Toronto Junction 1890-91*, under the heading "Societies" as being at 14 Dundas St. W. This placed it in the Campbell Block on the northwest corner of Dundas and Keele Streets.

The list of board members for 1888 reads like a who's who of Junction civic leaders and luminaries: President: Robert L. McCormack, a councillor and fuel merchant; Vice-President: Dr. George W. Clendenan, cousin of the reeve, CPR doctor and later mayor; Directors: David Lapp, councillor and chairman of the Board of Works, builder; F. A. Brooks, painter; Daniel W. Clendenan, reeve of the village, later mayor, lawyer, land developer; Dr. John T. Gilmour, MPP; Thomas J. Peake, councillor and hardware merchant; Rev. A. C. Miles of St. John's Anglican Church; Rev. James A. Grant of Victoria Presbyterian Church, and finally A. J. Reading, occupation unknown.

Walter Thring was the Secretary-Librarian from 1888-1893, and clearly it was a part-time job. The Tribune newspaper, dated November 22, 1890, listed the hours as : Open every evening from 7 to 10 P.M. Miss Elizabeth M. McCallum was the town's first full-time librarian. Her arrival in 1893 meant that the library was open longer hours — afternoons and evenings every weekday except holidays. A. B. Rice later described her as:

"Diminutive of size, widely known, highly esteemed in the community and a most efficient librarian . . . There was no printed catalogue and such an aid to library operation was unnecessary, for every volume with its location was registered on the tablets of Miss McCallum's wonderful memory."

By 1894 the library had moved its premises to the second floor of the Kilburn building at the northwest corner of Van Horne (now Heintzman) and Dundas Streets, facing the Occidental Hotel on the northeast corner, where it remained until 1908, when the owners of the Kilburn Block expressed a desire to renovate the building and charge higher rents.

In response to this, the library board wrote to philanthropist Andrew Carnegie, asking for a grant to build a new library. His response was in the affirmative, and the present structure at 145 Annette Street was officially opened on September 28, 1909. Rice also reported that Miss McCallum was worried that her job was finished when the new library opened, thinking that she would be supplanted by a man librarian. But the townspeople wanted her to remain, and so she did for many years.

Upon amalgamation with the City of Toronto in 1909, the Junction's civic employees all enjoyed substantial raises in pay. No less so for Miss McCallum. Her annual salary in 1909 was $120. One year later it was $420. She remained as branch head until 1917 and, because the library had no pension plan, remained in a lesser capacity until 1928.

The Most Attractive Resort in the Town is also the title of the Toronto Public Library's history of the Annette Street Library, written by Barbara Forsyth and Barbara Myrvold and reprinted in 2004.

TOP
West Toronto Public Library 1909.

BOTTOM
Ad for Walter Thring. *Charlton's West Toronto Junction Directory 1891-2, p. 158.*

Ravina Gardens: Gift of the Humber Watershed

by Diana Fancher

THE HISTORY OF Ravina Gardens park begins in glacial times when the Humber River delta extended along the shores of a much larger Lake Ontario. This area was under water at the mouth of the river. The ravine begins at the head of Laws Street, near Dundas, and extends all the way to Grenadier Pond. The watercourse is mostly underground at present, but still very close to the surface.

The first "users" of the ravine were wealthy local entrepreneurs who built large homes overlooking it. David Kennedy, a retired lumber merchant, was the first in the 1870s with an estate known as Lakeview Park. Kennedy dammed the stream to form a series of ponds which he stocked with trout, and also stocked the fenced-in grounds with English hare. Weekend hunting and fishing parties entertained guests on the 104-acre preserve.

North of Kennedy's land, this part of the ravine at the foot of Laws at Annette Street was known as "the Junction beauty spot", according to local historian A. B. Rice. In the 1890s three large homes dominated it: T. A. Heintzman's "The Birches", which still stands at 288 Annette Street, R. L. McCormack's "Oaklands" on the northwest corner, and Edward Lawson's mansion on the site of what is now the Annette Recreation Centre with Ravina Gardens as its grounds. Lawson was a tea merchant and land speculator whose business did not survive the depression of the early 1890s. He sold his house to Archibald Campbell, the proprietor of the Campbell Flour Mills and soon-to-be-returned Member of Parliament.

Some of the Ravina Gardens property was sold for unpaid taxes and picked up at various times by brothers Joseph and Jesse Smith, who were actively buying and selling lots in this area from the late 1890s. Jesse was a grain buyer and became mayor of the Town of Toronto Junction 1905-6. The brothers built a recreation facility which opened in 1907 as Ravina Park. The emphasis was on winter sports: hockey, curling and pleasure skating, although a swimming pool was eventually added. Separately-owned tennis courts were built at the foot of the park.

In 1952 the city bought the Ravina

property, closed the swimming pool and turned rink operations over to the Kiwanis Club. In 1954 the tennis courts were also acquired by the city. The rink was demolished in 1961 due to structural problems caused by underground water. The present park facility opened the same year. During the 1960s the houses on Annette Street were acquired and demolished, the bend in the road was changed and the Annette Recreation Centre built in 1967.

Ravina Gardens celebrated its 80th birthday as a popular recreation centre in 1997. It is entirely appropriate that a mural project for its retaining walls, a joint undertaking between the city and the local public and separate schools, features the history of the area it continues to serve.

TOP
The Lawson-Campbell House, built in 1887, demolished in the 1960s. It was on the site of the Annette Recreation Centre.
Courtesy of Anna Mirette Campbell Darling

BOTTOM
Aerial view from early 1920s, showing lower part of Ravina Gardens in relation to Annette School (top), Heintzman House (top left corner), and Humberside Collegiate (right). Glendonwynne Road is in the right foreground. Clendenan Avenue runs north-south at centre.
Archives of Ontario

Brilliant Hockey at West End Rink

"Ravina Gardens is one of the most popular covered arenas there is anywhere. Our League has played at Ravina for most of the 48 years since the Toronto Hockey League was first formed as the Beaches League on December 29, 1911. A great number of the early games were played in the former natural-ice rink and in later years in the modern artificial rink," wrote League Secretary-Treasurer Frank Smith in 1959, two years before Ravina Gardens was demolished and replaced by the George Bell Arena in Runnymede Park.

In 1925, just before the new artificial ice arena was built, *West Toronto Weekly* described the park as "four and three-quarters acres of land on which there is a covered hockey arena, a curling rink, club building and swimming tank . . . a large open-air skating rink is also operated".

In the days before artificial ice, the hockey season began the first week in January and finished in early March so that the playoffs could take place before melt down. Then as now, Toronto winters were unpredictable. Players had to be versatile enough to skate in "heavy going" (mush) if necessary.

Organization could also be a problem. In 1923 the hockey season began

January 3rd, practices along with pleasure skating two weeks earlier. The Victoria Presbyterians had just selected a coach at the end of December, and the various branches of the Toronto Industrial League (TIA), playing on open and covered rinks around the city, finally set up their schedule about the same time.

In 1923, two senior divisions of the TIA played at Ravina, one on Thursday nights and the other on Fridays. The local paper promoted the games as comparable to senior Ontario Hockey Association (OHA) hockey. The 1922 champion was local employer Willys-Overland.

However, the biggest draw at Ravina was the Saturday night double-header of the Mercantile League. Formed sometime between 1906 and 1911, in 1923 the League consisted of Gunn's, Kodak, Ford, and Canadian General Electric (CGE) — all employing substantial numbers of local residents — all four teams on the ice every Saturday night.

At the intermediate OHA level, the Victoria Presbyterians won the divisional championship in 1923. Their home games were at Ravina on Wednesday nights. St. John's Anglican won a divisional championship in 1923, but the weekly paper didn't note which league they were playing in or where.

Humberside Collegiate also played high school hockey. In addition to the "fast real hockey", there were just-for-fun teams like the Dundas Street South Side Clerks, who played the North Side Clerks on Wednesday afternoons (when Junction stores were closed) in 1923.

In 1924 demand for ice time along with increasing numbers of spectators resulted in plans for a new

artificial-ice arena and more complete, better-written coverage of the sport by *West Toronto Weekly*.

"It is not unusual that the west end of Toronto is solidly behind industrial sport. This has been caused by the fact that Ravina Rink is situated in the Junction, and the fans nearby have naturally become accustomed to watching brilliant contests at the west end plant," gushed the paper in January of that year.

Manager Norman Smith stated that he had been considering the proposition (for a new rink) for some time, but had reached a definite decision after a Saturday night double-header that started on perfect ice and finished on mud. He also declared that it was "a case of Ravina Rink erecting the plant or another party stepping in ahead," the paper reported.

Manager Smith, who hoped to build the largest rink in Eastern Canada, anticipated that one of the fastest senior teams in the OHA would be persuaded to play in the new rink and added that he was going after a professional franchise as well.

Meanwhile back on the ice, the Mercantile League had stolen Canadian Cycle and Motor (CCM) of Weston from the TIA to replace Gunn's. CCM, which actually manufactured sporting equipment, won the championship two years in a row, losing its third try in a 1926 play-off upset. K&S Rubber, playing at Ravina for the TIA, went on to win both its division and the overall industrial championship, the Toronto Star Trophy, in 1924.

The Smith Brothers, as the local paper referred to the owners, were not able to finance their dreams of glory that year, and the 1925 season was often played on soft ice. However, the teams and leagues were fully organized by early November. Advertising and press coverage also increased.

The Toronto Hockey League (THL) playing on Monday nights, seldom reported in the two previous years, was joined by a newly-formed local junior team from the West Side Athletic Club. Kodak's moved into the senior THL ranks, along with the CPR. The TIA, lacking any local teams, was assigned to oblivion by the local press.

1925 also marked the debut of the West Toronto Amateur Athletic Asso-

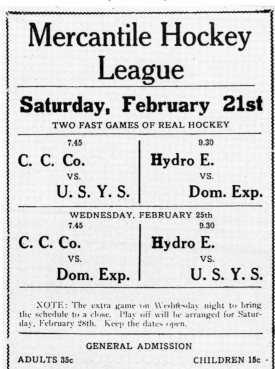

Mercantile Hockey League

Saturday, February 21st

TWO FAST GAMES OF REAL HOCKEY

7.45	9.30
C. C. Co.	Hydro E.
VS.	VS.
U. S. Y. S.	Dom. Exp.

WEDNESDAY, FEBRUARY 25th

7.45	9.30
C. C. Co.	Hydro E.
VS.	VS.
Dom. Exp.	U. S. Y. S.

NOTE: The extra game on Wednesday night to bring the schedule to a close. Play off will be arranged for Saturday, February 28th. Keep the dates open.

GENERAL ADMISSION

ADULTS 35c   CHILDREN 15c

*West Toronto Weekly
February 19, 1925*

ciation, which put together an intermediate OHA team to replace the now-defunct Victoria Presbyterians. They were narrowly defeated by Brampton for the divisional title that year. The West End YMCA organized Bantam and Midget Leagues to give "boys work" a place at the rink.

But the big news continued to be the Mercantile League, which had obtained permission for two senior OHA players to be on each of the four teams. Opening night featured Russian "fancy skaters", along with the Weston Boys' Band. Jack Wilson, manager of the J. M. Mounds Company, donated a silver cup for the team playing the cleanest hockey. However, in the third period of the first game, "play was going at such a clip that several players got the gate for being too strenuous.... Near the close play became very rough, but continued fast. Hydro's tried hard to equal the score (2-1 CCM) but it was to no avail."

The other two teams in the Mercantile League that year were a combine of Stock Yards/Swifts and Dominion Express. Penalty standings were reported in February and, although the actual number of penalties varied considerably, the total number of minutes awarded against each team was remarkably similar. Nothing further was heard about the "Clean" trophy. Kodak came back to play an exhibition game against Hydro. CCM won the title again but was defeated by A. R. Clarke Hides from the TIA for the all-industrial Toronto Star Trophy.

A scaled-down version of the original rink proposal was finally underway in the fall of 1925. However, the work went slowly and the 1926 season started a week or two later than usual.

Two games every night (except Sunday of course) made up for the delay, although it took a while to get ice conditions under control at the new plant. A "rolling puck" made it "hard for players to keep it in its proper balance" in one early game.

A bewildering array of interrelated leagues included Junior and Intermediate OHA; Midget and Bantam Inter Church League; Midget, Intermediate and Senior THL; the Toronto and York Industrial League (T&Y), formerly known as the TIA, playing two divisions at Ravina, and of course the traditional Saturday night double-header of the Mercantile League. Kodak returned to the league in 1926, replacing Dominion Express.

No surprise that the playoffs did not begin until late March, finishing in April. Runnymede United, the Midget champs of the Inter Church League, defeated the THL champs to take the city midget title. CCM attempted to finish another "brilliant" season, but slowed down toward the end and lost to Stock Yards in the Mercantile finals. A. R. Clarke defeated Stock Yards for the all-city title.

Attendance was low at the final game, in which Stock Yards had to borrow goal tender Claude Harris from their opponents! Harris did a spectacular job against his teammates, "as though he had been reared in the stock yards nets," and became Clarke's regular goal tender the following year.

In anticipation of an early start to the 1926-27 season, the annual scramble to line up teams and players in the various leagues was completed well in

advance. CCM moved back to the T&Y to replace K&S Rubber. T&Y double-headers continued to occupy Friday nights, while the "Big Four", now constituted as Stock Yards, Kodak's, City Hall (?), and Imperial Oil, continued to provide Hockey Night in the Junction as usual.

Perhaps piqued at not being able to take over the coveted Saturday night spot, T&Y made a big point of stating that, "this league is strictly an industrial one and all the members playing in it have to be bona-fide employees of the firms for whom they are playing. It is the only all-industrial loop in the city, outside of the THL commercial groups that this ruling prevails." However, since many if not most of the companies hired large numbers of not necessarily skilled workers, and virtually all of their team members had OHA experience, the distinction was a fine one. CCM's line-up included wingman Eddie Burke, who had left his Sault Ste. Marie team just as it turned pro for a steady job in Toronto. Another CCM all-star was centre Red Armstrong, whose junior OHA team had played in the Dominion championships. He had been working/playing for CNR the year before. Rearguard Pete LaRoche came from North Bay senior OHA to Gunn's and finally to CCM.

On December 11 the "Big Four" opened in the new arena, "crowded with perhaps the greatest crowd of all time," with another exhibition of "fancy skating", this time by Canadi-

LEFT
West Toronto Weekly Thursday, January 1, 1925

RIGHT
West Toronto Weekly December 9, 1926.

ans, with the Weston Boys' Band for intermission. The home town boys, Kodak's and Stock Yards, won the opener. Hockey coverage by the *West Toronto Weekly* approached professional-quality sports reporting; star players began to have their pictures in the paper (an honour previously reserved for politicians and obituaries), and the semi-pro status of industrial hockey which climaxed in the 1930s was fast becoming a reality.

Editor's note: This material was almost entirely gleaned from back issues of West Toronto Weekly, 1922-26. All unattributed quotes are from that paper.

Rave Review
Excerpted from West Toronto Weekly, *January 7, 1926*

The new Ravina Rink is one of the most modern equipped hockey cushions in Canada. Excellently situated, it is built of the best materials that could be obtained. It is not only solidly built and prepossessing looking but it is also fire-proof.

No longer will people go to work with a dislocated neck, the result of trying to obtain a view of the ice around a post.... A welcome sight to hundreds of people will be the radia-

tors generously placed around the building. Another welcome sight will be the seats. No longer will people tramp all over your feet. The seats are separate and lift up like the seats in school. In fact the students will probably think they are in school and be afraid to cheer for the team....

A new type of light has come on the market and will be used in the new rink. The spectators will not be able to see the bulbs so they will be able to see the offsides better than the referee. The roof of the building is to be white so that all the light will be directed onto the ice.

OPENING GAME AT THE RAVINA RINK
Splendid view of the spacious ice surface at the Ravina, which promises to be a decided acquisition to the many artificial ice rinks in the province.

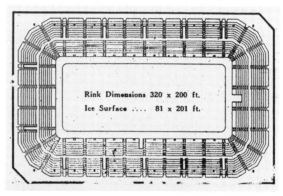

Rink Dimensions 320 x 200 ft.
Ice Surface .... 81 x 201 ft.

TOP
West Toronto Weekly January 21, 1926

MIDDLE
West Toronto Weekly May 22, 1924

BOTTOM
The Toronto Ravina's Hockey Club at the arena in 1928. The team existed for one year and no names were provided in source material. *Turofsky Collection, Hockey Hall of Fame*

The ice surface covers an area 190 x 80 ft., while the building overall is 258 x 138 ft.

A very interesting part of the new structure is downstairs in the west end of the building. The huge ice plant takes up nearly all one end. There are two great 40-horsepower engines which run the ammonia compressors. The ammonia is compressed and sent through pipes to the cooler. Here it is circulated around pipes which contain the brine.

From the cooler the brine is forced into large pipes which take it to all the various pipes which run side-by-side the length of the hockey cushion. There will be all together under the ice just seven and one-half miles of inch-and-a-quarter pipes.

The building is now rapidly nearing completion and ice-making will begin in a day or two. The Frick Co. are installing the ice plant and are practically finished. Just keep an eye on the papers and then when you get the chance make use of it and see some real snappy hockey in a real good rink that Toronto may well be proud of.

Rink in a Ravine

The long-awaited artificial-ice rink at Ravina Gardens was designed by A. W. Connor Co. and built in the winter of 1925-6. It followed all the latest trends in arena construction. Steel trussed arches, similar to a scissors truss, carried the weight of the roof without interior columns. The exterior walls were terra cotta tile panels between brick piers, and the gable-end walls were cement on metal lath.

The builders took advantage of the ravine. B. Patterson, who played hockey there in the 1950s, remembers that the entrance was from the parking lot into the upper deck. The concession booths were also at this level. Spectators then descended to their seats.

However, as a 1954 engineering report noted, the ravine was also the ultimate cause of the rink's demise. "There are indications that large volumes of water enter this area from the east side. Drainage from the north is also toward the building . . . on the west side . . . large volumes of water run down the bank and lay in the horizontal passageway beside the building." A high water table was also noted. The report concluded that the soil needed to be tested, also that excessive water under the ice surface must be drained and that a drainage system would be expensive.

LEFT
Ravina Gardens,
south entrance in
1952. To the right is
Rowland St. The
house of Joseph
Smith is partially
visible through the
trees, closest to the
arena.
*The Toronto
Telegram Collection,
courtesy of Toronto
Sun*

River Romance

by Diana Fancher

THE HUMBER RIVER has been a favourite recreational destination for local residents since Jean-Baptiste Rousseaux established a summer trading post at its mouth in the late 1700s. The Bâby family bought land beside the river for fishing expeditions in 1820, continuing their association with the river into the 20th century.

The Iroquois founded Taiaiagon even earlier, followed by French traders and explorers, the Mississaugas, and then the early English mill operators — Fisher, Scarlett, Howland, Cooper and Gamble. All have left their indelible traces along the river's winding course. Many are commemorated by plaques, adding a further historical component to today's pleasurable outings.

TOP
A Sunday excursion along the Humber River, after church of course, probably along the railroad right-of-way near the old street-railway bridge north of Dundas St, ca. 1915. On the left is Gladys Boxall (later Tizzard) who lived on Miller Avenue, and on the far right is her cousin Alfie Finley, who had recently moved to Glenlake Ave.
Courtesy of Ruth Tizzard Huff

BOTTOM
The Wigwam, on the west side of the Humber in 1916. There was another similar place called the Juanita as well. They sold ice cream and rented canoes.
Courtesy of Vera Downey Fitzgerald

The Belt Line railway provided a popular excursion route along the valley in 1892-4 and the Toronto Suburban street railway made it possible for people to picnic at Lambton Park, even going so far as to provide cutlery and tableware.

Footings for the street railway bridge and the site of the Lambton Park picnic area are still easy to find. Near these sites on Old Dundas Street, the Lambton Tavern, which provided a watering place for people and horses beginning in 1848, is now a community centre. Hurricane Hazel brought tragedy to the river in 1954 and illustrated the peril of residential building on a flood plain.

At the turn of the 20th century canoeing the Humber was a popular summer activity. Canoes could be rented along the navigable portion of the river south of the Lambton Tavern, or kept at Dean's Boathouse in Swansea. Corn roasts in the Humber River park system were popular with young people in the Junction during the 1920s and 1930s. Fishing continues to draw boys of all ages, even though the fish cannot be eaten at present.

Junction residents who grew up in the early years of the 20th century remember the river fondly, among them little Mary Norman, whose father Dr. Hugh Norman used to drop her and her sister Gertrude off to play at a shallow spot beside the Humber while he made house calls.

These photographs were taken of and by early Junction residents at their leisure along the river.

TOP
Amy Mills, age 14, Kodak Brownie Camera in hand, crossing the Humber River at Lawrence Ave., Weston in 1922. *Courtesy of Amy Mills Down*

MIDDLE LEFT
Vera Downey and Beth Agar saying good-bye to summer with the caption, "The last paddle with we two," in 1916. The Downey family, who lived on Runnymede Road, kept a double canoe at Dean's Boathouse. Vera's brother taught her to paddle and she always loved it. *Courtesy of Vera Downey Fitzgerald*

MIDDLE RIGHT
Opening day at the Old Mill Bridge in 1916. (L-R) Marjorie, Ethel and Mrs. Pugh of 633 Annette St. *Courtesy of Ida Reid Sanders*

BOTTOM
Charles Tizzard paddling a two-seat kayak on the Humber in 1918. Charles belonged to a rowing club in Parkdale and kept his own war canoe as well. *Courtesy of Ruth Tizzard Huff*

UNION STOCK YARDS, TORONTO, C

AS SEEN FR

ADA'S LEADING LIVE STOCK MARKET.
N AEROPLANE

The Queen City Mills:
The Big Flour Establishment by Electric Light

by A. B. Rice [attributed],
Daily Tribune, *Toronto Junction,*
October 7, 1893

ALTHOUGH QUITE AN informal affair, the visit of the Councillors and other citizens to the Queen City Mills last evening was an event of considerable importance, for to most of those present it was a revelation. It revealed a volume of business being done in our midst daily very far in excess of the popular estimate, while the interchange of views by those so fortunate as to be present must result in increased hopefulness.

Mr. Campbell sent out no formal invitations, except to the Council, but he made it known that any citizens who would be interested in the mill would be heartily welcome. Among those who attended were: Mayor Pears, Councillors Laughton, Heydon, Brown, Gillespie, Blundall and Wright, Dr. Clendenan, J. F. Holden, C. W. Batt, T. B. Phepoe, C. C. Going, A. H. Royce, R. C. Jennings, J. A. Ellis, H. C. Fowler, F. Wilcox, R. C. Eccleston, J. T. Jackson, F. N. Wallis, J. C. Willard and others.

The visitors were shown all over the premises by Mr. Campbell the proprietor and Mr. Enos Campbell his manager, both of whom spared no pains in describing the process of manufacture, packing, etc. The first place visited was the cooper shop and there some of those present, whose hair is streaked with silver threads of declining years, confessed that it was their initiation into the mysteries of barrel making. It is an interesting work – the making of barrels – and the company lingered long to watch the coopers

Archibald Campbell.
Tribune, Souvenir Edition, 1901, p. 12

deftly manipulate the staves and the hoops and with surprising rapidity turn out the finished receptacles for the matchless product of the model mill which these days knows no rest, but grinds unceasingly night and day – not slowly like the proverbial mills of the gods – but very fast although "exceeding fine," supplying the staff of life not only for the teeming masses in the great bustling Queen City, but also for the lonely fisherman down by the sounding sea as well as all sorts and conditions of men beyond the broad Atlantic.

Six hundred barrels every day!! Three thousand six hundred barrels every week!!!! Just think of the length of time that a barrel of flour will last the average family and you can form some idea as to the enormous number of people that the Queen City Mills are supplying with the most important article of daily food. But we are digressing. As the visitors went from floor to floor, viewing the fine machinery moving with the precision of clockwork, marvelling at the ponderous wheel of the magnificent engine and the expanse of the enormous belt which generates electricity that literally makes one's hair stand on end, and extracts a weird blue flame from the hand that is held near it, admiring the brilliancy of the incandescent light manufactured on the premises, noting the delicate texture of the silk through which the spotless flour is "bolted," in short noting the perfection of detail both of construction and operation of the model mill of this unparalleled age of human invention, it is not to be wondered at that the vocabulary of adjectives denoting admiration was completely exhausted.

After completing the tour of inspection the visitors were conducted into Mr. Campbell's spacious offices where, removed from the hum of the machinery, and the dust, the brain work of the man of business and statesman is performed, and it was at once apparent that the man's mind is not always engrossed with his enormous business and the affairs of the nation for he proved himself equal to a graceful discharge of social functions, and a "jolly good fellow" generally.

In proposing the first toast, "Mr. Campbell and continued prosperity to the Queen City Mills," Mayor Pears said that the prosperity of Toronto

Junction was entirely dependent upon the success of such industries.

After the assemblage had sung "He's a jolly good fellow" with great unction, Mr. Campbell said: "Mr. Mayor and Gentlemen: I desire to thank you heartily for the honour done me in paying this visit to the Queen City Mills and for the good wishes expressed. If the mill is beneficial to the town, and I hope it is, you have in a great measure to thank the Mayor and Council of last year. In looking for a site for the mill I did not think seriously of locating in Toronto Junction till I had met the Mayor and heard from his lips such glowing descriptions of the town's advantages and prospects. I do not regret the choice I made (cheers). The Junction's prospects are unrivalled. I don't believe there is a place with like advantages for factories in Ontario. The receipts of wheat from farmers here are very gratifying and far beyond my expectations. It is also gratifying to me that I have been able to find a ready market for the large output of the mill – 600 barrels a day. This is very important, for one week's product of the mill would fill an enormous storeroom. In fact I have found it somewhat difficult to supply the demand for the goods and I expect this state of affairs to continue till the close of navigation, when it may be expected to be dull for a time, but next year we hope to run the mill full capacity night and day, the year round.

"We are at present employing about 35 men. I trust that this industry, about which you have said so many kind things, may be the means of stimulating local business. Farmers are coming 26 miles with wheat for the mill. Some of them have never been here before but as they get to know the town we may reasonably hope that they will get in the habit of doing their shopping here. Next year we hope to buy coarse grains at our elevator here and stop all the barley, oats, peas, etc., passing down these roads as we are at present stopping the wheat. I again thank you all gentlemen for turning out tonight and for the good wishes expressed (cheers)."

Councillor Laughton knew of two farmers who had already opened bank accounts in town as a direct result of the mill being started here. This he concluded was an indication

The Campbell Flour
Mills, looking north-
east from the (Old)
Weston Road bridge
ca. 1920.
*City of Toronto
Archives*

that the farmers would eventually make the Junction their headquarters for business. Mr. Laughton also referred to the rise and progress of the Junction, the site of which was 12 years ago a wilderness.

Mr. J. F. Holden said that Mr. Campbell's fame as a businessman had preceded him and tonight's visit showed that the good reports had been justified. As a colleague on the High School Board he had found Mr. Campbell's advice good. As the means of conveying telegraphic advices between Mr. Campbell and his distant customers he found that the latter were in love with the goods. They did not try to cut down the prices. Their anxiety was to get enough of the goods.

Councillor Blundall after expressing his astonishment and admiration at the extensiveness of the mill, turned his attention to the pessimists who are damaging the town. Referring

to the oft repeated slander that factory employees do not reside here the speaker said that 60 employees of the Heintzman company are bona fide residents, while Mr. Heintzman and his four sons all have fine houses here and are large taxpayers. "If you can't speak of the Junction in encouraging terms, for God's sake don't speak of it at all," said Mr. Blundall.

Councillor Gillespie concurred with all that had been said.

Mr. R. C. Jennings, manager of the local branch of the Canadian Bank of Commerce, said that it was the mill that had led to that great monetary institution opening business here and he knew that other industries were sure to come. He was in correspondence with parties who will probably engage in the pork packing industry. His faith in the Junction was shown by his purchase of a home here.

Mr. Enos Campbell, Jas. A. Ellis, C. W. Batt, F. Wilcox and H. C. Fowler

each spoke in eulogistic terms of the mill, the town, its environments and its prospects. The sentiments were uniformly loyal and hopeful. Mr. Wilcox, a representative CPR man, testified to the enormous amount of shipping from the mill, which it is understood is represented by a freight bill of $200 daily.

In proposing the health of the Mayor and Council, Mr. Campbell expressed the hope that the personnel of next year's Board would be unchanged.

Mayor Pears in referring to the Town's affairs said that although the debt is large, it is not a debt that the Town can't carry, and carry with a considerable amount of ease. People slandered the Town on the subject of the rate of taxation, although Guelph, St. Catharines, Lindsay and other places paid 22 mills as against our 16 and had a higher assessment, and yet this town had made all its improvements in five years. We have fine waterworks, fire protection and sidewalks, the latter all paid for. People were inclined to blame the Council for the rate but it should be remembered that of the 16 mills, 10 mills is for debt contracted by popular vote, 3 mills for the School Board and only 3 mills for controllable expenditure. Regarding Mr. Campbell's wish re third term, His Worship said that he personally had intended to retire, but might change his mind before the close of the year. He was in the hands of his friends.

Postscript

Archibald Campbell was Liberal MP for Kent at the time this article was written. He got on so well with the town's leading lights, both political and financial, that he was elected MP for West York in 1901. He was appointed to the senate in 1907. Pears, however, did not seek a third term as mayor. Among those present, Laughton and Clendenan were future Mayors, Batt owned a planing mill, Ellis was the town's most prolific architect, and Phepoe was a bank manager. The story of the town's hard times during the depression of the mid-1890s is told by A. B. Rice in *West Toronto Junction Revisited*.

Part of Plate 3 of the *Insurance Plan of Toronto Junction*. Toronto: Charles E. Goad Co, 1903, revised 1912. WTJHS collection

Junction Bricks Exposed

by Diana Fancher

BRICKMAKING IS THE OLDEST organized industry in West Toronto Junction, dating from the 1870s. Before that, the earliest brick houses in the area were made from local clay, custom-made either on the premises or at the Brown family's small-scale pottery and brick works. Today, examples of the industrial product can be found on the exteriors of most buildings in the Junction. And, although bricks are no longer made in the vicinity, there are still unmined deposits of clay on those industrial sites.

The 1871 census for our area lists a two-horsepower brick making establishment, owned by the township, operating seven months of the year with six employees, turning out 400,000 bricks annually. In 1882 (the earliest year assessment rolls are available for York West), ten property owners or tenant voters were listed specifically as brick makers, employees of George Townsley being the most numerous. The Carleton brick yards, located north of St. Clair and into York Township, are well defined on maps of the period. The *Mail* newspaper reported that the average wage for brickmakers rose 15% that year to $2 a day for men and 75¢ for boys, and that there were 80 employees at the combined Yorkville and Carleton yards.

Only three years later, the five firms established in Carleton during the 1870s and early 1880s employed 85 people, and produced 8,000,000 bricks, and more than 2,000,000 sewer and agricultural drainage pipes in their yards alone. Booth and Pears, owners of the Yorkville and Carlton Brick Manufacturing Company, boasted "all the modern appliances", including steam-driven machinery, although George Townsley, who added a steam engine to his yard in 1884, was still the largest producer overall. William Pears went on to become mayor of Toronto Junction in 1892–3.

A report from the Ontario Bureau of Mines dated 1906 lists a Carlton West group of large manufacturers producing one to three million bricks a year. It includes: Wakefield Brothers, C. Mason, J. W. Lainson, James Lochrie, Edward Wakefield, J. Brown, and Thomas Norton. Mr. Lochrie was the largest producer.

Another group of smaller manufacturers produced one million or fewer per year. These were: Hinde Brothers, Lainson and Son, William Bushell, Titley and Frost, Smith and Crang, and the Brown Brothers.

The Brown family had by this time been in the business for more than 40 years; the Wakefield yard had been founded in 1873.

The Ontario Paving Brick Company

However, the most notable business, which produced a product much in

"Machine Gang for 1911 at Hine's [Hinde] Bros Lower Yard, West Toronto". *Courtesy of Doug Church*

Machine Gang for 1911 at
Hines Bros Lower Yard
West Toronto

demand at the turn of the century, was the Ontario Paving Brick Company Ltd., located on the east side of Weston Road, north of McCormack Street, and managed by company president William Pears. Unlike the other local brickyards, most of the raw material, Hudson Valley shale, was not dug on the site. However, the red clay component was undoubtedly brought from the producing yard 1200 feet to the northeast in which Pears had an interest.

In 1906, annual production at this large facility totaled 5,000,000 paving bricks for sidewalks, sewers and roads, as well as 4,000,000 building bricks. Paving bricks were used between streetcar tracks and also to pave the Union Stock Yards. The current Swiss Chalet on Keele Street has incorporated some of these bricks, found during the excavation of their building site, into the wall to the left of its bar area.

Among the most durable of paving surfaces, they were also noisy. Accordingly the bricks were made larger to reduce the number of joints per square yard, since it was the rattle of

wheels over the joints that caused the noise. The whole manufacturing process for paving brick, once the clay had been dried over the winter, seems to have taken about two weeks and quite a lot of machinery.

"Red enough for the most aesthetic taste"

Brick in the Toronto area came in two colours, red and gray, although orange-red and yellow are perhaps better colour descriptions. According to the Bureau of Mines in 1906, the raw clay represented an accumulation of re-sorted glacial clay. "The red clay is found on top of the gray, both being quite mild and containing a great deal of sand, remarkably free from boulders and pebbles". Junction brickyards produced red brick noted as being of "a splendid colour". The 1882 article on brickmaking in the *Mail* had gone so far as to say that they were "red enough to suit the most aesthetic taste, not even excepting that of Oscar Wilde".

West Toronto Junction, like the city of Toronto, had a stringent building

code, requiring after 1889 that almost all buildings be constructed of brick. The exceptions were outbuildings and private residences standing far enough apart not to be considered a fire hazard. Bricklayers were also much in demand; as many as 40 of them were temporarily lodged on Dundas Street near James Hall while building the half-block east from Pacific Avenue in 1888-9.

The variety of grades of brick available in the late 1880s was remarkable. The Heintzman house at Laws and Annette incorporates high-quality brick that has remained fresh and impervious for more than 100 years. Other buildings from the period are constructed of cheaper, softer brick which now requires special care and restoration. On Lavender Road a few years ago, the bricks of a small Gothic cottage were temporarily exposed before new siding once again hid them from view. Their non-standard size and colour (a mottled pink) made them look very much as though they were early products of a one- or two-horsepower operation.

"Standard construction gang on the Dodge Pulley Works job, West Toronto 1911".
Courtesy of Doug Church

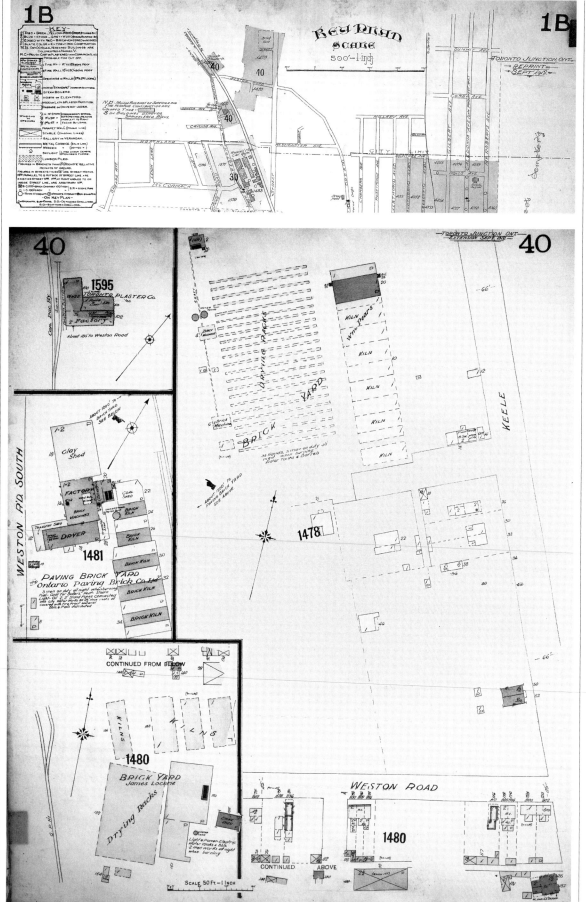

TOP
Part of Plate 1B (index) of the *Insurance Plan of Toronto Junction*. Toronto: Charles E. Goad Co, 1903, revised 1912. *WTJHS collection*

BOTTOM
The different premises of the Ontario Paving Brick Company in 1912. Streets near and in the valley have been much altered since. Plate 40 of the *Insurance Plan of Toronto Junction*. Toronto: Charles E. Goad Co, 1903, revised 1912. *WTJHS collection*

Driving for the Russell Motor Company

Excerpt from the memoirs of James Turkington

JAMES TURKINGTON came to West Toronto from Ireland in 1912. He was in his 90s at the time he corresponded with and was interviewed by the WTJHS and *Old Auto Tales*. He worked for the Russell Motor Co. 1913-1915 for 25¢ an hour, trucking parts and road-testing the cars in and around the Junction before final assembly. The driver would be in an open seat, the box body filled with sand bags, and a canvas cover used for the engine hood. Gasoline was 11¢ a gallon at that time, he reported.

In his spare time, during those early days, Jim painted scenery for a stock company that played at the Beaver Theatre and walked down to Swansea to watch a movie company filming "Indians" canoeing on the Humber River. For excursions to Lambton, he hitched a ride on a boxcar along the CPR tracks.

TOP
A Russell Motors car, perhaps 1909-10 vintage, returned to the company for refitting in 1911. It looks much the same as the cars Jim Turkington test drove in 1913 — a wooden box substituted for the seat and a box of sand on the rear for weight.
Courtesy of Ernie Brutzki

MIDDLE LEFT
Jim Turkington, age 21 in 1916.
Courtesy of Jim Turkington

MIDDLE RIGHT
The 1914 Russell automobile
Courtesy of Jim Turkington

BOTTOM
Employees of the Russell Motor Co. in 1915. (L-R) Back row: Mr. Blaine, drophammer man; 6th over, tallest in the row, Jim Turkington, trucker of parts; Harry Ward, trucker of parts; Bert Clisholt, machine operator; 4th over, Mr. Chuckhurst, machine operator. Front and centre: in the suit with light-coloured hat, Ed Hall, foreman; on his left Bob Loudsboro, tracer clerk; on his right Algy the errand boy; behind Algy, Mr. Boynton. Towards left centre in light-coloured coats: Sid Goff, machine operator and behind him Dick Corbett, machinist. Two left of Dick with a pipe, Scotty Davidson, machine operator.

Courtesy of Jim Turkington

Watt Milling:
The Pictorial History of a Diversified Junction Firm

by Diana Fancher with the aid of Roland Jerry, Norman Hain and photos from M. K. Stainton

THE HISTORY of the Watt Milling Company begins in 1898 with John Watt, Jr. Although born in Carleton and educated at the Davenport School and Weston High School, he returned to his father's Peel County farm for several years, before relocating to Toronto Junction, where he started a small business wholesaling hay, grain and feed. In 1891 he had married Mary Rowntree, whose family connections in area business and farming were no doubt helpful in establishing the new enterprise. The Watts lived on Osler Street in the early years.

Meanwhile in 1900 at Shelburne, Ontario, his brother Allan and wife Sarah purchased a house on Owen Sound Street and Allan became a hay buyer. In 1902 The Watt & Watson Company was formed with Allan Watt, John Watt and Wesley Davis Watson as the owners. Watson lived on Hook Avenue near the original "mill" on (Old) Weston Road. In addition to their Toronto Junction facility, the company also purchased a lot on the south side of Wellington Street by the railway in Shelburne, adding "lumber merchants" to their list of business enterprises.

When the Watt Milling and Feed Co. was formed soon after, the directors included Alex Hain of Toronto Junction and Mary Ireland of Shelburne. Finally in January 1907, the business was incorporated as a limited company, with all the directors, except for Mary Ireland, resident in Toronto Junction. The business, however, was located just across the railway tracks in the City of Toronto, part of it beside the tracks on Osler Street at Royce Avenue (now Dupont Street), and part of it across the street on the south side of Royce Avenue. The Shelburne facility was sold in 1911, after a fire destroyed the plant.

About this time "the firm went into the wooden skewer manufacture for the British market, and the enterprise was so successful that inside of two years . . . they were delivering two carloads per month . . . (to England) and had orders in their books for two years ahead. . . .", according to biographical material in Middleton's 1923 history of Toronto. The write up goes on to say that the American competition bought out their interest in that line at a handsome profit and the company went on to other lines of production.

In 1923 the same source describes the business as having an elevator and storage capacity for five thousand tons of grain, along with a lumber yard and storehouses to accommodate two million board feet of lumber, as well as a splendidly up-to-date planing mill and cabinet shop, modernly and completely equipped.

A new company office was built in 1920 and contained, "four private offices, general office, all finished in different kinds of wood . . . all of the woodwork used therein was manufactured and finished by the company in its plant . . . an attractive demonstra-

The original mill on (Old) Weston Road opposite the CPR station opened around 1900 and was photographed ca. 1911.
Alexandra Photo Co. (probably L. J. Turofsky)

TOP
Grain-storage shed used by Watt & Watson circa 1904, John Watt sitting in the doorway just before demolition, circa 1911. The CPR express building attached to the rear of West Toronto Station was built on the site.
L. J. Turofsky, Alexandra Photo Co.

BOTTOM
Three storeys of Carleton brick on the south side of Royce Avenue (now Dupont St.), opposite Osler Street, photographed in 1910. Note the '& etc.' on the end of the products list.
L. J. Turofsky, Alexandra Photo Co.

tion of the quality of its products". Presumably this was the relocated office at 43 Osler Street, since part of the Royce Avenue building was demolished for underpass construction in 1925.

By 1908 Allan Watt lived at 224 Evelyn Avenue, while John had moved first to Murray Street (now Louther Avenue) in York Township, then to 470 Windermere Avenue, later to Keele Street and finally to 185 Colbeck Street. However, neither stayed long at any one home. Wesley Watson moved frequently as well. This pattern of urban "migration", is often associated with small-scale house building, and it quite possible that house building was a company sideline. Or they could have been buying and selling the homes as personal real estate investments.

John's son David worked for the company as a bookkeeper before becoming a missionary. His son John

Lloyd, a stationary engineer and later millwright, worked for the firm until it began to wind down, opening a hardware store at Dundas and Burnhamthorpe Road in Islington in 1927. John Watt died in 1931. Allan Watt left the company to become a salesman around 1934, leaving Alex Hain as president to see the company through bankruptcy proceedings the following year. Although the company's assets included $64,000 in real estate scattered across the city, the collapse of the real estate market during the depression meant that the properties could not be sold.

The Chevrolet interval

A particularly interesting sideline developed by the company around 1915 was, according to Roland Jerry, the production of Chevrolet car bodies. During that year the legendary W. C. Durant, who later formed General Motors, issued a flurry of news

releases claiming that a new Canadian plant would produce 15,000 Chevrolet 490s in the first year.

Durant's Canadian activities radiated from extensive production facilities located on the west side of Churchill (now Perth) Avenue immediately north of the CPR crossing. The substantial site, originally known as the Dominion Carriage Co. Ltd., consisted of two buildings erected earlier for the production of horse-drawn vehicles. Watt Milling Co., with its output of dressed lumber, woodwork, doors and trim was only two blocks away, sharing its buildings with Toronto Auto Top and Body. These buildings had precisely the sort of layout needed for the quantity output of the open-touring-car bodies of the day.

Norman Hain recently commented that the two-storey structure was identified for years as "the trim shop". Hain recalled that his grandfather Alex and

Subway construction in 1925 at Dundas and Dupont streets removed not only the level crossing, but two sections of the Watt building, as evidenced by their sign. The site is currently occupied by Viceroy Rubber.
Arthur S. Goss, City of Toronto Archives

his father John often remarked on the "Chevrolet interval" when this was a major activity involving many workers and a large part of the plant.

"I never thought to ask for more details, as I suppose I simply assumed they were bodies for Chevrolet and General Motors at Oshawa," Hain commented, "I wish I had, it all intrigues me now". One of his uncles, the late Dr. Cecil Hain, recalled that as a youngster of 10 or 12 he would watch horse-drawn wagons and drays leaving the Watt Milling property laden with open-touring-car bodies. They proceeded along Osler Street and turned off at Pelham Avenue. "The only place they could have been going was to the Dominion Carriage plant a block or so away," added Hain.

However, the production of Chevrolet 490s in the Junction was short-lived, a few hundred cars perhaps, which ended late in 1915 when the Oshawa plant went into production. As it happened, production began so quickly that tooling and facilities were most probably drawn from the Dominion Carriage plant

with bodies from Toronto Auto Top and Body, at least initially, until Oshawa could produce its own. It is also possible that Toronto Auto Top

and Body and Watt Milling produced bodies used by the Russell Motor Car Co. or by the Ford Motor Company of Canada at its Toronto assembly plant.

TOP
Advertisment.
The Shelburne Economist, March 2, 1911, p.8.

BOTTOM
The west side of Osler St. north of Royce Ave. (now Dupont St.) viewed from West Toronto CPR station in 1910, shows just how much the "& etc." included, namely automobile bodies, tops and trim. Part of the site has recently been converted to industrial lofts, with row houses built on the remainder.
L. J. Turofsky, Alexandra Photo Co.

=== THE ===

Watt Milling & Feed Co.

Manufacturers of and Dealers in all kinds of
Building Material, such as

Lumber, Lath, Shingles, Etc.

HAVING more than doubled the size of our factory limits, putting in a large up-to-date dry-kiln and new machinery, we have now the largest and most up-to-date factory between the lakes. We are prepared to furnish all kinds of kiln dried building material.

¶ All outside customers desiring to use their own material can have it kiln dried and properly manufactured at very moderate prices. Satisfaction guaranteed.

¶ Those intending to build would do well to place their order with us as early as possible and avoid the rush.

WANTED—A quantity of Cedar Posts and Shingle and Lath Timber.

Summer at the Doll Factory

by Diana Fancher

DOLLS AND DOLL CLOTHES bring back happy childhood memories for many women. But few remember them the way Ida Reid Sanders did, as a source of employment, adventure, and a trip to the Police Magistrate's Court.

Ever since Ida was born in 1904, Mrs. Reid had been buying, dressing and even making dolls for Ida, her cousins in New Brunswick and friends of the family who also lived in the Junction. She would go to Eaton's after Christmas to buy returned dolls for 50 cents to freshen up and redress for the next year. One Christmas Ida found that Santa had left seven dolls under the tree.

Ida herself learned to make doll clothes as a very young girl with help from a cousin who lived with the family and worked in the millinery department at Eaton's. Her dolls had fur collared coats and fancy ribbons on their dresses. The Eaton Beauty dolls that normally sold for $1.00 only had ruffles and trim on the front of their dresses, not the back, Ida remembered with disapproval.

But World War I ended the Eaton Beauty and the lovely china dolls with glass eyes that had been made in Germany. Lots of men, including Ida's father Arthur Reid, were making good money "shell busting" on swing shifts in the munitions factories, but dolls for Christmas were in short supply by 1917.

At this point Junction resident Bertram H. Eaton, a leather worker by trade, stepped in to fill the gap, with the help of Harry Ziegesman and an unknown seamstress. Early in the summer a sign went up in the papered-over window at 1907 (now 3047) Dundas St. W.: HELP WANTED, BOYS AND GIRLS, EASY WORK. Ida's older brother Jack was looking for a way to earn extra money, since he was small for 14 and found that golf caddying or fruit picking was exhausting and not particularly well paid. He and his friend Wilf Robinson applied and were hired immediately, reporting back that there were jobs for Ida and younger brother Bob, if they were interested. Ida was the only girl who turned up the first day, so she persuaded Hilda Ricketts and a girl named Lily to come to work with her the next day.

"There were papier mâché heads on the dolls and they lacquered them," Ida remembered. "The smell of the lacquer was awful, it really was. It took you the whole rest of the day after you quit work to get it out of your nose. This last girl, Lily, I didn't know her very well, she was a tender flower and couldn't take the smell of it.

"And then it was very noisy, there was a woman who ran the power machine that made the clothes. It jiggled the floor, and oh, it was noisy! My mother wouldn't have let me stay there if I'd told her the songs that woman sang while she was running her machine — all dirty parodies on songs that were popular at the time."

Jack and the boys processed the dolls, while Ida and Hilda looked after the strings of doll clothes that "were being turned out of the power machine like sausages" as they piled up on the floor. "We cut them apart, tied the threads, turned them right side out, pressed them with our hands and made them into bundles of a dozen. Jump suits for the boy dolls, panties and dresses for the girls. We were paid by the bundle, strictly piecework, it was a sweatshop, very hot that summer," Ida remembered. "Their faces were painted on, so shiny, so lacquered, staring into space with the silliest expression. They had cotton bodies stuffed with excelsior, the hands and feet were papier mâché and the shoes were painted, no toes."

"I enjoyed it because I was out in the world," said Ida with a twinkle in her eye, "It was exciting! The money at the end of the week was great, I didn't have an allowance."

Excitement picked up when the provincial factory inspector came to call. "We were all working and these men came in, three of them. One questioned Hilda and myself, another man questioned the boys in the back and another man talked to the owner. Of course when the inspector asked me how old I was, I was pleased to tell him.

He was nice, I wasn't afraid or anything."

Unfortunately for Eaton & Ziegesman, the provincial trades and labour office had picked 1917 to crack down on the child labour law. In order to check any possible increases, the bureau launched 12 court cases, none of which were actually prosecuted. The Superior Toy Company was duly charged with obstructing an inspector, no doubt the reason three men eventually gained entrance to this very small factory. They were also charged with employing child labour.

Jack and Ida were thrilled when several family members were summonsed to appear at the Police Magistrate's Court downtown at city hall, but young Bob cried all the way in on the streetcar, clutching his mother's hand. Hilda and her mother as well as Wilf and his mother also came along. At that time it was possible to shift a fine onto the parents of underaged workers, if it could be proved that they knowingly consented to the employment of children under 14. However, the owners apparently decided that line of defence was not worthwhile.

Jack and Ida were disappointed that no one was called to testify. "We wanted more drama," Ida confessed. The owner was fined $30 after being questioned briefly and everyone went home. "Jack and Wilf were all right, they were 14," Ida noted.

Soon after the trial Jack and Wilf came back again to ask if the girls would do the work at home, only a few blocks down the street at Dundas and St. John's Road. So they brought the bundles of doll clothes along in plain brown wrappers and "we all did it, my

A family photo in the summery backyard of the Reid home at 3237 Dundas St. W. (L-R) Ida, Mrs. Sarah, Mr. Arthur and Walter "Bun" Reid ca.1918.
Courtesy of Ida Reid Sanders

mother did it. She did lots of sewing, so she had lots of scissors and everything and everyone came to our house. There were eight of us altogether, we had a regular factory in our back kitchen. My mother made the best root beer in the summer, so we had no trouble getting people to come."

"The money was great, the only other job we could find was picking berries at Pellatt's Farm and you worked all day for very little." The patriotic appeal to Ontario's youth for help with getting in the crops, which was initiated by the Trades and Labour Bureau that year, fell on a few deaf ears. But the doll factory soon folded and it was back to berry picking for the girls next summer.

In later years these youthful partners in crime, eager to spend the summer in a fume-filled sweatshop to earn their pocket money, found more profitable legal pursuits. Jack Reid left school permanently that year and eventually became a top salesman for International Harvester. Wilf Robinson went to Detroit as a mechanic for Fisher Body and looked prosperous on return visits, according to Ida. Hilda Ricketts found a job at Woolworth's when she was 14, ending her career as a buyer to marry a very wealthy man. Shy Bob Reid worked on Heintzman pianos.

Ida herself was first in her class at Humberside Collegiate in 1918, but had to drop out in 1920 to look after her mother, who was very ill. She was a legal secretary at Anderson & McMaster during the 1920s, then married and lived at 9 Clendenan Avenue until her home was undermined by subway construction. The TTC exchanged it for another house in Etobicoke in 1970, where she told this amusing story on a hot summer afternoon.

Ethel (left) and Marjorie Pugh with their dolls in the garden at 633 Annette St. circa 1909. Their father built the doll house; Mrs. Pugh made the curtains and rugs. *Courtesy of Ida Reid Sanders*

The New Market Was Open Today

Toronto Daily Star, July 28, 1903

WITH A WONDERFUL amount of bustle the Union Stock Yards at Toronto Junction was formally opened for business this morning. About 150 cattle-dealers were on hand, and the number of cattle handled was exceedingly large. By 10:30 o'clock 111 cars of stock were in the yards, and 10 more had just arrived, and it was said that more cars would keep on coming all day. It was also said that more cars would have been on hand for the opening had the shippers at outside points been able to get CPR cars. Manager Hodgson estimated that at 10 o'clock there were over 2,000 cattle, 500 sheep, and 200 hogs in the yards.

Several of the prominent cattle men when interviewed said that today at the Union Stock Yards eclipsed even the best days at the city market. . . .

At the City Yards

While there was a stir at the Union Stock Yards, there was comparative quiet at the city yards. There were but 37 loads of cattle there. Five other loads went through. The 37 loads averaged 23 cattle to the car, making in all 851 head on hand. These were bought up quickly and more could have been sold had they been on hand. The news of Mr. Levack's leaving the city market and casting in his lot with the Junction yards caused much comment. . . .

The dealers at the city yards generally expressed the view that the managers of the junction yards had been gathering cattle for weeks in order to make a big spread at the opening and that the first big showing would not be maintained, that there would be a reaction, and that the city had no reason for alarm.

It is openly acknowledged around the City Hall that the departure of Mr. Wm. Levack from the western cattle market to the Union Stock Yards at Toronto Junction is a distinct loss to the city market, because Mr. Levack is the largest exporter and dealer in cattle in the Province. He purchases cattle from upwards of fifty different cattle raisers, and will now have his cattle shipped directly to the Junction market.

Notwithstanding this loss to the city market, however, Commissioner Fleming is confident that if his recommendations are carried out it will only be a matter of a few months until the city market will have the call, and although cattle men who may remove to the Junction may order their cattle to be shipped direct there, the extra inducements the city can offer will afford such a savings to the cattle raisers that they will ship to the city market, and despite the fact that the dealers may have their headquarters at the Junction, they will be compelled to come to the city market to do their business. Mr. Fleming believes

that the city market will face its strongest opposition during the next few weeks, now that it is known that the city intends to put up a fight to retain the trade and all that is needed now is confidence in the management of the market and the city will come out all right.

Civic Committee Meets

The Civic Property Committee met this afternoon to consider the recommendation of the Commissioner of Assessment and Property that the fees and cost of feed at the western cattle market be reduced as a means of counteracting the influence of the special inducements being offered by the Union Stock Yards at Toronto Junction. There was a difference of opinion as to the wisdom of the course, but the majority of the committee expressed themselves in favour of the proposition to give the Commissioner power to take such action along the lines suggested as will be necessary to detain the cattle trade for the city market. A recommendation along these lines will be forwarded on to the Board of Control.

The prices at the Union yards ran as follows: Export, $4.00 to $5.10; butchers, $4.00 to $4.10; mixed, $3.75 to $4.25; sheep, $3.80.

TOP
W. W. Hodgson, 1936
Courtesy of Shirley (Hodgson) Moorehouse

BOTTOM
CPR Alley, Union Stock Yards ca. 1910
Ontario Stock Yards Board

Mourning at the Junction—Town Is Grief Stricken

by Diana Fancher

IN THE EARLY MORNING HOURS of Friday, July 26, 1907, the Dalmine launch capsized in rough waters during a storm on the Humber Bay, drowning nine of the ten young men aboard, all from Toronto Junction. It was, according to the *Toronto Evening Telegram*, the worst accident of its kind in the area for decades, prompting coroner Dr. J. E. Elliott to call for an investigation into the handling and use of gasoline launches generally.

Survivor George Shields managed to cling to the overturned launch for three hours, battered against the boat by the waves, before it drifted into shallow water at Sunnyside. He then staggered home to Van Horne Street (now Heintzman) bruised, bleeding and incoherent.

Later he told how the engine had stopped approximately 300 yards from shore about 12:30 a.m. Almost immediately a wave hit broadside, turning the boat over and throwing everyone out. The two who could not swim were lost immediately, but at

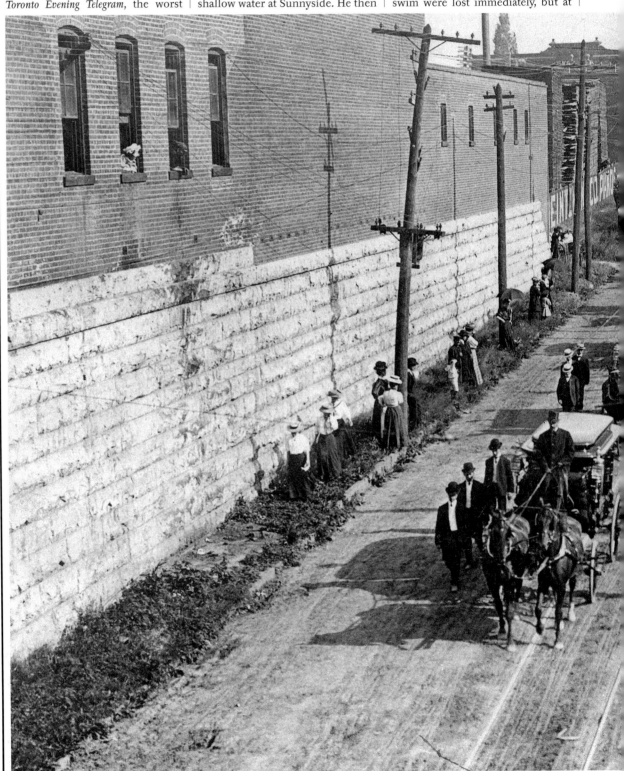

least eight of the others swam back to the launch and hung on for some time before being swallowed up by the lake. The Dalmine, right side up but full of water, along with the body of Walter Dundin, was found early Friday morning near the landing opposite the Swansea Bolt Works (just east of Windermere Avenue). The last of the bodies was recovered from the weeds further out on Sunday noon. Two of the victims, brothers Glen and Frank Daly, built the 18-foot launch themselves, with their father's help.

After saying good-bye to a chum on his way to Manitoba, the group took the launch across the bay to spend the evening at Hanlan's Point, where a sudden storm delayed their departure. Once the rain stopped they returned to the boat and headed for Devin's boathouse where the launch was kept. Police Constable McBurnie on duty at Hanlan's Point called out to them, "That boat's not balanced properly," he told the *Evening Telegram*. Someone called back that it would be all right once they got it started.

Weather reports placed the wind speed at 35 miles per hour. A Mr.

The Funeral Procession of July 29, 1907 is travelling north on Keele St.; the Heintzman piano factory is at left. The picture is taken from one of two postcards commemorating the occasion.
Courtesy of John E. Irvine

Lount reported seeing persons waving frantically from a boat low in the water, but could not find them again in the storm. Alf Preseley, the night watchman at the Swansea Bolt Works reported hearing cries around two or three o'clock, but could see nothing by his lantern light.

"It was no tragedy of luxury," the *Evening Telegram* advised, "The victims were all young chaps who knew what it was to earn a living by manly toil. They knew, too, all the better, the sweets of relaxation that follows such labour. . . . And they were all young. The oldest of the ten had not yet seen his thirtieth birthday." Six of the ten were CPR employees.

The *Evening Telegram* reported the reactions of grief-stricken families in detail. Councillor Irvine, whose son Joe was among the victims, left his work superintending the construction of a house at 100 Pacific Avenue (now 338 Pacific) to hire a horse and rig, first to drive to the morgue to say that the body washed up in Swansea was not his son's, then down to the beach where his son's coat was found.

Widower Joseph Daly, a CPR machinist who built a good part of the ill-fated Dalmine himself, fought back tears over the loss of his two sons. Mrs. Dundin cried, "My poor lad, my good lad, gone from me." The shock had completely unnerved her. Her son Walter also worked for the CPR.

Hugh Kyle, father of Frank, was the CPR engineer on the Myrtle train wreck. Mrs. Kyle told of losing a younger son in a street railway accident several years ago.

"On Saturday evening the streets were impassable and the police had no easy task to regulate pedestrian traffic," the *Evening Telegram* reported on Monday. "From the flagpoles on the town hall and the post office (Keele & Dundas) the Union Jack fluttered in the breeze and seemed to draw people from all quarters of the town, there to learn what there was to learn of the finding of more bodies. . . . All day long yesterday crowds poured into the nine homes and looked for the last time on the boys' faces."

Reg Miller was taken to Streetsville for burial and Gordon LaRoque's flower-covered casket, followed by many mourners, was taken to Mount Hope Cemetery after a service at St. Cecilia's Catholic Church on Monday

morning. A private service was held for Joe Irwin on Sunday evening and his body entrained for King on Monday morning.

The remaining six caskets were taken to Victoria Presbyterian Church for a public funeral service on Monday afternoon. Dr. Pidgeon and Dr. Hazelwood conducted the services, described by the *Evening Telegram* as ". . . beautifully simple and wonderfully pathetic. The row of caskets covered with flowers and the pews filled with black-clad mourners made a touching scene. (Two pews had been removed and the coffins placed side by side.)"

The fire bell tolled as a solemn funeral procession then took them away to Prospect Cemetery. Shops were closed and draped in black along Dundas Street and local factories closed at noon so that employees could attend the funeral. The CPR master mechanics issued a notice allowing their men to attend as well.

The procession was headed by mounted police and the Salvation Army Band and also included Mayor Whetter, members of town council, the school board and board of health, as well as town officials. The Shamrock Lacrosse Team, Rangers Club, Orange Lodge and CPR employees brought up the rear.

Postscript

In an unusual twist of fate, Joseph LaRocque, brother of Gordon and a CPR employee, nearly lost his life while trying to catch up his work after attending his brother's funeral. He

and William Greenshields were so intent on their job that they failed to notice the approach of the Muskoka express, barrelling down the track toward where they stood on a handcar. At the last possible minute the two young men leaped to safety as the handcar was annihilated.

Saved

George Shields, 19, CPR apprentice
45 Van Horne St. *(Heintzman St.)*

Drowned

Joseph Irwin, 20, bricklayer
68 Quebec Ave.

Reg Miller, 19, painter
39 Clendenan Ave.

Jack Irvine, 20, CPR employee
75 Clendenan Ave.

Walter Dundin, 20, CPR employee
77 Quebec Ave.

Frank Kyle, 18, CPR apprentice
19 Union St.
(Indian Grove, n. of Annette St.)

Glen Daly
49 Ontario St.
(Indian Grove s. of Annette St.)

Frank Daly, CPR apprentice
49 Ontario St.

Dawson Nehrgang, CPR switchman
143 Vine Ave.

Gordon LaRoque
Heintzman Co. apprentice
trainer for Shamrock Lacrosse Junior Team
143 Vine Ave.

Note: only the addresses on Vine Avenue are the same numbers as today. All of the young men, with the exception of the Daly brothers, lived north of Dundas St.

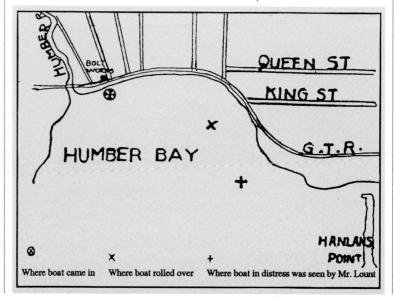

HUMBER BAY

QUEEN ST
KING ST
G.T.R.

BOLT WORKS

HANLAN'S POINT

⊗ Where boat came in   ✕ Where boat rolled over   ✚ Where boat in distress was seen by Mr. Lount

Toronto Evening Telegram, July 26, 1907

from **Junction Sonnets**

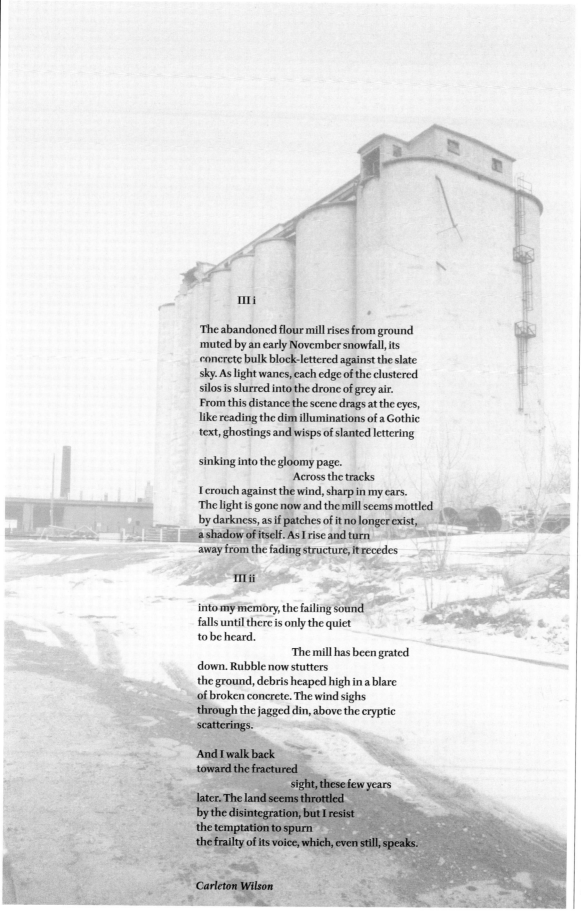

III i

The abandoned flour mill rises from ground
muted by an early November snowfall, its
concrete bulk block-lettered against the slate
sky. As light wanes, each edge of the clustered
silos is slurred into the drone of grey air.
From this distance the scene drags at the eyes,
like reading the dim illuminations of a Gothic
text, ghostings and wisps of slanted lettering

sinking into the gloomy page.
                              Across the tracks
I crouch against the wind, sharp in my ears.
The light is gone now and the mill seems mottled
by darkness, as if patches of it no longer exist,
a shadow of itself. As I rise and turn
away from the fading structure, it recedes

III ii

into my memory, the failing sound
falls until there is only the quiet
to be heard.
                   The mill has been grated
down. Rubble now stutters
the ground, debris heaped high in a blare
of broken concrete. The wind sighs
through the jagged din, above the cryptic
scatterings.

And I walk back
toward the fractured
                          sight, these few years
later. The land seems throttled
by the disintegration, but I resist
the temptation to spurn
the frailty of its voice, which, even still, speaks.

Carleton Wilson

*Photograph:
Larry Burak*

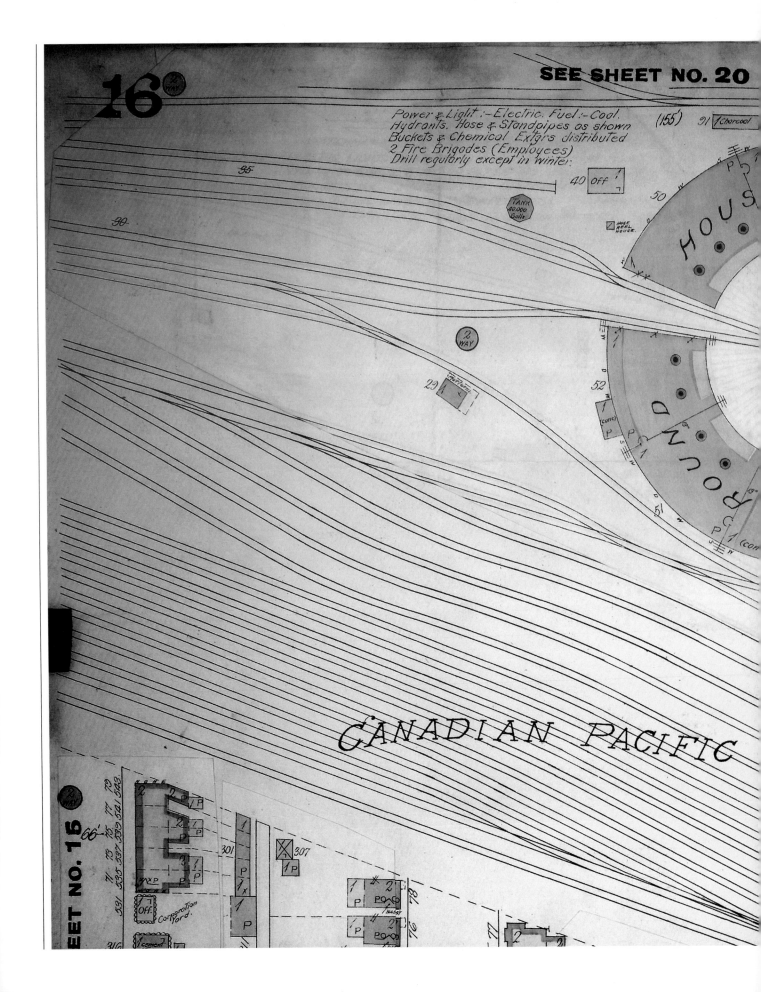

16

Power & Light :– Electric. Fuel :– Coal.
Hydrants. Hose & Standpipes as shown
Buckets & Chemical Extgrs distributed
2 Fire Brigades (Employees)
Drill regularly except in winter.

(155') 31 Charcoal

95

90

40 Off

50

TANK
40,000
Galls

HOSE
REEL
HOUSE.

HOUS

2
WAY

29 Charcoal

52

(conc)

ROUND

CANADIAN PACIFIC

EET NO. 15

66'

301

307

1 P

Corporation Yard.

Off.

cement

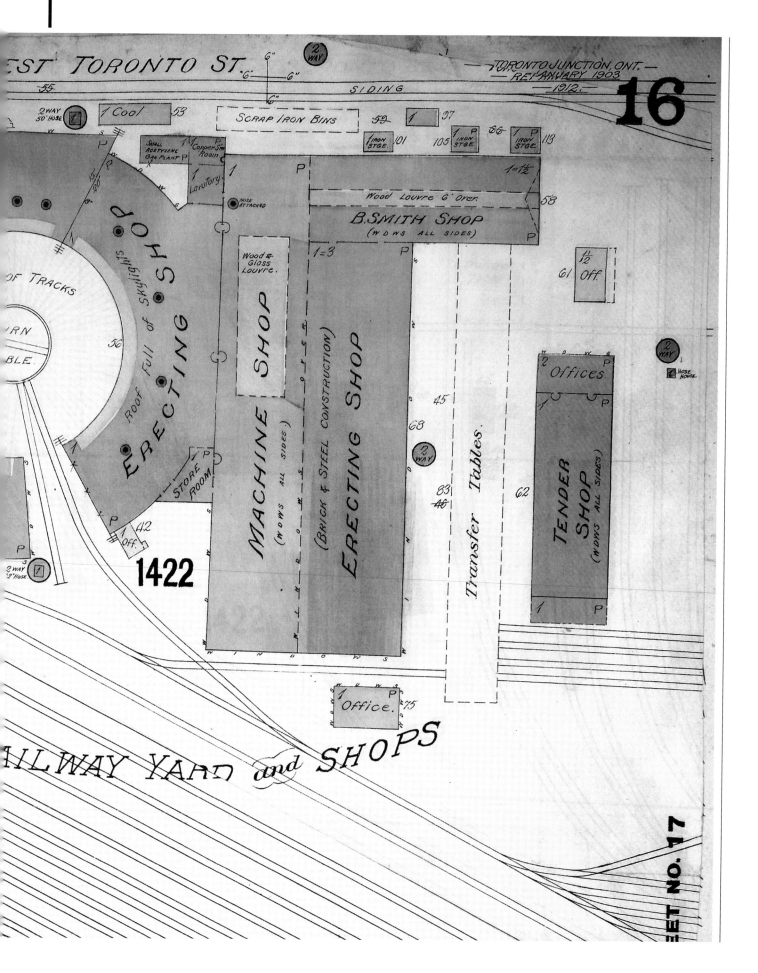

Mackenzie and
Mann's Toronto Rail-
way Company took
over the Toronto
Suburban Railway in
1911

RIGHT
Toronto Railway
Company ticket,
front (enlarged).
WTJHS collection

BELOW
Toronto Railway
Company ticket,
reverse (actual size).
WTJHS collection

STRIP.
233086

The Royce Family of Preston Villa: Unlikely Transit Entrepreneurs

by Ronald Stagg

TODAY, A POULTRY BUSINESS named after an abandoned street name, and a church which the family did not attend are the only noticeable reminders in West Toronto of a prominent, early family. For over seventy years the Royces were major figures in the area. The passing of some sixty years since they moved away has meant, however, that most people know little or nothing about the family and its role in the history of West Toronto.

The first member to arrive was Allan Royce, who was born in 1834 or early 1835 in Rutlandshire, England. The family was not particularly well off, although Allan's nephew would later become Sir Henry Royce, one of the founders of the Rolls-Royce Company, so Allan emigrated to Canada in 1856 to make a better life for himself. He joined his uncle, George Cooper, who was already established as a prosperous farmer in the area west of Toronto.

George and his brother William had settled in York (later Toronto), Upper Canada, in the mid-1820s. George drove the stage to Kingston while his brother ran a tavern. After William was killed in an accident, George married his brother's widow, and in 1831 and 1838 bought two farms of 200 acres each. These properties, lots 32 and 33 in the second concession from the Lake, ran from Dufferin Street to Dundas Street and from Bloor Street to St. Clair Avenue. Only Dundas Street and Davenport Road existed then. His early farm buildings were located near Bloor and Dundas. In 1854 he built a brick house, Preston Villa, using bricks made on the farm, on a height of land overlooking Davenport Road, a main East-west route (at the corner of what is now Lansdowne Avenue). He also built Davenport Station where the Northern Railway crossed his land, in order to have his mail delivered there. He continued to employ a number of men, and to farm on a large scale, although he did begin to sell off some of his property.

When Allan Royce arrived, he was put to work on the farm and soon rose to be manager. In 1863 he married Mrs. Cooper's niece, Sarah Jane Gilbert, and started to raise a family.

George Cooper died in 1884 and Allan Royce took over the farm, which by then consisted of just over 100 acres. As the area developed, he sold off more of the farm and invested money in mortgages and in real estate, in both Toronto and West Toronto. He also promoted the linking of the Carlton and Davenport communities to West Toronto Junction, serving as an alderman on the first council, after incorporation of the town in 1889.

In 1891 he joined with the major landholders along the whole length of Davenport Road to form the Davenport Street Railway Company. The company aimed to link Toronto, Toronto Junction and points west in order to promote development of subdivisions along the route. Allan Royce was a major shareholder. In 1894 that company and its competitor in the area, James Saurin McMurray's City and Suburban Street Railway Company, were taken over and forcibly amalgamated as the Toronto Street Railway Company (TSR) by the firm that was building both, and also owed money by both. The construction company then resold stock in the newly formed company back to the Royce family and a few of the other original Davenport investors.

By 1900 Allan Henry Royce (son of Allan), his law partner R. T. Henderson, Bracondale engineer Frank Turner, R. L. McCormack of Toronto Junction, along with E. P. Heaton and R. W. Smith of Toronto, controlled the company.

The Royce family were long-time supporters of the Davenport Methodist (later United) Church. George Cooper, had been an enthusiastic convert to Methodism, building the area's first Methodist church on his land, near Bloor and Dundas, and also providing the lot for the second church, on Davenport Road. Allan Royce, for his part, contributed heavily to the building of the third church, at the turn of the century. Mrs. Royce laid one of its two cornerstones Allan served for a long period as a church official. He was also a school trustee.

At his death in September 1902, following years of suffering from "pernicious anaemia", Allan Royce left an estate of about $74,000 — a sizeable amount for that time. All of it went to

85

TOP
Royce Monument, Prospect Cemetery
Larry Burak

BOTTOM
Preston Villa circa 1900-10. The back of the property at St. Clair Avenue was across from Prospect Cemetery.
Courtesy of Allan Royce

his wife Sarah who continued to reside in the house on Davenport. By then only 43 acres were left to the family farm, and more was sold off since the rest of the family members were not interested in farming.

Allan and Sarah Royce had six children: a girl who died in her first year and five boys. The youngest, Harold Thomas, b.1880, became a doctor and moved away from Toronto, later settling in New York, but the other four retained ties with West Toronto.

The oldest, George Cooper, b.1865, married Marguerite Mackie in 1889. He organized the Whaley Royce Musical Instrument Company with a store in Toronto which he operated until the turn of the century, and he also lived in the city. In 1902 he joined the TSR as a stockholder and general manager at the company office on Keele Street. He and his wife and their daughter, Georgia Marguerite, then moved to the house they had built at 364 Annette Street in 1905, only a few doors from another TSR investor, R. L. McCormack. In the years prior to World War I George also established the Ferranti Electric Meter and Transformer Company, which he headed until his death, and for a brief period had his own business, Royce & Co.,

which sold electrical supplies, both located on Dundas Street. George later set up Croyebert Financial Company and became its president. He also had a financial interest in Ontario gold mines, a very typical investment for an entrepreneur of the day.

After an earlier student membership during the 1880s, George Royce rejoined the Queen's Own Rifles in 1893 and had risen to the rank of major by the outbreak of the World War. After service as a commanding officer during the organization and training of militia units at the start of the War, and rising to the rank of Lieutenant-Colonel, he was given the command of a large prisoner of war camp at Kapuskasing. However, within a short time he left the camp to assume command of the 255th Battalion, Canadian Expeditionary Force, which he had organized, taking the small contingent of 250 men to England in 1916. In 1917, after the battalion was broken up to reinforce other units, he returned to Canada, where he rose to the rank of Colonel, briefly commanded the Queen's Own Rifles in 1920-21, before retiring in 1928. Upon his return from the War, he resumed his duties as general manager of the Toronto Suburban Street Railway Company, a position he held until the company was fully integrated with the Toronto Transit Commission in 1924.

The second son, Allan Henry, b.1867, graduated from the University of Toronto

and Osgoode Hall, becoming a lawyer in 1896. He continued to live at Preston Villa but practiced law in partnership with R. B. Henderson in central Toronto. He eventually became the president and principal shareholder of the TSR, which provided Toronto Junction's streetcar service, along with service to Lambton, Weston and other areas to the west. He was the first secretary-treasurer of the Canadian Street Railway Association in 1904, later acting as the association's legal counsel. After selling the TSR in 1911, he continued to do legal work for Mackenzie and Mann, the Toronto firm which added the TSR to its railway and street railway portfolio. The firm also owned the Northern Railway which passed though the Royce farm. Allan Henry died at age fifty in 1918, reportedly from overwork, and shortly after arranging the sale of Rolls Royce engines for use in US government vehicles and aircraft — clearly a project associated with his brother John Charles.

The third son, Gilbert, b.1870, became a doctor, practicing in Ottawa and then on College Street in Toronto. He too lived in the family home on Davenport. Like his older brother, he became a part-time soldier in the Canadian Army Medical Corps, beginning in 1901. During World War I he rose to the rank of Lieutenant-Colonel and commanded a military hospital in northern Greece. He was discharged in 1919 and returned to his medical practice in Toronto, working as a nose and throat specialist at the Toronto General Hospital, and teaching at the University of Toronto.

LEFT
Allan Royce as a young man.
Gerald Lynes

CENTRE
Allan Henry Royce.
*Toronto Star,
December 24, 1904*

RIGHT
Col. George Cooper Royce in his uniform as commandant of the Queen's Own Rifles, from a 1932 painting by Allan Barr.
Queen's Own Rifles Museum

The other son, James Charles, b. 1873, took a different path. He received a Master of Engineering from the Massachusetts Institute of Technology and after working for the Cramp Steel Company in Collingwood, set himself up as a consulting engineer in Toronto, although he too lived in the family home in West Toronto. By the end of World War I he was working for the Rolls-Royce Automobile Company in Toronto, soon afterwards joining his brother George's investment company, Croyebert Ltd., where he became secretary-treasurer of the firm.

The year 1920 marked the end of the Royce family's strong association with West Toronto. Allan H. had died in 1918. Gilbert married Winifred Stagg, whom he met during the war, and moved elsewhere in Toronto. Sarah Jane, her son James Charles and his wife Minto Campbell, who were the last occupants, moved as well. The farm was sold, and Preston Villa, along with the remaining property, became Earlscourt Park and a recreation centre. Even George Cooper Royce, although he continued to work

for the TSR until its demise, bought a house in the same general area (Rosedale-Deer Park) as the other members of the family.

Most of the people involved in the development of the communities which became the Town of West Toronto Junction in 1889 and the City of West Toronto in 1909, were associated with business and the professions. Names such as Gilmour, Heydon and Clendenan come to mind. Allan Royce was unusual in

that he was initially a farmer. While his property was technically outside the boundary of West Toronto Junction, he took an active role in the religious, educational and political life of the community. Two of his sons continued to contribute to the growth of that community for much of a generation after his death. As well, the family's varied and interconnected business enterprises were symbolic of an age of individual enterprise and initiative in Canada's history.

TOP
Cornerstone, Davenport United Church.
Larry Burak

BOTTOM
Toronto Suburban open-air Dundas Car 363 rounds the bend at (Old) Weston Road during work to change the gauge on the line, September 17, 1912.
TTC Archives

Dundas Street in the Junction: 30 Years Without Rails

by Stuart I. Westland

THE HISTORY OF PUBLIC TRANSIT on Dundas Street in the Junction is, overall, one of ascendancy followed by decline. For some 30-odd years the Junction had its own local streetcar system operated by the Toronto Suburban Railway (TSR), which was formed out of an early merger between the Davenport Street Railway and the City and Suburban Electric Railway.

The early TSR was a typical small-town trolley operation of the 1890s, using small, single-truck cars operating on single-track lines which travelled along a combination of centre street and side of the road tracks.

Expansion was rapid in the early years, with the various lines all focussed on the Keele and Dundas intersection. Following the Davenport line (to Bathurst) and a Humberside to Gilmour line on Dundas Street — both opened in the fall of 1892 — the Crescent line (to Fairview Avenue and Evelyn Crescent) came in 1893. The long Weston route followed in 1895, and a Gilmour to Lambton Park extension in 1896. Considerably later, in 1914, another lengthy extension carried the Weston line to Woodbridge.

In the meantime, the Toronto Railway Company's (TRC) Dundas line in the City of Toronto had been pushing westward, first as a horsecar line to Dufferin Street (Brockton) in 1882, and to Lansdowne Avenue in 1884. The TRC was electrified in 1892, and the tracks were extended to Bloor Street the same year. This was followed by a further extension in 1895 to the Toronto city limit at Humberside Avenue (College cars, which the Dundas cars replaced, had reached this point a year earlier). Finally an agreement was reached in late 1899 whereby the TRC Dundas cars would be extended to Keele Street. The company's single end equipment would then wye in the intersection, across the Toronto Suburban's single track from Dundas Street (west) to Keele Street (north).

Following a lengthy period of construction, the TSR inaugurated a dramatically different form of electric railway, a full scale US-style intercity line to Guelph, using big steel car equipment operating on a higher voltage (1,500 volts direct current). The

PCC-type streetcar turns onto Runnymede Road from Dundas, at the western terminus of the Dundas carline. Streetcars were removed from this section of Dundas during the night of May 10-11, 1968.
John D. Thompson

Guelph line directed traffic from a very large, if thinly-populated, catchment area to Keele and Dundas during its first years (line voltage was stepped down on city trackage). After the newly-formed Toronto Transportation Commission (TTC) took over the city portion of the TSR system in November 1923, the Canadian National Railway (CNR) became the owner of the non-city portions of the TSR system. In 1924 the CNR constructed a cutoff from Lambton Park by way of a route north of St. Clair Avenue, to a station at the northeast corner of Keele and St. Clair. This was ultimately a wasted effort, since the Guelph line ceased operation on August 15, 1931.

Returning to the principal focus of this article, it is well-known that the TTC, created in 1920, took over the entire operations of the dilapidated Toronto Railway Company system on September 1, 1921, immediately embarking upon a massive reconstruction and modernization program. In 1924 the reconstruction program continued into TSR city territory. This included the extension of double track along Dundas Street from Keele to Runnymede. The TSR line was temporarily relocated to the north side of the street; its final removal to follow shortly.

As part of the wholesale refurbishing of Toronto's streetcar system, the TTC ordered a total of 575 steel double-truck motor and trailer cars, all but 100 of which were equipped for operation in two-car trains. This equipment was placed on the Dundas route to Keele Street in early 1923, and to Runnymede Road in January 1924.

Thus commenced the halcyon period of transit operation on Dundas Street, a period when the TTC clearly considered the Dundas service to be one of its "big" lines, using essentially the same car equipment that was serving the Yonge, Bloor and various Queen Street lines. Junction residents could ride the big cars directly to the downtown loop behind City Hall, benefiting from the time efficiency inherent in a diagonal route.

A TTC system-wide service summary, dated March 17, 1924, in the author's transit collection, shows an intensive service level on the Dundas line, with three-minute headways (frequencies) in off-peak hours, and one minute 50 second headways in the p.m. rush. Another summary, dated May 28, 1930, shows only a slightly reduced service in this Depression year: four minutes off-peak and two minutes 13 seconds in the p.m. rush (a.m. rush headways were slightly wider in both cases.

In the meantime, feeder services in the area had changed. The TTC inaugurated its first bus route on September 20, 1921, from Dundas Street via Humberside, High Park and Annette to Runnymede, quickly killing off the TSR Crescent line. After several reroutings, this service was replaced by a Runnymede route, which operated from Bloor and Runnymede to Keele and Dundas, reinforcing the transit focus at the latter intersection.

The Township of York assumed ownership of the remainder of the Lambton line (Runnymede to Lambton Park), and the TTC operated it for them on a contract basis. This route was changed to bus operation on August 19, 1928, at the request of York Township. From 1929, two partially parallel bus services operated on Dundas Street. They were the Lambton (Keele and Dundas to Prince Edward in Etobicoke) and Islington (Runnymede to Islington Avenue) buses. These extra fare services were known as coach routes, since they used vehicles assigned to, and painted for, TTC subsidiary Gray Coach Lines.

On December 1, 1938, the two-car train operation was totally removed from the Dundas route and replaced by the new, one-man streamlined PCC cars. These cars ruled Dundas Street for almost 30 years, continuing

TTC Dundas streetcar is eastbound on Dundas at Keele St. in April 1968, shortly before trolley coaches took over service between Dundas West subway station and the Runnymede Loop. *John D. Thompson*

the Runnymede to downtown routing. This historic through service was abruptly terminated on May 10, 1968, when the Bloor-Danforth Subway was extended from Keele to Islington. Pursuant to one of the more unfortunate decisions ever taken by the TTC, the Dundas carline was truncated at Dundas West Station on Bloor Street and the relatively short Junction 40 trolley coach service commenced over the outer portion of the route, without any westward extension. The "trackless trolleys" gave way to the ubiquitous diesel buses in January 1992.

At the time of the Dundas West service change, TTC policy was still directed toward total streetcar abandonment by 1980, with some kind of Queen Street subway still in the picture. In the immediately ensuing years, however, there was mounting citizen pressure to keep the streetcars. This pressure was focussed in a very active group known as Streetcars for Toronto. The movement culminated in a landmark decision, taken at a Commission meeting on November 7, 1972, to preserve indefinitely what remained of Toronto's street car system. Plans soon followed for the purchase of new car equipment and the renewal of track systems based on long-term operation, rather than the former patchwork rehabilitation designed to keep the system operable until 1980.

Unfortunately, the renaissance came too late to save the Dundas carline in the Junction. The TTC's over-riding philosophy of "feed" the subway had strengthened a pattern of route alterations which began in the late 1940s, progressively de-emphasizing the Keele-Dundas transit centre. The Annette trolley coach had replaced the Runnymede bus on Annette Street in 1947. This east-west crosstown service bypassed the Keele-Dundas terminal point of the former Runnymede bus service. The Weston Road route, which had looped in the Keele-Annette intersection since conversion to trolley coach operation in September 1948, now carried its passengers down to Keele Station.

The buyout of West York Coach Lines and Roselands Bus Lines back in 1954 had resulted in immediate diversion of their routings away from their former Keele and Vine terminal point. The Lambton route no longer reached Keele Street by 1968. For a period it had been cut back to Runnymede Road and renamed Dundas. When it was again extended easterly, once more bearing the Lambton name, it was diverted down High Park Avenue to the subway.

In the meantime, through north-south bus routes had been developed on Jane, Runnymede and Scarlett Road — all crossing Dundas Street but delivering their passenger loads to the subway and Bloor West Village, not to the Junction.

Today's situation is a far cry from the heady days of the 1920s and 1930s, when the commodious Witt trains carried Junction residents downtown with a frequent service along a direct diagonal route. Toronto has few diagonal streets, and those that do exist tend to be of limited length, falling far short of the central area. By contrast, many other cities which are more liberally endowed with diagonals, such as Buffalo, Cleveland and Chicago, have preserved centripetal transit services on these streets. The TTC's infrastructure and routing pattern seem to say to the Junction area that the optimal route for residents travelling into downtown Toronto is by way of a two-transfer ride on crowded subway trains.

The relatively recent relocation of the lengthy and heavily travelled 41 Keele route from a southern diversion along Symington Avenue to Lansdowne Station, to a route entirely on Keele Street terminating at Keele Station, brings a significant new element of transit service to Keele and Dundas. However, it is not the Junction's "own" transit route, and it does not enhance Dundas Street, delivering riders, as usual, to the subway.

In the early 1990s the TTC considered a report on the feasibility of establishing streetcar service on three north-south routes (all south of Bloor-Danforth), ostensibly to utilize a car surplus. While these conversions did not in fact take place, they did raise the question of a better strategy, that of restoring the historic Dundas carline service to Runnymede Road, and possibly as far as Jane Street. Those business streets on which streetcars still operate, such as Queen, College, Roncesvalles and St. Clair, have a vibrancy and atmosphere which busses do not produce. Restoration of the old no-transfer route to downtown would not only be transit strategic in terms of subway relief, but would assist greatly in image revitalization for Dundas Street in the Junction.

FACING PAGE, TOP
Postcard view looking north at Keele and Dundas ca. 1914, showing a Toronto Railway Company Dundas streetcar wyeing for its return trip eastward. The car's conductor is guiding the trolley pole as the car backs up. The streetcar wires have been painted out by the artist who colourised the postcard.
WTJHS Collection

FACING PAGE, BOTTOM
The Weston car lays over at Dundas and Keele Sts., November 9, 1940.
TTC Archives

Double tracking in progress, while streetcar service continues on both Keele and Dundas, November 19, 1923. Cars and pedestrians are a different story.
TTC Archives

Cor. Keele and Dundas Streets, West Toronto, Ont., Canada

The Streetcar That Never Ran

by Raymond Kennedy

THE STORY OF THE STREETCAR that never ran ends in 1985 when reconstruction work at the Runnymede Road subway between Dundas Street and St. Clair Avenue revealed hints of this long forgotten trackage. When workmen began tearing up the road leading down under the railway yards in preparation for a new and wider underpass, they found steel rails and wooden ties buried under the pavement.

The streetcar tracks ran from Dundas and Runnymede north to St. Clair, towards land acquired by the TTC on both sides of Runnymede — from Henrietta Street south to Liverpool Street on the west side, Cobourg Place, Hagar Avenue and Britannia Avenue on the east side. The TTC had planned to build a new carbarn on the site (referred to as Britannia) to replace the carbarn on Lansdowne Avenue just north of Bloor.

When the tracks were laid, so the story goes, a streetcar was run through the subway under the watchful eye of a Board of Transport inspector, who promptly condemned the whole thing! The road was only wide enough for one vehicle at a time, both a streetcar and an automobile could not pass side-by-side. The narrowness of the underpass meant that if a streetcar became disabled for any reason, it would block the street so that a fire truck or an ambulance or a police car would be unable to get through, requiring a long detour to either Jane or Keele Street.

The tracks were paved over, the carbarns were never built, and the land lay vacant for many, many years. As a child I remember regularly walking across the open field from Henrietta towards St. Clair, as did hundreds of people daily until housing was built there in the 1960s

Only now, after many years of delays and false starts has the major task of rebuilding the underpass been accomplished, while the CPR still maintained freight operations above. To close even a portion of the railway tracks would have been impossible before 1964, when the main CPR yard was moved from West Toronto to Agincourt.

TOP
Trackwork in progress on Runnymede Road south from St. Clair Ave., November 18, 1927. Lambton Roundhouse is on the right. *TTC Archives*

BOTTOM
TTC Property at Runnymede Rd. and Henrietta St., May 11, 1934. *TTC Archives*

A Brief History of Public Transit on Annette Street

by John D. Thompson

THE FIRST RECORDED PROPOSAL for transit service on Annette Street was put forward in 1907 by the Toronto Suburban Railway (TSR), the privately-owned company that was then operating streetcar lines in West Toronto. A survey was made for a line to the Swansea Bolt Works (located near the lakeshore), extending from Dundas Street via Keele, Annette and Elizabeth (now Runnymede Road).

In 1908 the Swansea line was surveyed as an extension of the TSR's existing Crescent route, which extended south on Fairview from Dundas and terminated at Evelyn Crescent. The new route, presumably, would have split from the Crescent line where it crossed Annette, heading west on that street. However, the Toronto Junction town council opposed the laying of streetcar tracks on Annette, and the TSR dropped its proposal.

It was left to the newly-formed Toronto Transportation Commission (TTC), thirteen years later, to bring transit to Annette Street. Interestingly, this was provided by the TTC's first bus route, Humberside. It began at the intersection of Dundas and Humberside, where a small garage was constructed. Buses proceeded west on Humberside to High Park Avenue, north to Annette, and west to Runnymede, where they terminated. The Humberside bus route was originally intended to be a temporary measure, until the TTC could commit resources to lay streetcar tracks over the route. At this time bus operation was in its infancy. However, the Commission never did get around to building the Humberside streetcar route.

The four gasoline-powered busses ordered by the TTC were built by the Fifth Avenue Coach Company of New York City, and were similar to vehicles already operating in that city. They were of double deck design, to increase capacity, with an open top deck. Power was provided by a four-cylinder engine, developing a startling 35 horsepower. There were seats for 22 passengers inside and 29 on the top level. Solid rubber tires, typical of the era, meant a somewhat less than feather-smooth ride.

A fifth bus, built by the Leyland works in England,

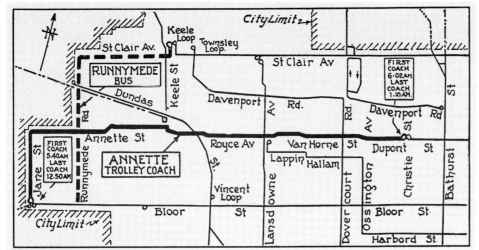

TOP
Annette Trolley Coach Route, October 6, 1947
TTC Archives

BOTTOM
Bus No.1 on the Humberside Annette route turns onto Humberside in front of the Dundas streetcar, May 7, 1923. Note the TTC and police uniforms, and the casual attitude toward traffic by local pedestrians.
TTC Archives

followed in December 1921. Three others, all from different manufacturers, joined the fleet in the coming months, giving the TTC a total of eight double deck busses. However, the double deck concept, popular to this day in Great Britain, never really caught on in North America, and single level busses soon replaced the earlier vehicles. Luckily, Bus One is preserved at the National Museum of Science and Technology in Ottawa.

On December 5, 1922, the Humberside route was extended west on Annette from Runnymede to Jane. Then on September 6, 1925, the route name was changed to High Park, starting at Keele and Dundas (looping on Mavety) and running via Annette and High Park Avenue to Bloor Street. Further route changes took place on November 29, 1925, with the new Runnymede and Jane bus routes replacing the High Park Annette line. The Runnymede line's ultimate routing began at Bloor and Runnymede, proceeding north on Runnymede to Annette, east to Mavety, north to Dundas, east to Keele, south to Annette, west to Runnymede and south to Bloor. The Jane bus commenced its journey at Bloor and Jane, heading north on the latter street to Annette, thence east along Annette to Runnymede and north to Dundas. Service was extended north to St. Clair and east to Keele on November 26, 1931.

Twenty-two years later, transit service on Annette underwent a major transformation, with the launching of the Annette trolley coach route (the TTC always tended to use this term

rather than calling them "trolley buses", as in other cities), on October 6, 1947. The coaches started at Christie Loop, on the northeast corner of Christie and Dupont Streets; this facility also served as the western terminus of the Dupont streetcar route. They travelled westward on Dupont and Annette to Jane, then south on Jane to the Jane Loop on the southeast corner of Jane and Bloor, where they connected with the Bloor streetcar line.

Short turn loops were located at Keele and at Runnymede. Service remained unchanged on the Annette route until February 28, 1963 when, coincident with the opening of the University Subway line, it was extended eastward on Dupont and Davenport to Bedford Road, and south to loop at St. George Station. Christie Loop was abandoned at this time, as the Dupont cars were withdrawn. Then on May 11, 1968, with the opening of the Jane subway station, the coaches began looping at the station and Jane Loop was closed.

The only other major changes to the Annette route were the changes to the vehicles used. Commencing about 1970, the original trolley coaches were replaced by new vehicles built by Winnipeg's Western Flyer. However, these coaches incorporated the motors and controls of their predecessors which dated from 1947-53. The Flyers provided service exclusively until the summer of 1990, when the TTC began mixing in trolley coaches leased from Edmonton, which had a surplus of these vehicles. The 40 Alberta coaches, easily spotted by

their blue and white paint scheme (the TTC was not about to spend thousands of dollars on painting the coaches), were newer than the Flyers, dating from the early 1980s, and generally superior vehicles, combining a standard General Motors bus body with electrical equipment from the firm of Brown Boveri.

However, in recent years the TTC has become increasingly disenchanted with trolley coaches, citing their higher purchase and operating costs, and lack of flexibility, as reasons for discontinuing their use and replacing them with diesel buses. This actually occurred on January 14, 1992, but as a result of political pressure centred on environmental concerns, the trolley coaches returned to the Annette and Bay Routes on September 6, 1992.

This proved to be only a temporary victory, as TTC management remained determined to remove them, using the Commission's current desperate financial situation as a lever to do so. The critical date was July 23, 1993, when the lease of coaches from Edmonton expired. The trolley coach era in Toronto had run its course.

FACING PAGE
Bus No. 8, the last in the TTC's original fleet of double deck buses on the Humberside route, shown at Dundas and Howard Park, December 11, 1923.
TTC Archives

LEFT
TTC trolley coach 9002, eastbound on Annette at Medland St., summer 1954, passing the "Western Branch" of the Toronto Public Library, now the Annette Street Library.
Canadian General Electric photo courtesy of Ray Corley

RIGHT
Edmonton Transit System trolley coach westbound on Annette St., in front of Victoria-Royce Presbyterian Church at Medland St. in June of 1993.
John D. Thompson

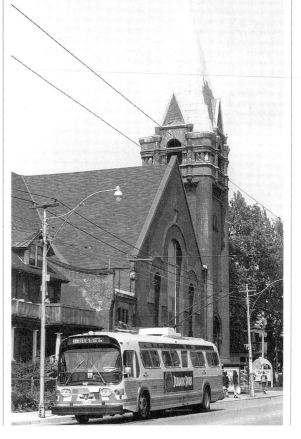

A Bridge to the Outside World

by Diana Fancher, with research contributions by Alec Keefer, Ian Wheal and David Cuming

IN THE EARLY YEARS of the 20th century, residential development was expanding rapidly into the area between Lansdowne and the CPR-CNR mainline, between Bloor Street and what is now Dupont Street immediately adjacent to Toronto Junction. There was little industrial development in this area, which roughly constitutes today's Junction Triangle, because of the tax exemptions offered by Toronto Junction which were not available to City of Toronto industries.

However, local residents were trapped in a "triangle" of railway tracks and level crossings on every side. Bloor Street did not extend west of Lansdowne Avenue and none of the roads were "improved". Getting to the streetcar at Lansdowne or Dundas could be both dirty and dangerous.

To remedy this, Ward Six Alderman James McGhie proposed in December 1904 that an overhead footbridge be constructed at Wallace Avenue to cross the rail corridor. This would deliver residents to the Dundas streetcar link into Toronto or alternatively to the Toronto Suburban streetcar into Toronto Junction and destinations north or west, as well as to the

CPR station, shopping along Dundas Street, and local industrial employment.

By 1905 alderman McGhie had got himself appointed chair of the Works Committee and was pushing strongly for the footbridge, along with Alderman John Graham, also serving on the Works Committee from Ward Six — the ward in which the bridge was to be located.

However, the city envisioned a cheap wooden footbridge as a temporary measure to tide residents over until the massive underpasses at Lansdowne and Dundas on Bloor Street and on Dupont Street could be constructed. The underpass projects

TOP
The Wallace Avenue Footbridge, looking southeast from Dundas Street, April 22, 1915. Note the Glidden smokestack at the far left and men at work on the railway tracks.
City of Toronto Archives

BOTTOM
Wallace Avenue Footbridge, looking northeast from Dundas Street, January 12, 1926. The Glidden paint factory has expanded considerably in the 11 years between photographs. Glenlake Avenue is in the foreground.
City of Toronto Archives

were also considered in 1905 and put on indefinite hold because of the cost. West of Dundas, Bloor Street was still a series of steep ascents and perilous descents into mudholes and streams.

The railways, on the other hand, insisted on a steel bridge. Negotiating and dithering over whether or not to declare a right of way for Wallace Avenue across the tracks to Dundas Street and consequent expropriation of property went on for most of 1905. In the end no highway was declared and no property expropriated. The City Engineer submitted a budget of $4,500 for the bridge in 1906 and tenders were called.

But no company willing to tender at that price could be found. By the end of 1906 the City Engineer in desperation was proposing to buy the requisite parts and build the bridge with day labour. Enter the newly-formed Ontario Bridge Company, with 23-year-old Fraser Matthews as chief engineer. The company submitted a design and a budget for $4,200 which was hastily approved by the city under "emergency" authority to suspend a further call for tenders.

City Engineer C. H. Rust also drew up plans for the 28 precisely placed concrete piers to support the steel structure according to the requirements of the two railways. That contract was let to E. C. Lewis Co. of Close Avenue. Those plans are still in the Public Works Department.

Possibly because he was fresh from engineering school with all the latest construction techniques at his fingertips, Fraser Matthews had the spans secured with rivets. Rivets were still an unknown quantity at the turn of the century. *Engineering & Contract Record* carried several articles about a road bridge in Quebec which collapsed because of the failure of a single rivet. However, around this time, the introduction of portable pneumatic tools revolutionized field rivetting to permit consistency and securely rivetted spans.

The two symmetrical cascades of 42 steps onto Dundas Street, another unique feature of the bridge (demolished) were built entirely on the Dundas Street road allowance to avoid the cost of expropriating property.

The Ontario Bridge Company went on to other projects in Toronto and around the province. Fraser Matthews became president and general manager as well as vice-president of Disher Steel Construction Co., before his death in 1954 at age 70. The Ontario Bridge Company ceased to exist five years after his death.

Immediately as the bridge was finished, industry began springing up along either side of the rail corridor, making the footbridge an integral part of local journey to work patterns. The City of West Toronto was annexed in 1909. The grading of Bloor Street west

to the Humber began in 1912, although the massive underpasses were not built until the 1920s.

Today, the demise of the Glidden Company, ITT Grinnell and other local track-side industry has lessened traffic on the footbridge. The Symington Avenue bus takes residents directly into the Dundas West subway station. However the bridge, rebuilt in an altered design, still provides local residents with quick access to the Dundas West subway stop with its two streetcar links, as well as to the Junction bus. In addition it provides school and neighbourhood links across the bridge.

Located close to studios on Wallace Avenue, the bridge has also been used as a location for films. In 1989 it was featured in the Bette Midler movie "Stella".

Postscript

Like other area pedestrian rail crossing structures in the west end, the simple and economical original design has been replaced by a structure which encourages graffiti and discourages pedestrian use. Interestingly, the "original" graffiti on the rebuilt bridge, which the city hastily scrambled to replace with commissioned art, was better designed than its officially sanctioned replacement. In fact many people mistake the official art for graffiti!

Stock Yards Railway

by Raymond Kennedy

BACK IN THE EARLY PART of the century railways were the only way to ship goods for any distance and they were vital to every business and industry. Rivalry existed then as now between the railways and it was this rivalry that almost led to the creation of another railway company right here in West Toronto Junction!

Beginning in 1884, the Canadian Pacific Railway (CPR) dominated West Toronto in every way — yards, shops, employment, freight sidings, passenger traffic, etc. The Grand Trunk Railway (GTR), on the other hand, just passed through on its way to other industrial centres where it supplied the main railway service. The Grand Trunk was not interested in being part of what it perceived to be a CPR town.

When the new Union Stock Yards was built in 1901-3 at a cost of $250,000 — a lot of money in those days — the GTR refused to build a 600-foot long siding into it, even though the stock yards agreed to pay the cost. Furthermore, the GTR refused to handle any shipments of live stock. This created considerable difficulty for the yards since, according to Manager Hodgson's article in the *Toronto Star*, three quarters of the province's livestock was shipped to market via the GTR.

Thus it came about that Andrew Dods, Morley Franklin Pumaville, Arno Linder Bitzer, Mervil MacDonald and Malcolm Dingwall sought a provincial charter to incorporate the Junction Terminal Railway Company to service the Union Stock Yards and "to operate over other railways". It was no doubt this latter request that alarmed the GTR most. The directors probably envisioned someone else's trains running downtown to the City of Toronto's Western Cattle Market at Wellington and Tecumseh Streets where the GTR did supply siding, as well as to other abattoirs.

The GTR opposed passage of the bill at Queen's Park, claiming that such a charter "was a violation of an existing freight agreement", whatever that might have been. The bill was withdrawn, but with the privilege of reintroduction at a later date. As a result of the application, the GTR agreed to build the siding but then refused to execute the agreement. Eventually, after further wrangling and intervention by the Railway Board, the siding was built.

The track crossed Keele Street on the south side of St. Clair Avenue, running west until it curved northwest across St. Clair to enter the vast complex of the former Canada Packers facilities. It then joined the CPR tracks running through Runnymede (Ryding Avenue) Park from the CPR's West Toronto yard.

At one time this track continued westward until it curved northwest across Jane Street to join the Toronto Belt Line Railway. The Belt Line came up from Swansea, swung eastward along the back of Corbett Avenue and along a Hydro right-of-way until it wound up back at the north of Canada Packers, crossing Weston Road on a bridge (demolished) and rejoining the GTR line back where it started.

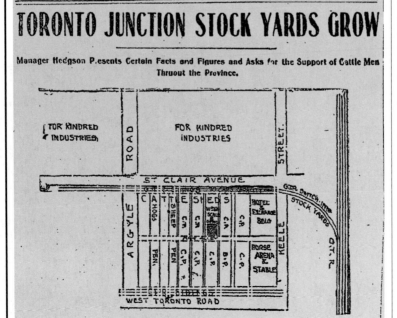

TOP
Aerial view of the Union Stock yards ca. 1920. The view is to the west with Keele Street in the foreground and St. Clair Avenue on the right. Across St. Clair in the extreme top corner is a portion of the Harris & Gunn complex, later amalgamated as Canada Packers.
Bishop-Barker Aeroplanes Ltd.

BOTTOM
"Map Showing Location of Toronto Junction Stock Yards and Proposed New Switch."
Toronto Daily Star, July 9, 1904

A Railway Family's Christmas

as told to Diana Fancher by Audrey Rutherford Addleton and Elinor Binns Jones

At the Rutherfords

AUDREY RUTHERFORD ADDLETON'S father, John William Rutherford, started with the CPR in Owen Sound and came to the Junction to begin his career as a fireman and locomotive engineer in 1886. When his first wife died, leaving him with three small children, he married Eleanor Fowley. They lived on Laws Street. Later he took the Ottawa evening train down to Havelock, the first 100 miles. He took the night run so he could help his wife during the day, since the family had grown to five children.

Audrey remembers:

"He was a perfectionist and everything had to be just perfect before he went on a run. He was called "Nifty" by his fellow engineers and firemen, because Mother washed his overalls every Monday, starched them and ironed them. And he was called Nifty because of that. He wore a typical engineer's hat and he always had a red cotton handkerchief in his pocket and he would come at the weekend with his pocket full of little tissue orders that the operator at the station would hand out. They were about the size of dollar bills, and my sister and I would play store with them.

"His schedule was two nights on a run, one night off. Two out of three nights he'd be working. He never got any regular holidays, he just worked all the time. When he took time off he wouldn't get paid for it at all.

"At Christmas, one thing used to bother us. Dad went out Christmas Eve on his run and he would always say he fixed the damper in the chimney, the fireplace grate, so Santa could get down; but we had to wait til he came home at nine or ten o'clock in the morning and had his breakfast before we could have our Christmas. Then after my eldest brother got married, we were only eight and nine, we had to wait until my brother and his wife went out to her family place to have their Christmas tree before we had ours. So it was kind of hard on small children.

"The gifts in those days were much smaller, I remember Peg and I exchanged hair ribbons and things like that. We always hung our stockings up and mother always put in an apple and an orange and a few dates or raisins and always those cream candies, pink and green and white and orange. You can still buy them.

"One year there were dolls for us under the tree, we thought they were just great. Later I realized that it was my same old doll that had been down to the dolls hospital and had been redone. Mother had dressed it up — part of its arm was off and the eyes had been pushed in. I still have that doll.

"We had lovely Christmas dinners. The usual turkey, cranberries, potatoes and turnips. Those were the days when there weren't too many green vegetables. You'd have turnips and carrots and things like that. We always had a plum pudding too."

With the Binns Brothers

In 1898 Elinor Binns Jones' father, Stanley Binns, moved to the Junction from Owen Sound with the CPR and boarded briefly with the Rutherfords. His brother Alan also worked for the CPR. The two brothers, who both became locomotive engineers, married the Barry sisters, Alice and Margaret, and the two families shared a house on Pacific Avenue.

Elinor remembers it as though she and her cousin Barry had two sets of parents. Christmas at their house was unpredictable.

"Being in a railroad family, my father wasn't always home at the right time for Christmas dinner. I can well remember my mother having a dinner ready and my uncle would be called out to a railway accident somewhere and Christmas would be shot. You never were sure whether everybody would be home or not.

"There was one accident on the 24th and my uncle had to go. So he ordered turkeys and mince pies for the clean-up crew, because they would be away all Christmas Day. I can remember Uncle Alan phoning that. The accident was up around McTier."

TOP
(L-R) Audrey and Margaret Rutherford are already counting the days until Christmas. They are standing in the front yard of their home at 62 Laws St. in 1916. *Courtesy of Audrey Rutherford Addleton*

BOTTOM
(L-R) Helen and Alan Binns with niece Elinor, Margaret and Stanley Binns with nephew Barry, in front of their house at 268 Pacific Ave. *Courtesy of Elinor Binns Jones*

CPR's Lambton Roundhouse: A Rail Fan's Memoir

by John D. Thompson, with thanks to Newton Rossiter, CPR (retired)

FOR 48 YEARS, from 1912 to 1960, the Canadian Pacific Railway's Lambton Roundhouse dominated the southwest corner of St. Clair Ave. W. and Runnymede Road. At this facility, located beside the railway's Lambton freight yard and Toronto–Windsor main line, routine maintenance, called "running repairs", was performed on locomotives assigned to pulling freight trains in and out of Toronto, as well as engines that switched freight cars in the yard and at West Toronto industries.

Physically, Lambton Roundhouse was an imposing structure. As its name implies, the building was circular, with 30 tracks, called stalls, each with space for a single "iron horse". It was built of concrete, with a wooden roof, surmounted by high wooden smokestacks to better disperse smoke from engines being fired up. Each stack had a number on the top, representing the number of the stall beneath; thus, when an engine arrived after dropping off its train, an employee, called a "hostler", would be instructed to put it into stall 10, for example, which could be readily identified by the number.

In the centre of the roundhouse, in the open air, was a circular pit containing an 80-foot long turntable. The turntable was a bridge-like structure with a single track; it could be rotated by means of an air-operated engine to line up with the tracks leading into any of the stalls, and the tracks heading westward, away from the roundhouse. When a locomotive arrived, it would move onto the turntable. An operator would then rotate the table to the appropriate stall, line up the tracks, and the locomotive would be run, front first, into the roundhouse. The procedure was reversed when a locomotive was being taken out.

A tall brick smokestack at the west side of the roundhouse indicated the location of the steam heating building, where steam was generated for heating the roundhouse and other nearby buildings, such as the offices on the north side of the property, beside St. Clair Avenue. A 50 x 90 foot addition housed a machine shop. Each stall contained a 65-foot-long inspection pit for performing maintenance beneath the locomotives.

About a thousand feet west of the roundhouse stood the coaling tower. The massive structure, as its name implies, provided coal for the locomotives. The coal fed by gravity, via metal chutes, into the locomotive tenders. Originally a wooden structure, this tower was replaced by a more durable concrete and brick structure. Coal,

In the summer of 1960 a handful of steam locomotives are still inside Lambton Roundhouse, among them No. 2414 and a Royal Hudson. Both were scrapped soon after this photo was taken *Raymond Kennedy*

often from Pennsylvania, would be loaded into the tower from hopper cars spotted beside it; the coal would be taken up into the top of the tower by a conveyor belt bucket arrangement.

Sand for the locomotives was also provided at this location. Piped into a dome atop the boiler, the engineer would release it onto the rails when starting a train to provide better traction for the drive wheels.

A black water tower stood over near St. Clair, close to the coaling tower. The locomotives were watered from standpipes in the yard — unique devices that were swung over openings in the locomotive tenders, which held as much as 12,000 gallons.

After a locomotive arrived at Lambton, it would be stopped over an outside pit. The firebox was opened

TOP
CPR Pacific-type locomotive 2203 is about to have its fire dumped at Lambton Roundhouse, September 3, 1959. Note spout of water column at left, conveyor belt from ash pit at right and roundhouse with open door and smokestacks. View is toward the northeast.
John D. Thompson

BOTTOM
Locomotives No. 1057 and 2414 leave Lambton Roundhouse on their way to pull a Farewell to Steam excursion, May 15, 1960. No. 1057 was the last engine to leave the roundhouse and is now part of the South Simcoe Railway fleet at Tottenham, Ontario.
Courtesy of Raymond Kennedy

and the blazing coals dumped into the pit. Later the ashes would go up a conveyor belt into a dump car, and be recycled for use as ballast beneath the tracks on branch lines and sidings.

Before being put away in the roundhouse — even without a fire, the boiler would retain enough steam pressure to move the engine — the locomotive would be inspected and greased. If any defects had shown up in the locomotive's operation, the engineer would advise the roundhouse staff of these so that they could be corrected before the next trip.

Lambton Roundhouse employed maintenance workers having a variety of skills, such as machinists, boilermakers, pipefitters, electricians, steamfitters, and mechanics, to name a few. They were capable of making repairs to boiler tubes, gauges, the running gear, fireboxes, dynamos, headlights, etc., and repairing minor collision damage, as well as washing out the boiler at prescribed intervals. For major overhauls, engines were sent to the nearby West Toronto Shops or to the company's Angus Shops in Montreal.

When a locomotive was ordered for a train, it would take several hours to raise steam, since about 200 pounds per square inch, on average, was operating pressure. A layer of coal would be spread evenly throughout the bottom of the firebox on the grates. Kindling wood or creosote-soaked wooden blocks would be used as a base; then kerosene-soaked cotton waste would be thrown in and lit to get the fire burning. In a few moments the coal would catch, and the firebox interior became a raging inferno.

As the boiler pressure needle climbed, the engine would come alive, transformed from a cold, dead piece of machinery into a panting, thumping, sighing creature — the most marvellous of man's creations. A whine atop the boiler, as the turbo generator kicked in, and the cab glowed with warm, yellow light. A cough, a wheeze, and then the locomotive's air pumps on the side of the engine started their rhythmic cycle, pumping up the air system.

Finally, the steam pressure gauge showed enough steam to move the engine out. The hostler climbed into the cab and took his place on the right hand seatbox at the controls A lazy sigh of air sounded as he put the engine's valve gear in reverse. Outside, the turntable was lined up for the stall. Then, his gloved hand went for the brass engine brake handle, releasing the brakes. The melodic bell sounded a warning to any workers around to stand clear. The hostler pulled back on the throttle and live steam roared into the cylinders.

Slowly, almost imperceptibly, the giant of the rails began moving, easing onto the turntable with a massive thump as over 200 tons of dead weight passed over th gap between the table and solid ground. Coming off the table and heading for the departure track, the hostler opened the cylinder cocks, letting condensate spew out from the cylinders in great white clouds. After coaling and a final inspection, the engineer and fireman would board the locomotive. It would then be coupled onto its freight train and start earning revenue for the CPR, heading for Windsor or Sudbury or Montreal, or a multitude of other destinations.

In 1912 Lambton Roundhouse was at the edge of development, being mostly surrounded by open fields. These were gradually filled in with houses and stores, except for the vacant lot at the northeast corner of Runnymede and St. Clair, which remained empty until about 1960. That year, in the autumn, Lambton Roundhouse fell to the wrecker's ball as diesel engines replaced steam locomotives. The CPR subsequently built new diesel facilities at Agincourt Yard.

I became familiar with Lambton in the Indian Summer of its life — Labour Day weekend, 1959, was my first visit. As a budding rail fan, age 13, I visited the office of the genial foreman, the late Don Cochrane, and signed a release of liability form. I was thus free to wander at will throughout the engine terminal and roundhouse.

For an impressionable teenager, who had been fascinated by steam locomotives and railways from earliest recollections, it was like entering the inner sanctum. I had gone past the

Two-part view of Lambton Yard looking east toward Runnymede Road with St. Clair Ave. W. at left, during the summer of 1960. At the far left is a bunkhouse where London-based engineers and firemen stayed. Next, a large steel water tank which fed trackside stand pipes (already removed) to refill steam locomotives, followed by the stores building and the office building. Its boiler room shared a chimney stack with the machine shop, which in turn was attached to the roundhouse.
Raymond Kennedy

roundhouse in cars on numerous occasions, looking through the windows at the fronts of locomotives, the yellowish headlight reflectors catching my eye.

It was a sunny Saturday afternoon, the brightness outside contrasting with the cool gloom of the roundhouse. I walked through the structure, gazing upon perhaps a dozen steam locomotives but, alas, none of them had steam up, nor, I was told, were any to be fired up that afternoon. I was wondering if it was a wild goose chase — by that time steam operation was a rarity — and walked over to the west end of the terminal, past the coaling tower. Looking down the track, I almost jumped for joy as I saw a steam locomotive moving slowly toward the tower a lazy wisp of smoke drifting skyward. It halted beside the coal tower, and I immediately went into action with my brand-new Kodak Pony IV camera. As luck would have it, the very first picture I ever shot with it was of an operating steam locomotive.

Then the hostler invited me up into the cab to ride into the roundhouse — what a thrill! I didn't realize it then, of course, but that fateful lucky Saturday marked the beginning of an absorbing, lifelong hobby. There would be more visits to Lambton, and each time Lady Luck smiled on me, providing one or more of CPR's dwindling reserve of steam locomotives for me to watch and photograph. On a rainy

Remembrance Day visit that fall, I encountered a fellow rail enthusiast, Ted Wickson, who became a lifelong friend and even, for several years, a co-worker at the TTC. On that occasion I had a brief cab ride on one of CPR's finest locomotives, G3g class Pacific 2399.

Then, on sunny December 31, 1959, the ground thick with recent snow, the phone rang in my house on Melrose Avenue in North Toronto. It was Don Cochrane, telling me that the last scheduled steam locomotive was about to depart on a freight for Montreal. I hustled out to Lambton, dreading that I would be too late. The Runnymede bus at the corner of Keele and St. Clair seemed to take forever to arrive. As we neared the familiar bulk of the roundhouse, I spotted a column of grayish smoke.

I leaped off the bus and raced up the stairs to the yard as Mikado-type locomotive Number 5411, a sleek, massive machine just 19 years old, glided past and coupled onto its train. The roundhouse crew had done themselves proud, polishing and shining the boiler until it gleamed in the cold winter sun. Newspaper photographers and yours truly recorded the event. I climbed up into the cab, enjoying the cosy warmth.

Then, shortly after three o'clock, it was time to step down and take up position for my farewell photos. There was the familiar lazy sigh of air as the brakes were released, then I saw

the engineer's gauntleted hand pulling back on the throttle. The 5411 came to life, the drivers revolving ever more slowly, then gaining momentum. Smoke shot skyward as the engine passed me, the thunder of the exhaust shattering the sky. I shot pictures feverishly, for I knew this would be one of the most exhilarating, and saddest, experiences I would ever have.

On June 5, 1960, Lambton Roundhouse echoed to the sounds of a steam locomotive for the last time. One of the magnificent Royal Hudson passenger locomotives, No. 2857, beautifully repainted and polished, was sent down to Union Station to pull a Farewell to Steam excursion to Port McNicoll. It was the end of an era.

Two months later, a diesel yard switcher removed what was likely the last steam locomotive, Number 1057. This veteran, ironically constructed the same year as the roundhouse, was destined, not for scrap, but for display at Regal Stationery on Eglinton Ave. E., Leaside. Today, Lambton's last engine operates periodically at the South Simcoe Railway at Tottenham, Ontario.

In 1993 the Lambton Roundhouse site was occupied by a trucking concern, virtually all traces of its former use had vanished. However, for myself and countless other rail CPR's fans who were lucky enough to be there, the roundhouse will remain forever bright in our memories.

Mary Etta Cherry: An Educator to Remember

by Jonathon Reid

One of Toronto's best known teachers has been borne to the grave . . . after a brilliant career. . . . She is mourned by hundreds of students.

Front page article from West Toronto Weekly, *February 26, 1942*

MARY ETTA CHERRY, the first principal of Western Avenue School, died at her home at 243 Keele Street, on February 18, 1942, after a brief illness. She left no immediate family. She had lived in West Toronto Junction for nearly 50 years, for 27 of them principal of the school so many had hoped would one day bear her name.

Miss Cherry in her prime, 1907.
Courtesy of Gwen Couture

She was born in the mid-1860s, in Dundas, Ontario, the child of Margaret and William Cherry who had immigrated from Ireland. The family moved around, and Mary attended schools in Strabane, Orillia and Galt before receiving her Teacher's Certificate from the Toronto Normal School in June 1887. Her early teaching career took her to Ivanhoe, Rawden and Uxbridge, before being appointed in 1891 to the staff of Carlton School on Davenport Road, where she remained for eleven and a half years.

In 1901, having proved her worth at Carlton, Miss Cherry was put in charge of the new school on Western Avenue as *de facto* principal, officially overseen by Principal Wilson of Annette Street School. In 1905 Miss Cherry was confirmed as principal of Western Avenue School, a position she held until her retirement in June 1928.

From the evidence, Mary Cherry, not yet 40, approached this stage of her life and work with a fully formed, comprehensive educational philosophy.

Healthy growth of the intellect and the body were twin and inseparable goals. Inculcating recognition of duty and commitment to doing a job properly were givens. Brewing in young minds a wonder and excitement at life and its possibilities was a central responsibility of all teachers. And school was not a closed system. It was an integral part of the larger community which for Miss Cherry included, church, charity and missionary endeavours, along with the work-a-day reality of the agricultural, business and professional worlds towards which the young people under her tutelage were making their way.

Miss Cherry's own words, recorded in the foreword of *The Yesteryears of our Community*, published by Runnymede School in 1939, are worth repeating. She began by translating the word "education" from Latin: "Duco - I lead; e - out of; tion - the act of doing, - 'I lead out of the act of doing.' Education," she continued, "means leading the young mind out to an understanding and an appreciation of the vibrant glorious world. That was the teacher's ideal definition of the word "Education" 50 years ago. It caught my fancy then, and still holds it. Modern trends in education all have their origin in a

vital past. You can't get away from the fact that you can build no superstructure which will stand, save one – a superstructure on a solid foundation. . . . Begin where you find the child – *exactly* where you find him, and from his living present experiences lead him into the storied past and the beckoning future where he is to live and move and have his being."

Miss Cherry added to this philosophy a dimension of enlightenment ahead of its time: her open respect for the young, and her readiness to fight on their behalf. She spoke out on the subject of children's rights, emphasizing that recreation, which would develop children socially, educationally and ethically, was the right of every child. Early on she successfully lobbied against the Board of Education's policy of locking school recreational areas after school hours and during the summer. Many years later, in his book *The Toronto That Used To Be*, Rae Corelli wrote that summer in the Junction wasn't just a time for kids to play, but also a time to remember Mary Etta Cherry for making the playgrounds available.

In 1911 Western's cadets, under Miss Cherry's command, won the highly esteemed Lord Strathcona's medal for overall excellence. Western's sports teams were unstoppable for the same reason. As Maynard Metcalf, an Annette Street School graduate, recalled in his autobiography, *One Man's Word For It*, ". . . the primary education of the budding geniuses and politicians of the town was provided by four public schools: Annette, Western, Carlton and St. Clair. The athletic event of the year was the school field day, and Western usually walked off with the championship because, so it was said, of the aggressive character of the principal of the school, affectionately known to her 'subjects' as 'Madame' rather than Miss Cherry. 'Madame' Cherry pioneered organized sports and athletics as a regular part of school activities. Hence her pupils were better prepared for the interscholastic field days which came once a year."

Miss Cherry's approach to academics was just as vigorous. A feature article on Western Avenue School, published in the *Toronto Star Weekly* in November 1917, recorded the inventiveness of the reading instruction, the success of the story-telling approach to spelling and word definition, and Miss Cherry's emphasis on map-making as a means of learning geography. Discipline in the school — at 700 students the largest school in Toronto with a woman principal, as the reporter trumpeted in his headline — was excellent. Integration of school and community was also noted. The large auditorium seating 500 was described as "the fruits of Miss Cherry's campaign to make the school the social centre of the district," and the success of Western's Mothers' Association, founded by Miss Cherry, was acknowledged.

Her commitment to service within the church and in her private life was equally robust. She was a devoted member of St. John's Anglican Church and, being without family, often welcomed young boarders in need of a home who received the added benefit of her wisdom and guidance. I know of one young man,

Robert Harris, a school drop-out at the age of 12, who, under her influence, returned to finish high school in 1909 when he was 20. He then proceeded to medical school at the University of Toronto, where he graduated at the top of his class, and ultimately became the leading Canadian orthopaedic surgeon of his time. Dr. R. I. Harris never lost touch with her, and the "Legend of Miss Cherry" continues in his family to this day, three generations later.

In April 1928, as her retirement approached, large deputations of West Toronto supporters, armed with petitions, appeared three times before Toronto trustees, lobbying heatedly to have the school named after her — all to no avail. Apparently they feared setting a dangerous precedent.

Dr. Minerva Reid, a founder of Women's College Hospital and its past surgeon-in-chief, replied for the deputation: "The only objection I have heard to the change is that Miss

Cherry is not *dead*! That objection will always stand, for her name will never die in Ward Seven. If you ask the pupils what school they attend," Reid thundered, "they do not say 'Western Avenue School,' but 'Miss Cherry's school'!"

During the controversy, much-publicized in the press where support also ran strongly in favour of her name being given to the school, Miss Cherry remained serenely above the fray, and in tendering her resignation showed not the slightest hard feelings, speaking only of her indebtedness to the board, "for constant helpfulness and courteous consideration throughout my long period of service."

The Board graciously returned the compliment. Their official minutes record the following: ". . . in accepting the resignation of Miss Mary E. Cherry, an esteemed Principal, a great educator and an outstanding woman who has for many years given of herself unsparingly in the cause of educa

Kindergarten at Western Avenue Public School, 1919. Verna Swan, 2nd from right in 2nd row.
Courtesy of Verna Swan Lynes

tion as Principal of Western Avenue School, this Board desires to express its appreciation of her splendid services in the cause of education and her faithful attention to duty. This well-beloved Principal has had a most distinguished career in the work, she has

been always an inspiration to her pupils and a wonderful asset to the neighbourhood."

It is a lesson for us to consider that a century ago in December 1901, Miss Cherry and Miss Barnes — excited, optimistic and full of the task at hand

— welcomed the first children into the classrooms of Western Avenue Public School. One hundred years later we are celebrating what they began. In doing so we are all part of what Miss Cherry so deeply believed: All education has its origins in a vital past.

TOP
Young athletes of Western Avenue Public School in 1911.
Indian Road Crescent Public School

BOTTOM
Western Avenue Public School ca. 1917.
Toronto Board of Education Archives

Courage: The Artist as a Young Man

by R. M. "Mel" McLean

Mel McLean grew up on Gillespie Avenue and graduated from Carleton Public School, after which he went to the Ontario College of Art in 1925. The following is an account of his experience with the largest art work ever painted by a member of the Group of Seven – the five-piece mural painted for Humberside Collegiate, which was recently restored by the school, with the help of the West Toronto Junction Historical Society.

IN 1925 I WAS FORTUNATE to have enrolled in day classes at the Ontario College of Art (OCA) where Arthur Lismer was the Vice-Principal. Later in the course I became an assistant to Lismer, operating the projector for his "History of Art" lectures at the Toronto Art Gallery and the University of Toronto extension classes, as well as lectures for the summer teachers courses at OCA. I also helped in his studio when the centre panel for the mural at Humberside was painted and installed in 1928 on the wall of the original auditorium at Humberside.

When Mr. Lismer first began preparing to paint the centre mural, he had a carpenter build wooden trestles to hold the large frame that the linen canvas would be stretched on. The carpenter also built a painting stand from which to paint the high parts of the mural. It was a platform about three feet square and about five or six feet high with a railing on three sides. The carpenter then built steps up one side with railings. This platform was moved around and the painter could reach any part of the mural.

The mural was eighteen feet high by ten feet wide and Lismer's studio was only fifteen feet high. The frame for the mural had to have three-foot sections, one for the top and the other for the bottom. This made it possible to turn the bottom section up while the top was being painted. To paint the bottom section, the top was bent down and the mural was raised so that the bottom could be painted. Raising the mural and securing the bottom section was a difficult job because of the weight.

After the frame was assembled it was lifted to the top of the trestles the carpenter had made, then the Belgian linen was stretched over the frame and then sized with a hot gelatin coating. When it was dry, a coat of paint was applied by brush to the linen. The paint was made from lead, boiled oil, turpentine, and dryers. When it was dry, we carried the canvas on the frame to the east wall, with both the top and the bottom section turned up.

Mr. Lismer first painted a preliminary painting about 40 inches by 70 inches on a separate canvas with a few figures on it. I still have the canvas, having saved it when he was moving from the house to the studio. It had been discarded.

The next time I was in the studio helping was when the mural was near completion. I posed for the figure with the garment on, holding a staff. In the frieze at the bottom it is called "Courage". The woman on the right called "Beauty" was painted, but Lismer was not satisfied with her left leg. He used my left leg as a model, so I have my left leg in the mural as well.

When the top section was completed and dry, our next problem was to bend down the top three-foot section so the mural could be raised up with the bottom frieze section at ground level. The bottom section was the frieze with the ribbon scroll and names of the figures.

When Lismer was completely satisfied with the painting of the mural and it was dry, we had to lift the mural down and put it on the trestles. The tacks were removed from the sides of the canvas where it was attached to the frame. The next problem was to trim the sides of the canvas to the ten-foot width. Then the mural was rolled up from the & ready to be transported to Humberside Collegiate Institute. When we arrived in the auditorium at Humberside, Board of Education men had built a large wood scaffolding.

The wall that the mural was to be put on was a rough-cast sand plaster trowelled to a smooth surface. It did not have a white plaster finish. The plaster wall had to be sealed with a paint sealer which my father, a decorating contractor, painted. When the paint was dry, a mixture of white lead, enamel and turpentine was prepared to coat the wall so that the mural could be fastened to it.

Two of us held the rolled up mural from the centre platform as two men pulled the top up and fastened it to the wall. We gradually rolled it down while pressing the mural to the wall with cloths until it was secured. We noticed at different places small bubbles of white paint would come through on a nose or different parts of the mural. These were wiped off and Mr. Lismer used the paints from his palette to touch up the spots.

I was away from Toronto when the rest of the mural was painted and installed. A student by the name of Harold Kihl worked on some of the pieces and I am sure that his signature is on one of the sections to the left of the centre one.

Any of Lismer's students who are still living will be delighted to learn that Humberside has restored the murals and that they honoured him by naming the auditorium Lismer Hall.

Mel McLean poses for the figure "Courage" in the centre panel of Arthur Lismer's mural. This drawing shows the 18 x 10 foot canvas folded over.

Crashed and Spiked: School Daze in the Junction

by Joe Alexandroff

WE MOVED IN 1913 from the last house [north] on Quebec Avenue to 110 Maria Street which my father built. A short time later I started at Strathcona Public School on St. John's Road at Runnymede. My favourite subject, next to recess, was Manual Training, which we had to take at Annette Street Public School, as it had the proper equipment and set-up. One morning each week in our last two grades, we were allowed to leave Strathcona, after checking in, and sent to Annette.

Accident between schools

On one of these occasions, as we straggled noisily in little groups along St. John's Road, we heard shouting behind us. Looking back, we were quickly galvanized into action, heading for the safety of verandahs or between houses. Racing toward us was a runaway team of horses dragging a wagon emitting sparks as its iron tires hit the curb. When the horses passed us, one was on the lawn, the other running on the sidewalk. But they came to a sudden terrifying halt as they straddled a post between them. The impact pulled the horses around and their heads banged together. The post broke, but was held up by the overhead wires, as the centre shaft smashed, one piece piercing the first horse, which kicked feebly and then lay still. The other horse raised its head a few times and whinnied, but could not get to its feet.

We approached the horses very carefully and just stood there looking.

Soon we were joined by the driver who was out of breath and crying. He was not much older than we were and our emotions were in a turmoil also. As a crowd started to gather, we remembered that we had a deadline, so we tore ourselves away. A police patrol wagon passed us going to the scene and shortly after we rounded Clendenan Avenue, we winced as we heard a shot and knew that the other horse was also dead.

Manual training just dragged and dragged that day. When it was over we ran most of the way back and got there just in time to see a team of horses pull the second horse on top of the first, which was already on the Dead Animal Wagon.

I guess this is so clear in my mind because my father had a lot of horses in his lumberyard for use in his building, wrecking and lumber activities. He also always had a horse or two stabled at our house in the backyard, as well as a small buggy and a larger family-sized one.

Orating at Humberside Collegiate

The biggest change in my life in 1921 was becoming a pupil at Humberside Collegiate Institute. Suddenly I was "Alexandroff", instead of the more familiar "Joe". There was a great overcrowding of new high school pupils and my form, 1G, was in the portables along with three other classes. These were on the south side of the school, close to Clendenan Avenue. Because of the overcrowding, many retired teachers were pressed back into serv-

ice. For a few weeks we had a retired inspectress whose classes were most interesting and different. I remember discussing news events and other items in the daily newspapers.

But what fixed her in my memory forever was the day I had to give my first oral composition. We had to orate in alphabetical order of our names and I was to be second. We could choose our own subject. I chose to speak on Russia, the cruel regime that forced my parents to leave and look for a better life in Canada in 1906. Maybe you can imagine my torment as I sat there, when the first student, a girl, was called up. She addressed the teacher, the pupils, then looked around scared, started to cry and ran into the cloakroom!

I don't know how I got up there, I think I floated up, there was no feeling in my legs. I addressed the teacher, the pupils, and then just stood there looking helplessly at her with my mind a complete blank.

"It's OK, watch this," she said. Then to my horror she pulled out her desk drawer and took out a hammer and a four inch spike. She walked to the back of the room, reached up and tapped the spike into the wall. She came back and asked me if I could see the nail. When I said yes, she told me to speak to the nail and never take my eyes off of it. I did and had very little trouble.

I have many times stood up in moments of business or club stress and nailed home a good point while remembering this moment!

III

FACING PAGE, TOP
Humberside Collegiate as it looked during the 1920s.
Courtesy of Les Stringer

FACING PAGE, BOTTOM
Strathcona Public School ca. 1914.
Valentine & Co. postcard

LEFT
Joe Alexandroff 1986.
Courtesy of Joe Alexandroff

RIGHT
Jewish Boys Club, Toronto Junction Branch 1926-7, photographed in the gym of Humberside Collegiate where they used the facilities under the care of the West Toronto YMCA. (L-R) Back row: an Alspector, Hymie Usprich, –, a Culiner, an Usprich, Max Alexandroff, a Culiner –, Dutchy Jacobs. Second row down: Joe Alexandroff left end, an Alspector second from right, "Babe" Pearlstone right end. Third row down: a Leibel toward centre in striped sweater, an Usprich in diamond sweater, two Greenblatts second and third from right end. Front row: fourth over "Shoom", right end "Itzy" Salkin.
Courtesy of Joe Alexandroff

A Question of Patriotism: Harry Lee and the Great War

by David Roberts

I N THE FOYER of Annette Street School is an old-looking, cast-metal plaque erected in 1917 by the Board of Education to commemorate the death the previous year of Harry Erland Lee, the first public-school teacher from Toronto to "make the supreme sacrifice" for King and Country in World War I. A large portrait of Lee, donated to the school by its teachers and students at the same time, has since disappeared. So too has memory of the controversy surrounding Harry Lee's troubled response to the war.

Of Loyalist-Methodist background, Harry was born in 1889 on the family farm at Stoney Creek near Hamilton, a son of Marcus and Ida Lee; he was named after his uncle. He attended the local public and high schools, Hamilton Collegiate, and in 1907-8 the faculty of education at the University of Toronto. His aunt, three first cousins, and probably other relatives had all gone into teaching. In keeping too with the family tradition of military service, he spent time in the Wentworth County militia in 1913 and trained at infantry schools in Niagara-on-the-Lake and Hamilton and at the musketry school in Ottawa. One close cousin followed a similar path of military preparation.

Lee taught at the Victoria Industrial School in Mimico before transferring in September 1914, just a month after the outbreak of war, to the newly rebuilt Annette, then known as "the railway man's school" after its working-class locale. Part of a staff of about 25, he was given the junior fourth class; in addition, he took on a position in the night school at Ogden School downtown. Of middle height and dark complexion, the young bachelor lived in a boarding house at 137 Medland Street. In the eulogies that would attend the plaque's unveiling, the outspoken teacher took a genuine interest in students' welfare. Whatever he said and did in his classroom at Annette School in late December or early January drew him into the vortex of anti-German paranoia, which demanded blatant fidelity from all of Toronto's teachers.

The evidence is murky and layered in bias, with few direct statements from Lee. As directed by the board, he initiated "war talks" or discussions of the war in his class. Apparently he had a reputation for being argumentative, with a tendency to philosophical and socialistic points of view. Often ill-defined and splintered, the socialist movement was just one of the ideological currents of radical reform that were making public authorities uneasy, especially so at the start of the conflict. Other than his past militia affiliations, Lee belonged to no known organizations. According to his principal, William Wilson, the people at his boarding house, where he talked about the war, were bored with his views. At no point did Lee explain his classroom discussions. Whatever was said, two or three students mentioned the discussions to their parents, who, perhaps with axes to grind, complained to their local trustee, Dr. R. R. Hopkins. He immediately set out to rid the board of Harry Lee.

The campaign of vilification began on the evening of January 7, when Hopkins interviewed Lee and quickly came to the conclusion that, because of his "pro-German sentiments," he should be dismissed from Annette School as "unfit to discuss the war before loyal British children." The press was so informed. Lee offered an explanation but was temporarily suspended by Inspector J. W. Rogers, and the next night Hopkins explained the summary dismissal before a meeting at Annette of the Ward Seven Ratepayers' Association. Questioned by the *Globe*, Principal Wilson came down hard on Lee as a teacher — he had supposedly tried to steer him away from controversy — but Wilson was befuddled when the newspaper asked him how Lee could be a socialist and still support the German kaiser, a question that turned on socialist opposition in Germany to war before conflict erupted.

On January 12, Lee was questioned and then reinstated by chief inspector Robert H. Cowley. Lee blamed two

Valentine & Co. postcard showing Annette Street Public School, sent May 9, 1914.
Courtesy of Donald Harlock

Annette Street, Public School, West Toronto, Ont., Canada

students who had been "a constant source of annoyance to him" and whose parents, he maintained, had complained spitefully to Hopkins. Since the whole episode was deemed "irregular," with no clear process, some questioned whether the matter had to go to the board's management committee, but that is where it landed for further investigation. At a public meeting of the committee on the 14th, Hopkins tabled his written charges: Lee claimed to be a Teuton and familiar with German "Socialistic writers," his teachings and explanations of hostilities were pro-German, and his classroom duties were being neglected. After an inconclusive debate about legal responsibility for investigation, and vague reports of "alien enemies" elsewhere in the board's staff, the committee deferred action until Lee, Hopkins, the two inspectors, and Annette's principal could be brought together the following week. In the meantime, Lee had resigned his position at Ogden School.

Whatever Harry Lee felt to this point, he was not prepared to sink in the mire of patriotic innuendo, school-based antagonisms, and unclear board procedure. On January 19 he appeared before a special meeting of management committee. The crowded audience included about a dozen students from Lee's class. Appearing on his behalf was Thomas Cowper Robinette, KC. Though Hopkins also had counsel, board solicitor E. Percival Brown, some members of committee took umbrage at Lee's representation by one of Canada's foremost criminal lawyers. The hearing, which lasted three hours, was inconclusive but the lines were clearly drawn. Hopkins and Wilson remained convinced that Lee was a "strong Socialist." "My knowledge of Socialistic writers in Germany is meagre," Lee retorted in a statement that reflected Robinette's careful legal coaching, and he reiterated his full support for the allies. The *Globe*, in its report of the hearing, caught a revealing distinction in his testimony: though he backed the allies, he hated militarism.

Conscious that some staff at the board's technical school had been singled out for their German origins but were being aggressively defended by their principal, management committee met again at the end of the month

to review the evidence against Lee, who had again been placed under suspension. It calmly reached certain conclusions. Lee was no German; his "war talks," though not as gung-ho on loyalty as some wished, had not instilled anti-British ideas into the minds of his students; concerns about his ability as a teacher should come forward "through the proper channels"; and he should be returned to his classroom on 1 February, pending the chief inspector's examination of his teaching record. Though some trustees still pushed for Lee's resignation, the board accepted the committee's finding on February 4. Lee was certainly not the newly elected board's only concern: the accidental shooting of a student at Kent School on January 23 had alarmed many.

On February 18, the very day that the inspectorial report on Lee's teaching ability was slated to go to the board, Harry Lee went down to the military camp at Toronto's exhibition grounds, enlisted, and applied for a leave of absence from the board. The *Globe* found his timing "a curious coincidence," though the report would not actually be tabled until March, by which time attention focussed on Lee's status as a probationary teacher and salary. Why did Harry Lee enlist? Was it to avoid further embarrassment or harassment? Was he, consistent with his past military training and professed patriotism, doing his duty, or taking the "acid test" as the *Globe* put it? Lee's exact motivation remains unclear. For the board of education, the difficult problems of unpatriotic and Germanic association could be shelved, although more instances would arise. At Annette, students turned with vigour to supporting the war effort by

working towards certificates from the Canadian Red Cross.

On enlisting, Lee joined the 4th Canadian Mounted Rifles as a private. In July he went overseas to England. His time there was not pleasant: between September and December he was hospitalized with gonorrhoea. After a spell with the Fort Garry Horse, he transferred in February 1916 to the 1st Canadian Motor Machine-Gun Battalion, and with it went to France at the end of June. Several weeks later, while manning his gun with B Battery on the night of September16-17 during the battle of Courcelette, Harry E. Lee, service number 109447, was killed by shell fire. He was buried in a British cemetery 500 yards southwest of the small village of Pozières, near Albert.

Lee was recognized as the first Toronto teacher to die in the Great War, though many others enlisted, saw service, and died later. Another Annette teacher, Donald S. Macpherson, enlisted in 1916 and would live to see his war diaries published. Later that same year, a motion by the board to erect a plaque in Harry Lee's memory was evidently voted down on the grounds that one plaque should be put up at war's end to honour all the serving teachers who died. Annette could erect its own memorial. The board quietly reversed its position, however, and in December it authorized three trustees to purchase an appropriate tablet for installation at Annette.

The plaque and portrait of Lee, commissioned by the school from an unknown artist, were hung in the main corridor of the school in early May

PTE·HARRY E·LEE
EDUCATION

IN MEMORY OF
Gunner
Harry Erland Lee,
WHO FELL
FIGHTING FOR THE EMPIRE
AT
COURCELETTE,
SEPT. 16. 1916.
THE FIRST TORONTO TEACHER
TO MAKE
THE SUPREME SACRIFICE.

LEFT
Harry E. Lee, undated graduation photo.

RIGHT
This plaque is mounted in the entrance foyer at Annette School.
Larry Burak

Local Boy Makes Good

1917. At a ceremony in the auditorium on 22 June, district commander Major-General William Alexander Logie, who knew the "fighting" Lee family, officially unveiled the plaque and portrait in the presence of members of the family and a "large company" of parents, teachers, and students. Apart from the unveiling, the *Mail and Empire* reported, "the evening was a military one, [with] appropriate songs and recitations tending to stir up the patriotic sentiments of the audience." In death, "Gunner Lee" was assigned sterling qualities. Board chairman Miles Vokes described him as having been a teacher "beloved by his scholars." Sparing no superlative, the superintendent of the Mimico industrial school, Chester Ferrier, recalled Lee's courageous and unselfish work there. Logie, conscious of Lee's controversial convictions in 1915, said it was his actions and sacrifice that mattered. Even his former antagonists, trustee Hopkins and principal Wilson, sang his praises. Later in 1917, and again in 1920, Marcus Lee endured the painful process of helping the University of Toronto complete its roll of service on his son.

Lee's example resurfaced in January 1918, the last year of the war, not in eulogistic terms, but in the context of critical debate in the case of Freda Held of Carlton Street School. Pilloried by Hopkins and others for suspected disloyalty, here too with vague notions of lurking socialism, she resigned, with the board refusing to investigate. One supporter remembered how Harry Lee had almost been "driven out of the schools for thinking a little for himself." Another defender, Professor C. B. Sissons from the university, thought the plaque to Lee "should stand as a warning to those who mistake loyalty to convention for loyalty to country. Above all things, our teachers must feel free to think for themselves, and if at times they are in error, should expect warning and guidance, rather than the methods of the Star Chamber."

Perhaps this is what Hopkins and Wilson thought they had tried to do with the headstrong teacher at Annette Street School. Lee, however, did not meet the board's criteria for inculcating patriotism. Loyalty became a vital quality for teachers, and Harry Erland Lee had to enlist and give his life to achieve the standard.

by John K. Barnes

MY MEMORIES OF Carleton, Davenport and Osler Schools are many and varied. They go back to when I, as a lad in 1909, enrolled in Carlton School under the principalship of Mr. Hancock.

Of the first few years much is almost beyond recall. I do, however, remember the old school facing the north. The playground to the south was elevated above the street level and made of wooden planks. This platform sounded like thunder when the pupils, most with heavy boots, assembled and marched into the school. At other times, like recess and dismissal, the thunder was somewhat compounded.

I went through the usual grades, from Junior First on. One of the events I do remember was carrying our books and supplies to the new Carlton School. My teacher was Mr. Armstrong, who enlisted in the army before the term ended. Miss Chantler took over for the rest of the year.

I recall when some of the pupils attended St. Mark's [Anglican] Church Sunday school in a wooden building facing Ford Street. Mr. Hancock was the superintendent. Most of us behaved fairly well in Sunday school because we had the feeling that if we misbehaved on Sunday, Monday would bring a reckoning. I have no proof that it did, but most of us had that feeling!

Mr. Hancock, as superintendent, often put on entertainments in the Sunday School Hall which anyone could attend. On one occasion I recall, as a member of the Boys Brigade Bugle Band, we "entertained" the audience with our version of:

Here comes the Boys Brigade
All smothered in marmalade
A tu'penny ha'penny pill box
And a half yard of braid.

In Senior Fourth I was taught arithmetic and grammar by Mr. Hancock and the other subjects by Miss Henderson. My final year was an outstanding one in many ways. Aside from being promoted, the big events had to do with the achievements of the Cadet Corps of which I was a proud member. The corps won the city championship in military drill and in rifle shooting. Both events took place in the Armouries on University Avenue. We practised our shooting at targets properly placed in the school basement. Our proudest moment arrived when we took part in the march past down University Avenue on Empire Day.

With a lapse of several years to further my education, I returned to Carlton in 1926 as an occasional teacher, filling in for Mr. Ed Smith. It was then that opportunity knocked for me. Mr. Hancock was opening a new class and asked me if I would like to take over. My career was launched! My appointment, after a certification from the lady inspector, Dr. Marty, and the Board of Education, was signed for $1,625 a year. The staff adopted me as a local boy who had succeeded. They helped me over many a rough spot in the years that followed.

There were a few irritants along the way. The size of the classes seldom slid below 48. One year I had an extra pupil sitting at my desk. Doing away with sharp pen nibs and ink wells was a blessing.

Relaxing from the ups and downs of classroom routine, we as a staff found time to bowl at the Dufferin Street bowling alleys. A number of us played badminton morning, noon and after school. We used the kindergarten then. We had social gatherings, picnics, etc. We even had a dinner at the posh Granite Club.

Carlton and Davenport pupils did very well in athletics. The high point in soccer came in 1936, when the bantam, junior and senior teams each won the city championships in their division. In 1933 a group of pupils took part in a city-wide physical culture demonstration in front of the grandstand at Exhibition Park. It was in honour of the visit to Toronto of Lord Bessborough, Governor General of Canada.

With the retirement of Mr. Hancock, there followed several short-term principals. When Perth Senior School opened, Mr. Carter and I moved there. We spent several years at Perth under Mr. Stiver and then we went on to Osler when it opened.

At Osler, Mr. Carter and I fitted in very well with the second floor group — Miss Dorse, Dave Reese, Dave Coulter and Marv Lipton. It was a pleasant and rewarding ending to my career in an almost high school atmosphere.

My final memory (1966) was being on the platform of farewell when the temperature in the auditorium was at the melting point. In many ways it was a truly a memorable farewell!

E. Hancock

TOP LEFT
Mr. E. W. Hancock principal and coach of the Carlton School Rifle Team, City and District Champions in 1926.
(Note: his name is misspelled on the photo!)
Courtesy of Earl McLean

TOP RIGHT
John K. Barnes, in his classroom at Carlton School, 1938.
Courtesy of John K. Barnes

BOTTOM
Empire Day tableau on the steps of Carlton Public School ca. 1900.
Toronto Board of Education Archives

Life on the Streets

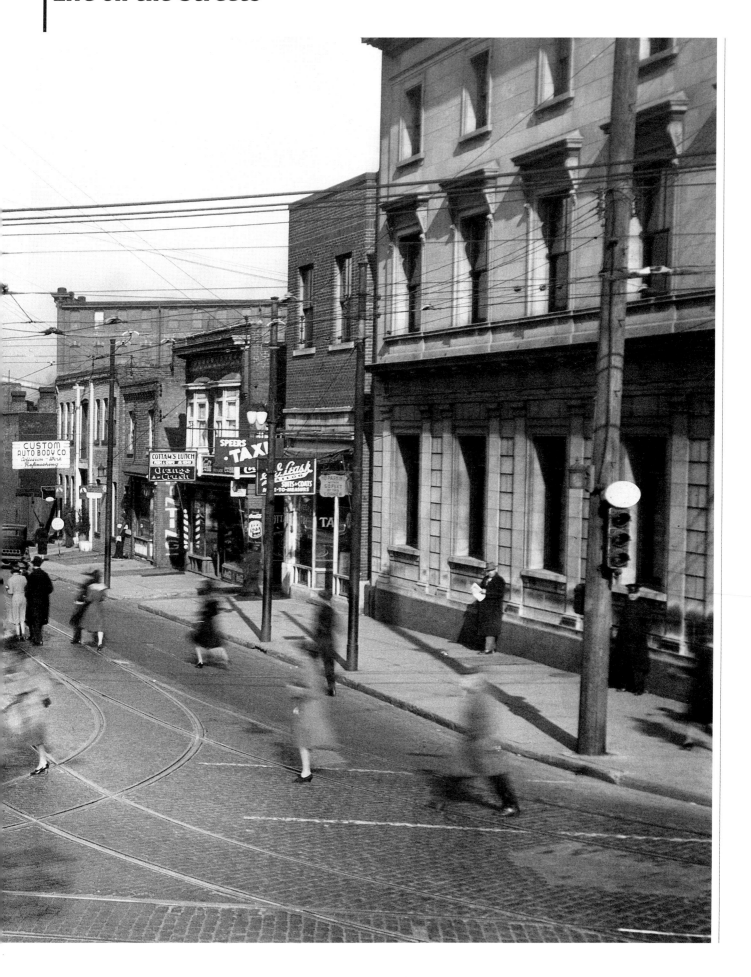

Roughing It on Runnymede Road

118

by Vera Downey Fitzgerald

I WAS BORN IN 1900. I had four brothers and I was the only girl and the youngest. We moved out to 181 Elizabeth Street (renamed Runnymede Road) in 1901. Out here was called the country then, it was so far west, and all my relatives would bring their friends out on Sunday and they would say, come on, we're going to the country. That was Runnymede Road. The lots were big and the house that my father bought was the mayor's house, Jimmy Bond, I think it was.

There were very few houses on Runnymede Road, perhaps two houses from Annette down to Bloor. Bloor Street was just a mud hole. My father was always fond of skating and he would flood the part of the lot north of the house, where there were no trees, with a hose and the boys would come from a long distance away to play hockey.

The house looked like a farmhouse, it had the peak, two bedrooms in the front with shutters on the windows, but we never closed them. There was a veranda all the way across the front of the house. All the rooms were very large, with a dining room that was the

whole length of the house. We had no bathroom when we first moved there, but my father had one of the bedrooms made into a bathroom.

We never had servants, my mother was very healthy, you know. And my father, he was retired when he came out (from the dairy business). He used to do all the outside work, all the gardening and things like that, and mother did the work inside. She was used to it, from the farm.

We had cherry trees, apple trees and pear trees and a big barn. Will Shaver and his sister, they were relatives of ours, came every morning during the week from Islington, drove down in a horse and buggy and left the horse and buggy at our place, because we had a big barn and a big yard and you could just drive in. From our house they walked to Humberside Collegiate. They graduated from there.

We had lamps in the house when we first moved there, just lamps, and then next we got gas in the house and there was a big post outside. The streets were lit with gas. There was a huge thick rope and it was tied on the bottom of the post on a hook. The man would come around about five o'clock or just before dark and pull

that down, take the rope and pull the light down and light it and pull it up again.

So one time the boys undid the rope and they were skipping with it, having a great time, even though they

weren't supposed to touch it, of course. Mother didn't know anything about it until a few days later a policeman came to our door and said, "Mrs. Downey?" We had company, you know, and to see a policeman come to the door, that was really awful. He told her about the boys playing with the rope and to make sure they didn't touch it again. I don't know how old I was when we got electricity, perhaps eight or nine, but I thought, "Oh, I'll be able to play out all night," because it was so bright.

We used to skate Tuesday, Thursday and Saturday at Ravina Rink. There would be crowds on Saturday night. And of course we'd hold, you know, our arms close together, and we had really good skaters there. We had a three piece band in even the coldest weather, it could be zero weather and they'd come out on the verandah and play and then go back in and get warm.

One time I was skating with a really good skater and we were going around, just in a circle, and right at our feet a couple ahead of us fell. The rink was crowded and we had to think quickly, and we jumped them. We didn't hit them and we didn't fall. That was Charlie Barber, one of the chaps I skated with a lot, he was a wonderful skater.

I skated at Ravina from the time I was eight or nine years old. They had "bands", and someone would come up and say, "Will you give me a band?" and I would say, "Well, I have one," and they'd come up and get you. I generally had my bands all full. We had intermissions between the bands.

I must have been about eight or ten years old the year the stock yards were on fire and we could see the smoke from our place, even though it was away up on St. Clair Avenue. We could see the smoke, so my girl friend said, "Let's go to the fire!" I asked my mother or dad, one of them and they said, "No, you can't go, that's too far away." Finally my girl friend said,

"we'll just go to Evelyn Avenue." So they said, all right, don't walk any further than that.

We just kept on going and walked to St. Clair Avenue, and by this time it was dark. But I'm glad we went, because I never saw a fire like it. The stock yards were on fire and three houses were burnt. People were coming out with pillows in their hands and mattresses and then the roof would go flat — I never saw a fire like it. We didn't get home until about ten o'clock and as soon as I went in, my father slapped me across the face, they were so worried about me going there. But I'm glad I didn't miss it.

Postscript

The stock yards fire in 1908 was so extensive that the stock yards had to be entirely rebuilt. The house at 557-9 Runnymede Road is still there, but has been completely refronted and divided into apartments.

Postcard.
Courtesy of Howard Thompson

Growing Up on Old Weston Road

by Tom Wogden

WHEN MY PARENTS, Tom Wogden and Amelia Lomax, came to Toronto in 1912 from Derbyshire England, they were on their honeymoon, although they never went back, not even for a visit. For a short time they lived on McMurray Avenue in the Junction. A sales slip from Birkett's Grocery Store at the corner of McMurray and Dundas shows that at the time $1.83 would buy almost a week's supply of groceries.

After two or three months, they moved to 314 Weston Road North (now Old Weston Road) where my maternal grandparents, Mr. And Mrs. Edward Lomax, had purchased one of the four-room, semi-detached houses on the west side of the street between Davenport Road and St. Clair Avenue. Along with mother's brother, Edward Jr., they lived in that house until I was born on December 7, 1916, and then for two years afterwards. At this time my father built a bungalow on Bernice Crescent on what was then called the Scarlett Plains in York Township.

In 1921 we moved back to Weston Road North, where my father built a home at 326. My uncle Ed Jr. had married by this time and built his house at 324 a little later on. The property for these houses was purchased from Mrs. Brown, who had a grocery store which sold everything from ice cream to coal-oil. The store was all frame construction and very old. It was completely lighted by coal-oil lamps and heated with coal stoves. However, it did have one of the few telephones in the district and people would give her a nickel or a dime to use it.

Mrs. Brown was from Jamaica. She and her husband, who passed away in 1913, owned land from the store at 320 to about 330. There were fruit trees on the property as well — two apple trees ended up in my uncle's back yard and a pear tree in ours. One year Mrs. Brown sold the apples from these trees in her store and set aside the proceeds to purchase a pair of fur-trimmed galoshes for my cousin who was about two at the time.

Mrs. Brown died in about 1928 or 1929. After her sister and cousin came up from New York to settle her estate, the store was demolished. The slightly higher ground on which it had been standing was levelled, and two semi-detached brick houses were erected. Coincidentally, people by the name of White moved into one of them.

The field between the houses and the railway tracks was used for awhile by the Gurney Foundry for slag dumping; presumably it was railway land originally. Eventually it was purchased in about 1950 by the John T. Hepburn Co. for one of their manufacturing plants. Directly behind these houses was the Albert Kerr Co. (hides, wool, furs) which later housed Cadet Cleaners. In a larger house next door to this building a Mr. Dafoe ran a printing shop. However, it was demolished to provide an outdoor eating area for Cadet employees.

It was not unusual to see cattle being driven along Old Weston Road from the stock yards to the small abattoirs in the southwest end of the city. We were also treated to some of the local fife-and-drum marchers who went through the streets practising for the Glorious Twelfth (of July) parade.

Change on the Road

If you ever wonder why Old Weston Road is called by that name, this is the explanation. There used to be a Weston Road North, from the beginning of the Street at Dundas to its intersection with present-day Weston Road. There was also Weston Road South, continuing from that point north. Needless to say, there was considerable confusion at the post office; people often got mail for south instead of north and vice versa. Then Rogers Road was extended to Weston Road South, whereas it used to stop at Weston Road North. Finally, the powers that be decided to call Weston Road North "Old Weston Road" as it is today, stopping it at Rogers Road, instead of continuing along to the other Weston Road where Rogers Road now intersects it.

There have also been changes to the south end of the street. During the centennial of Carleton Village School in 1989, I conducted several walkabouts of the district with school classes. One of our stops was at the grounds of the Metro Pumping Station where we could see and discuss the remains of the Old Weston Road bridge. This bridge provided the most convenient north-south route over the railway tracks for all users, linking Dundas Street to the northern residential and industrial areas. Now people have to take lengthy east or west detours.

The bridge was built in 1911, closed in 1970 and demolished in 1982. One bright lad on a tour asked me: "How come if people want it, and it was so useful, that it hasn't been replaced by a subway or something, because in a democracy, the people should be heard." I heard him all right, but after some thought I replied, "I don't know."

Riding the radials

Before 1923 the Davenport streetcar line ran west along Davenport Road, north on Ford Street to St. Clair

Amelia Lomax Wogden holding young Tom and standing with a neighbour on the front porch of 314 Weston Road North, late spring 1917.
Courtesy of Tom Wogden

Apple blossom time: spring 1927 in the backyard at 324 Weston Road North.

LEFT
Mrs. Brown who had a store and lived next door.

RIGHT
The three children are Tom Wogden standing behind Millie Lomax, a cousin who lived in the house, and seated, his brother Harry. Grandfather Edward Lomax Sr. is standing under the tree.
Courtesy of Tom Wogden

BOTTOM
Another pair of semis, 294 and 296 Old Weston Road, 1989 (compare to the older view of 314 on the facing page); although missing the front railing, the house on the left appears much the same as it did when this subdivision of workmen's homes was built in 1909-10.
Courtesy of Debbie Cox

Avenue, and west on St. Clair to Keele Street. I remember travelling on this line to Casa Loma with my mother. After 1923 the line went north from Davenport along Old Weston Road to St. Clair Avenue, and looped at Townsley Street. It meant that the people on Old Weston Road were deprived of their lovely little boulevard.

The Free Car for Sunnyside Beach started at the car stop on the corner of St. Clair and Old Weston Road, as the Townsley Loop was right behind the Heydon House Hotel. This familiar historic site is where I helped a chum, Bill Tait, sell papers at two cents each: the *Star* and the *Telegram*. Several of the residents of the hotel bought papers which we delivered to them. The garage at the back of the hotel was where horses and cars were kept for guests. My recollection is that there was an athletic club on part of the second floor at one time. The main store in the building at this time was Moore's Drug Store on the corner.

The Guelph radial car ended at Keele Street, instead of crossing to the carbarns, located just behind our house at 326 Old Weston Road. It cost my parents 10 cents each and 5 cents for the children to visit my relatives on Scarlett Road, travelling on this line. The regular TTC fares were four for a quarter for adults and ten for a quarter for children. The carbarns were eventually sold by the TTC and, after use by various transportation companies and other businesses, were removed when John T. Hepburn took over the property. In addition to the Townsley loop, there were car loops for short turn cars, etc. at Caledonia, Prescott, Keele and Northlands.

Ed Seedhouse, who ran a bus line to the west, sold it and started West York Motors which ultimately grew to encompass the south side of St. Clair from east of Osler to Ford Street, after the removal of several houses and two gas stations.

Fuel for love

At one time there were five gas stations located very close together — the only one which survived was on the southwest corner of Weston Road and St. Clair Avenue (all now demolished). The old Red Indian Station at the foot of Ford Street on Davenport Road was run by Herb Rawlinson

whose younger daughter Helen became my wife in 1949.

The people living in the area in those days bore such names as Hall, Tait, Thompson, O'Gorman, Redish, Beeton, Byford, Lainson, Hughes, Hume, Harley, White, Rumble, Bagg, King, Galer, Dunham, Jemmet — and all the adults spoke with a British accent of some sort. It was even odd to hear a so-called Canadian accent among them. Names like Ossosky, Jamendoff and Sala had begun to creep in, however, and today the residents form a veritable League of Nations, with even a Sikh Temple built on the land directly opposite where I used to live.

All those residents were hard-working, industrious people, employed with the railways, packing houses, stock yards, street-car companies, Campbell Flour, Gurney Foundry, Dodge Pulley and other local industries. None of them were ever well known or had streets named after them, but they were the "salt of the earth" to whom we owe a lot of praise. My uncle worked for over fifty-one years at Gunns Ltd. (later part of Canadian Packers) and my father worked thirty-eight years at Swift Canadian. Even my grandfather, who was over 50 years old when he came to Canada, worked 14 years for Canada Packers.

We enjoyed good health, fun and exercise, picnics, sports, games, walks, hikes. We did not realize that we were poor or that we were missing anything. The policeman walked his beat or rode his

"Planet" bicycle. We were familiar with him and felt safe, even after dark. There did not appear to be as much crime in those days.

My brother and myself are both happily retired grandfathers now, but we sometimes wonder if times are really better today than they were in our younger days, or only different.

Postscript:

There have been many changes in the Old Weston Road and St. Clair Avenue area since this article was written in 1993. The abutments of the bridge were demolished completely, in spite of an attempt by the WTJHS to have them incorporated into a park in order to take advantage of their exceptional view of the rail junction. Historical preservation and the

Toronto Public Works Department remain incompatible — as does democracy and federal funding for bridge replacement. Cadet Cleaners has closed. The John T. Hepburn Company is gone, replaced on the east end by the Delta bingo hall. The last traces of the stock yards and meat packing industry are almost obliterated as well, replaced by big box stores, a housing subdivision, and a shopping plaza.

TOP
Looking north toward the intersection of Old Weston Road and St. Clair Ave., December 12, 1944. Three of the five gas stations within a block of each other are visible, along with the tower of the Heydon House Hotel.
Courtesy of Tom Wogden

BOTTOM
View of the Old Weston Road bridge in the 1920s, looking south from Junction Road.
City of Toronto Archives

St. John's Road Revisited

by Diana Fancher

ALTHOUGH ST. JOHN'S ROAD is featured indirectly in several articles and some of its more prominent buildings are catalogued in the Nabob's Retreat walking tour brochure, few people are aware that it is one of the oldest streets in the area, predated only by the major highways.

In 1853 John Major bought 151 acres from John Scarlett and three years later filed a plan of subdivision which he named Runnymede, taking the name of the Scarlett house on the north side of the Dundas Highway, opposite the point of intersection with St. John's Road. At that time it was named Louisa Street, probably after Scarlett's third wife, Louisa Maria Henroid. Maria Street was also part of Plan 166.

Unfortunately for John Major and his investors, no settlement followed and they were eventually foreclosed by the City Bank, beginning a pattern all too familiar to local land speculators.

Twenty-five years later there was renewed interest in the subdivision when the Credit Valley Railway (CVR) located its station in the general vicinity, north of its right-of-way. James Saurin McMurray, an officer of the CVR, also bought, then sold, lots on the south part of the Runnymede Estate property in 1879. Both John Major and James McMurray had wives named Jane, but it was probably the latter who gave her name to Jane Street. The CVR was bought out by Canadian Pacific in 1883.

In 1881 landowners Fisken and Wadsworth donated the lot for St. John's Anglican Church. The congregation had been meeting at various homes in the area since 1879. Fisken Avenue also resulted from this partnership, as did Vernon Street, named for Vernon Wadsworth. Both streets are one block long and one block from the intersection of Louisa and Elizabeth Streets. There are so many local landowners with wives or daughters named Elizabeth, including the wives of both Fisken and Wadsworth, that it is impossible to determine which of them gave her name to the street. In 1909 it was renamed Runnymede Road.

The close connection between this area of York Township and neighbouring Etobicoke had already been established by the Scarletts, who originally owned at least 1,800 acres of land from Old Weston Road (at Dundas) to the west side of the Humber River, from south of Dundas Street to north of St. Clair Avenue (at Jane) and then north to the Town of Weston along the Humber River.

In 1882 Daniel Webster Clendenan had begun buying and selling land near Louisa and Elizabeth Streets, eventually taking a seat on the county council. That year, he and his wife Clara donated the land for a school on the southwest corner. Similar to the split personality of Carleton and Davenport, the school and church were located here, while the taverns and shopping were ten to twelve blocks away at Keele/Dundas/(Old) Weston Road. Suburban sprawl was the rule rather than the exception in West York. However, in this case the school and church were located so as to be most accessible to the rural populace as far south as Swansea, rather than because of any aversion to taverns.

There were very few residents on Louisa Street during this period, one or two on the section west of Elizabeth Street, including John Clark on the northwest corner. John Daniels had a market garden on 12 acres with a modest frame house at what is now 149 (southwest corner of Fairview Avenue). The corner house had an extra wide lot because Daniels' "wood house and outhouse" stood close to

Part of plate 44, showing registered subdivision plans in 1890. *Atlas of the City of Toronto and Vicinity,* Second Edition. Toronto: Charles E. Goad Co, 1890. *Toronto Reference Library*

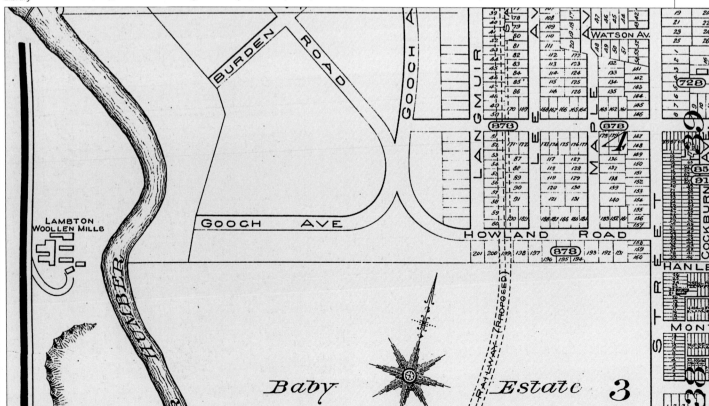

the street on what is now lawn. Another market garden occupied the land between Dundas and Louisa, along the east side of Elizabeth Street.

The first assessment for the Village of West Toronto Junction lists Daniels, 65, as resident with Dr. Gilmour, the MPP, and J. D. Spears, village councillor and local developer, as the owners. Daniels is gone the following year, and a new subdivision which includes

Gilmour and Fairview Avenues is registered. Also in 1888-9 three modest frame dwellings were put up close to St. John's Anglican Church at No. 104, 108 and 112 by Matthew Lawless, a mail clerk, who moved into No. 104. Reflecting the close proximity of the Canadian Pacific railyards, George Hubert, the first in a long list of resident CPR employees, became a tenant at No. 108.

The new building code for 1889 virtually outlawed frame construction in the town and no more frame houses were built on the Junction portion of Louisa Street. Two of these three were demolished soon after the turn of the century, while No. 108 was removed to an undisclosed location in York Township in 1908, where frame construction continued to be permitted. In general, the nine blocks of Louisa Street in York remained undeveloped for some time. The housing also tended to be more modest when it was built.

1889 was the beginning of a three-year building boom in the Junction, during which suburban villas were scattered along Louisa Street by small-scale developers with widely varied financial resources. Those with insufficient capital lost their investment in the depression which followed, while those who did not overextend themselves came out ahead, much as is the case today.

Numbers 142, 156, 166, 196, 77, 81, 167 and 171 were built during this period with 258 following in 1892. After that nothing else was built for almost ten years until the next economic upswing just after 1900. Number 156 was demolished in the 1930s and No. 258 was demolished and

LEFT
188 St. John's Road. The reproduction shows faint traces of the Crescent Car Line streetcar wire overhead. *Tribune Souvenir Edition, 1901.*

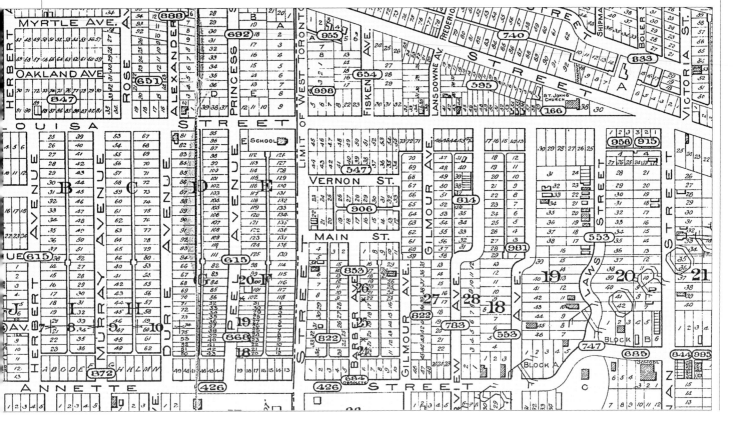

replaced by the heating plant for Runnymede Hospital. Most of the other homes are described in the Nabob's Retreat walking tour brochure. Villa residents during this period were mainly professional people from the town within walking distance of their offices, but at the same time removed from the bustle of town life on a quiet residential street.

Close relationships developed between the residents at No. 196 and 188. Besides being next door to each other, the first two owners sat on town council in 1891 and were both on the council committee which established the local Ball Electric Co. That same year, W. H. Millichamp operated a brickyard in Carleton and dabbled in speculative building. Joseph Campbell made his living in real estate, bringing friends and family into his speculative ventures, which included building Kilburn Hall on Dundas Street.

Another neighbour, Joshua Horner, at No. 156, was on town council as well and was also an active real estate agent. At 26, Campbell was the youngest member of council, Millichamp was 28, and Horner in his 30s. It is easy to imagine the three young men bringing out the maps after dinner and planning the town's development. However, their influence was short-lived. Campbell and Horner saw their fortunes reverse in the depression and Millichamp moved on to other pursuits elsewhere. Campbell and Horner both changed their profession to that of travelling salesman, although Campbell abandoned his impressive home to move in with relatives on Rose Avenue in Toronto, never to return. Horner simply moved across the street to a more modest home at No. 171. The difference was that Horner's relatives lived nearby.

The next residents of Nos. 196 and 188 were also both politicians, this time both were also lawyers. John Baird, the Grand Trunk Railway agent, and his son William, who eventually became town councillor and then mayor, moved into No. 196 in 1893. William married the daughter of town councillor George Gilbert in 1896. Next door A. J. Anderson rented from Campbell for a few years before buying the house. Both men were prominent local Conservatives with long political careers. Both served as aldermen for the area after amalgama-

tion with Toronto in 1909. Both were on the city's parks committee and were responsible for the enlargement and naming of Baird Park. Anderson went on to four terms as MP, while Baird was a long-serving MPP.

The Bairds lived at No. 196 for only three years, however; the first truly long-term resident was Dr. J. T. Kerr, a veterinarian. Interestingly, the Andersons sold No. 188 to Dr. James Dow in 1913. He established a medical practice at his home and lived there until the 1950s. The Dows were mentioned regularly in *West Toronto Weekly* social columns during the 1920s.

The most stylish house from this period, No.142, also housed two important members of the town's business and intellectual élite. Thomas Beresford Phepoe, the handsome Irish manager of the town's first and most important Molson's Bank, bought the house soon after it was built. Since the bank handled the town's accounts, it is easy to imagine him discussing town business over after-dinner coffee and cigars, perhaps a shot of rye for good measure, with the three town councillors who lived less than half a block away.

Phepoe was transferred to Winnipeg during the depression and rented the house to bank employees until the economy improved. In 1898 he picked up the lot next door at a tax sale and sold both to Louisa Street's best known resident, Franklin C. Colbeck, the principal of West Toronto High School, which became Humberside Collegiate. He and his wife Maggie lived out the rest of their lives in the house, and he spent much of his spare time gardening on the large property. Colbeck Street was named for him in 1909.

Colbeck was also a well-known scholar who set the normal school (teacher training) exams in classics and was on the senate of both Victoria College and the University of Toronto. He was a Victoria College graduate and four daughters were Victoria alumnae as well. Two taught at local schools.

Another Victoria alumnus, the first West Toronto High School principal, J. C. Robertson, left that post to become a professor, then Dean of Victoria College. Colbeck spent his summers with classics professors, mostly University of Toronto graduates like himself, on Georgian Bay. They were part of a group which formed the Madawaska Club around Go Home Bay. Another Victoria alumnus, Humberside math teacher Richard Gourlay, was also part of the group.

Soon after the turn of the century, the four blocks east of Elizabeth Street were almost entirely built upon. Large comfortable, flat-fronted detached houses with columned front porches were the style, broken now and again by a semi-detached, a gambrel roof, or a slightly different front porch. Strathcona School was built in 1908-9, then enlarged in 1914 and 1918 to accommodate rapid growth in the area.

The 1908 assessment gives an interesting variety of occupations for resident voters, all men of course, on Louisa Street. Nine were railway employees, including six CPR engineers, an air brake inspector and two conductors. The CPR's West Toronto Roundhouse and repair facilities were in full swing and the land had already been purchased for Lambton Roundhouse.

There were two or three factory workers, but by and large the rest were storekeepers or professionals, including Strathcona School principal J. H. Colvin. There were two lawyers, a druggist, a real estate broker, five spinsters looking after their own households and five "gentlemen".

Another gentleman, Henry McKillop, 59, owned a house that had originally fronted on Dundas Street beside the church. However, either because the railyard and street traffic had become too noisy or because he hoped to develop commercial frontage there, McKillop bought the irregular 38-foot lot behind the house, disposed of the frame house on that property, moved his own large brick house backward to conform to the setback, renumbered it No. 104 Louisa Street, and rented it to druggist W. Howell in 1908. The house never quite recovered from having its backside exposed to public view and has a slightly odd look about it even today.

With amalgamation in 1909, the town's north and west boundaries became the boundaries of Toronto and street names were changed so as not to duplicate those of Toronto streets. St. John's Road was named for the church, although former MPP John Wesley St. John was no doubt happy to recommend the name as well.

St. John's Church was demolished in 1923 when the congregation chose to move to a more Anglican neighbourhood at Quebec and Humberside Avenues. The small houses east of No. 104 were built on the site soon after. St. John's 1911 parish hall survived as a YWCA until 1979, when Toronto's Parks and Recreation Department decided that green space was more desirable than the basketball court gym it housed. Unfortunately the Raptors were not around to disagree.

In 1912 York Township finally outgrew the school D. W. Clendenan had founded and built George V Public School on the north side of St. John's Road further west. The "Elizabeth Street School" was used as a garage for a time and torn down in the 1920s when the pace of development accelerated. Runnymede Road officially recognized the long connection of that name with the district. However, as we have seen, it never did lead to John Scarlett's house.

Runnymede Collegiate at the corner of St. John's and Jane Street was built by the township in 1927. By that time St. John's Road was fully developed from east to west.

TOP
The Colbeck residence at 142 St. John's Road ca. 1916. *Courtesy of Margaret Belcher*

BOTTOM
Lucinda Colbeck picking fruit in the summer while a University of Toronto student ca. 1915-18. *Courtesy of Leslie Tomlinson*

Daughter of St. John's Road: The Sequel

by Barbara Large Whaley

EVER SINCE READING "St. John's Road Revisited", I have been anxious to contribute details of the street where I lived from 1909 to the end of World War II, except for short absences to Edmonton before the war and a stint in Ottawa in 1941, before my husband went overseas.

The last time I was in Toronto, the daughter of a first cousin drove me past 166 St. John's Road. It sported a fire escape and it occurred to me that it was probably now a fourplex. The basement is high with plenty of windows and so is the attic, formerly the storeroom for my maiden aunt's barrels of dishes, steamer trunks full of old clothes too special to throw away, and large portraits of elderly relatives long deceased.

I was a baby when we moved from what used to be Western Avenue (now Indian Road Crescent) to 166 St. John's Road. My brother Victor was five and a half years older. My parents G. Herbert Large and Marian, née Barnes, had married at Toronto Junction in 1898. My father first worked at Heintzman's and then established his own business buying houses to renovate for rent or resale. He also sold insurance. They both sang in the Methodist Church choir. I have a silk square on which is printed an appreciation and thanks to my mother for her services as a soloist.

As you can see from the picture of my home, the upstairs over the porch was a sunroom, and incidentally my playroom — home to my large family of dolls. Apparently I was a bossy kid and one day mother found Alyse Van Dusen in tears because I was washing her teddy bear, which I insisted needed it.

Marian and Herbert Large flank their children Victor and Barbara at the front steps of 166 St. John's Road ca. 1910. Barbara's aunt, Rachel Barnes, is to the right.
Courtesy of Barbara Large Whaley

In those days women called on friends and left calling cards if the resident was not at home. When the Dow family moved to St. John's Road in 1910, Mrs. Dow came to visit as a newcomer, bringing her daughter Jean. While the two ladies were having tea, I took Jean up to my playroom. There shortly followed an altercation from above, then silence and mother said, "I see that I can relax now, since your child seems to be able to cope with mine." Although she was some months younger, she sure could. Jean was so bright at school that her teacher had her try the high school entrance examination when she was in Grade 7 (known then as Junior 4th), and at the age of 10 she passed highest in Toronto.

Jean's father, Dr. James Dow, originally from Fergus, had also been a brilliant student who taught for several years until he could save enough money to attend the University of Toronto medical school. Later he returned to Toronto to be in a university city — all of his very bright family of five graduated from the University of Toronto as well.

The very long block in which I lived stretched from Gilmour Avenue to Dundas. The corner house was occupied by the Blewets, who patiently listened to Jean and me, frequent visitors, as we warbled our latest songs with enthusiasm, but no training. In between the Blewets and my family were the Davidsons, whose daughter Dorothy was a schoolmate and friend of mine.

Next door to the east of us at No. 158 (now demolished) in a huge old house, with gas lighting and a stables at the rear, were the Mercers. They were gentlefolk of Scottish descent, the youngest member famous as being the first Canadian general to be killed in World War I. I believe that, unlike the modern practice, he was up at the front with his men to see how they were faring. The family were mostly unmarried, all elderly and greatly grieving over the loss of their youngest member. Frank Mercer, retired teacher from a boys' school, was lame from a riding accident, necessitating the use of a cane and elevated boot. He took a particular interest in Jean Dow and me and the two of us felt free to run into their home to watch the two brothers play checkers

and eat chocolate-covered ginger candies. I have a collection of snapshots Frank Mercer took of Jean and me, lasting until 12 years of age. After he and his brother died, his sister Helene moved to a boarding house in the downtown part of the city, where Jean and I were invited to have tea. To my amazement, Jean and I were each presented with a filigree brooch with a diamond, that Frank had left to us as a remembrance.

Next to the Mercers was a newer home at No. 150, where a retired Anglican minister lived with his family, and next to them the Colbecks at No. 142. Jean and I would call with the shameless query, "Is Lucy in?" after one of their many parties and were always invited in to feast on the leftovers. Lucy was the domestic science teacher at Annette Street Public School, where Strathcona pupils went once a week for the girls to learn cooking and the boys manual training.

In the next house was Miss Inglehart, who taught at Strathcona and, amid much excitement, married while there. Of course she had to quit teaching immediately. Then there were a couple of CPR families whose names elude me, and then the Woodburns, whose son Chris was best friend to John Dow and also friends with my brother Victor. Still further east was Tom Hackett, who went to dental college with my brother.

Across the street at No. 103–5 was a building which housed the Inglehart Nursing Home, which was, I think, run by a sister to my school teacher. Next to them were the Thompsons at No. 97 with three little girls, one of whom inscribed in my birthday book, "To Barbara on her eighth birthday from her little friend Edith". Further east were the Normans, where I remember a birthday party for Hugh

Norman at a very tender age. Margaret and Helen Colvin, Jean Dow and I were all invited and had new dresses for the occasion, which I recall was a glorious, uproarious success.

Next door east of the Normans was a family of two girls, and I remember to my shame attending a lovely party there where I accepted a cigarette, which I smoked flamboyantly to show sophistication — something I had not been permitted to do at home. There were also the Hargreaves, whose son Teddy was a playmate to Bruce Whaley. Bruce lived at No. 117, the southeast corner of Fairview Avenue. Although we weren't particularly playmates as youngsters, I later married him. The Wileys lived on the southwest corner of Fairview.

A good many families whose men worked for the railway lived on St. John's. They kept pretty much to themselves as their hours were irregular, but their children of course mingled with the others at school. The Watsons, Roseveares, Libbys and Tolmans lived between Fairview and Gilmour. Miss Rowntree and the Englishes, who kept a pair of delightful identical Sealyham terriers, were in two of the older houses at Nos. 167 and 171, amongst those occupied by the railroad families. Next to the Watsons there were residents no one

Frank Mercer in front of 158 St. John's Road, although it's the porch of No.150 in the background. "He was a master at a boys private school at one time, and who had been in a riding accident and wore an elevated shoe to compensate for the difference in the length of his legs from the accident." *Courtesy of Barbara Large Whaley*

knew. It was rumoured they were bootleggers. A large truck was frequently parked in front of the house and Miss Helene Mercer didn't think it suitable on a residential street and complained, I don't know to what authority. It was removed! Later the occupants departed and were replaced by a pleasant family whose daughter, Margaret Todd, became a schoolmate of mine.

Next to the Roseveares were the Smiths — I knew Rose, an older sister of Chris — then Woodburns and Arnolds. Mr. Arnold was a civil servant. Their little girl was named Gladys, and Jean and I spent hours there playing with her from babyhood on, watching all the traffic from their porch swing.

The Dows lived for three or four years at the southeast corner of Gilmour, but moved to the larger house at No. 188 when the opportunity came. I thought the Casselmans lived there for a couple of years after the Andersons, but anyway my best recollections were when the Dows lived there. Dr. Dow's older brother moved with his wife and two daughters from a farm near Fergus to retire to a house opposite No. 188. The older daughter, Laura, taught school and the younger attended Humberside Collegiate.

Next door to the Dows at No. 196 were the Rowes. My father knew Mr. Rowe from early prospecting days in Cobalt and Porcupine. The two girls became professional singers with magnificent voices and the boys, as I recall, were deeply into the stock market. The middle sister Molly was always in the background, quietly and efficiently serving any guests who dropped in. She married a nose and throat specialist.

I believe the Carsons were next door to the Rowes; they were a railroad family with two bright, red-headed boys, one of whom was tragically killed while on a summer job at a fashionable resort — by stepping back into an open elevator shaft — something which could never happen today. Another CPR family lived next door and, although I can't recall their name, I do recall their later account of my visit to them. I rang the bell and announced that I was, "Mr. Large's little girl, and this," pointing to our little Yorkshire terrier, "is Tatters Large".

Strathcona School grounds, now Runnymede Hospital, included the property from Fisken Avenue to Runnymede Road, and the caretaker's house (demolished) was occupied in my day by the Cross family, whose sons all joined the army in World War I, including the youngest — a strapping big lad named Norman — who lied about his age, which was 14!

On the south side of the street one of the larger homes on a double lot at No. 222, belonged to John T. Moore, who had two attractive daughters as well. Then followed a dozen or so smaller houses and finally a fair-sized house at No. 275, the home of the Colvins, whose father was principal of Strathcona School before he moved to High Park Avenue and became principal of Annette School.

Like Mrs. Dow, his wife called to introduce their two little girls, Margaret and Helen, to me. Mr. Colvin's two maiden sisters lived next door to him and moved to High Park Avenue at the same time he did. They were well-to-do business women who had a dry goods store on the south side of Dundas Street near Keele. Next to their home were two stores on the corner of Runnymede, one dry goods and the other a convenience store, also run by two sisters, where most of the pupils of Strathcona School perched on a stool at one time or another, deliberating lengthily over the choice of penny candy.

In retrospect, I feel that the street from Clendenan Avenue to Runnymede Road was like a small village. There was drama, lots of gossip and much activity. Gilmour Avenue took a decided jog to the west at Vernon Street, resulting in a parkette which was the playground for us all. One winter it had an igloo, complete with entrance tunnel built by the active and enterprising youngsters. I also remember a small bakery on Vernon where bread was sold from a house. There was a lane behind the homes on St. John's west from Gilmour, so that residents with no driveways could in later years have garages for their cars.

How well I remember my eight years at Strathcona School, where we lined up regimentally in assigned places for each class on the boarded part of the playground and on a signal marched into our classroom to the accompaniment of a vigorous piano piece played by one of the staff. It was a different era from today. The teacher was supreme, any disciplinary problems were dealt with by the principal, drugs unheard of, and the annual school concert the well-attended highlight of the year!

Later I attended Humberside Collegiate where my uncle and aunt graduated long before I was born. Aunt Rachel, mother's younger sister, who lived with us on St. John's Road, taught at Strathcona, then Annette and finally at Keele Street Public School. Uncle Charlie Barnes taught classics at Humberside before moving to Jarvis Collegiate. My first cousin Alfred L. Burt was a Humberside graduate and Rhodes Scholar who became an historian and moved to Minneapolis — another of my academic family whose pattern I certainly did not follow!

LEFT
Barbara Large, 1927.
Courtesy of Barbara Large Whaley

RIGHT
Bruce Whaley, about 12 at the time, with his little dog, in front of 117 St. John's Road in 1919.
Courtesy of Barbara Whaley

St. John's Road Part III: A Visit to the Doctors

by Diana Fancher, based on material contributed by Mary McRuer Gaby and Mary Norman Gourlay

The Dow Family

DR. JAMES DOW and his wife Katherine, née Armstrong, came to the Junction and to St. John's Road in 1910 when their eldest daughter Mary Rowena was 16, so that the five children in the family would be able to live at home and attend the University of Toronto. They were also close to an excellent high school, Humberside Collegiate, attended by the younger members of the family.

It was a somewhat daring move for Dr. Dow, then in his late 40s with a well-established medical practice in Belwood, near Fergus, Ontario. However, he quickly reestablished a thriving practice in the Junction, which he continued until a few days before his 90th birthday in 1952. Mary Gaby remembers that he was particularly fond of his Maltese patients who, he said, always paid their bills promptly and gave him wonderful bread and other baked goods which he very much enjoyed. She remembers his office in the house at 188 St. John's Road, which had a curtained-off section containing his dispensary and a roll top desk with a large stuffed owl perched on top. There was also an electric fireplace in the room.

Katherine Dow quickly established herself in social and political circles in the Junction, where her lively if somewhat "intimidating" intellect was put to use in organizational activity. Among other accomplishments, she was president of the High Park Women's Liberal Association, president of the Women's Auxiliary of the West End YMCA and president of The Runnymede Travel Club. The travel club joined the Status of Women in 1912, soon after her arrival. According to her granddaughter, Mary, she was particularly interested in the constitution and several times journeyed to Ottawa to discuss it. She even taught a teenage boys' Bible class at Victoria Presbyterian Church. Both she and Dr. Dow were from a Scottish background, something they had in common with many other turn-of-the-century Junction residents.

Katherine had grown up in Selbina, Missouri, although her father was originally Canadian, and she had returned to Toronto to study music at the Royal Conservatory, where she met James, a medical student at the time. They married in 1893. Her father came to visit regularly, when he also bought sheep for his farm. And, in 1929, when Katherine came into a small inheritance, she invested in the stock market to accumulate enough money for an extended solo trip to Italy. Her last paper for the travel club was on atomic energy. She died in 1954, aged 87. Dr. Dow died in 1958, aged 96.

By 1916 the Dows had moved into the elegant home at 188 St. John's Road, where their eldest daughter, Mary Rowena, posed with her wedding party in 1919. She had started to study at the University of Toronto, but left to do secretarial work in Ottawa during World War I and then returned to marry James McRuer, whose family lived at 79 Gothic Avenue. He had courted her for six years, according to a *Globe & Mail* article. Later she returned to university part-time and graduated with a B.A. in 1943, the same year her two daughters graduated from Queen's University in Kingston and the University of Toronto.

In the meantime, Mary Rowena's husband ran for the federal Liberals in High Park riding in 1935, narrowly losing to the incumbent, Conservative A. J. Anderson who, as readers will recall, also lived at 188 St. John's Road for a number of years. Later McRuer became Chief Justice of the Supreme Court of Ontario and chaired several royal commissions.

Son William Wilfred followed in his father's footsteps, graduating from the University of Toronto and becoming a family doctor in Toronto. Daughter Margaret played hockey during her years at the University of Toronto, finishing with an M.A. in psychology, and taught for several years. She married P. C. Anderson. Son John Armstrong received a B.Eng. from the University of Toronto and moved to Detroit. Finally Jean, the youngest, the smartest and, according to Mary, "the flapper and the black sheep of the family", acquired her B.A. then

September 28, 1919: Mary Dow McRuer's wedding party in the front yard of 188 St. John's Road. (L-R) the irrepressible Jean Dow, Margaret Dow, Mary the bride, and next-door neighbour Alice Rowe. Remnants of the spirea hedge still survive today although the last of the trees was recently cut down.
Courtesy of Mary McRuer Gaby

left to take up a variety of glamorous occupations as well as life in the fast lane in New York City.

The Norman Family

Mary Norman Gourlay's mother, Elizabeth Cutts, was also born in the United States. Her parents came to Toronto from Maine in the 1890s, eventually settling on Woodside Avenue. Her father opened a hardware store on the northwest corner of Pacific Avenue and Dundas Street. Elizabeth met Hugh Norman at McMaster University where they were both students, and then studied music at the Royal Conservatory. They married in 1907, when Hugh received his M. D. and set up a practice in the Junction. In 1912 they built the house at 35 St. John's Road, on the southwest corner of Laws Street, which featured a separate office and waiting room opening onto Laws Street.

Although Dr. Norman had the usual family practice, he was probably a pediatrician at heart. Not only did he take his own children with him on house calls, but when they got to be too old to enjoy the trip, he took the neighbourhood children with him instead. Mary remembered that he regularly invited the neighbourhood boys up to the sun room to play billiards, also suggesting that if they cut the grass neatly, they might be allowed to wash his car. There was always an extra child invited to the cottage in the summer as well.

Mary also remembered that her father was a fabulous storyteller with wonderful, scary stories about wolves coming down the chimney. He also had a fund of adult stories about life on the family farm near Shomberg. Another favourite story was about the time he was asked to make a house call at Bâby Point. He put on his best clothes for the occasion, only to find that the patient was the housemaid.

Dr. Norman's patients were mainly railway families in the area. He kept office hours every day but Sunday, which was by appointment only. The morning was for house calls, with two hours in the office in the afternoon, and two more after dinner. He was an active Liberal, although the local association was never able to persuade him to become a candidate. He was also an active member of the Oddfellows and instrumental in having the local lodge hall built on Keele just north of Annette Street in the 1920s.

Like the Dows, both Mary's parents and grandparents were strong believers in the value of education. She and her brother Hugh, who also became a doctor, and sister Gertrude were expected to do well at school and go on to university — whether they wanted to or not. They were coached in their lessons at home. Mary began attending Annette Street Public School at four, went to Humberside Collegiate at 11, and at 16 on to Victoria College, University of Toronto, where her soon-to-be husband's father, Richard Gourlay, had also graduated. She met her husband Don, a University of Toronto medical student who lived on Evelyn Avenue, on the streetcar ride to the university. His father died before they were married.

Don's mother, Ida Gertrude Gourlay, née Eastwood, also a doctor's daughter, had been in the first class of women admitted to the University of Toronto in 1885, and was on the first

West Toronto Junction High School staff until her marriage. She read and wrote poetry extensively and was active in the Runnymede Travel Club, whose members considered themselves the élite of West Toronto, according to Mary.

Soon after their marriage in 1935, Don and Mary Gourlay established their home and Don's medical practice at 62 Jane Street, where they lived until the 1980s. Their son Richard's children returned to Humberside Collegiate to continue the family's traditional involvement with the school, even though his family lived in Etobicoke. Richard was president of the Parents' Association in 1985.

Both the Dows and the Normans continue to have doctors in the family, male and female.

Afternoon
Feby 15th
Mrs Hudson

1947-48

...... Mrs. G. T. Clarkson
. Mrs. M. J. McHenry
..... Mrs. V. S. Stevens
.. Mrs. George Rapsey
..... Mrs. Renwick Bell
.... Mrs. S. Andrews
. Mrs. Charles Hudson
.... Miss D. Colbeck
Mrs. W. H. Kirkpatrick
..... Mrs. P. T. Jermyn
Mrs. W. J. Cryderman
.... Mrs. James Dow
..... Mrs. P. E. Heeney
.... Mrs. John Young
. Mrs. C. S. Patterson
..... Miss Mary Watson

MEMBERS

Mrs. Sydney Andrews, 222 Rosedale Heights Drive ...... HY. 2395
Miss Norah T. Belcher, 12 Walmer Road .... KI. 0745
Mrs. Renwick Bell, 5 Elm Grove Ave. .... LA. 3284
Mrs. J. Lennox Dest, 995 Avenue Road .... HY. 7422
Miss Georgina Bog, 80 Lowther Avenue .... KI. 7809
Mrs. W. H. Butt, 54 Oakmount Road .... JU. 2769
Mrs. A. W. Campbell, 343 Annette St. .... LY. 1734
Mrs. Arthur Cherry, 198 Dunn Avenue .... LA. 4187
Mrs. G. T. Clarkson, 45 Wychwood Park .... LA. 9515
Miss Dorothy Colbeck, 69 Humbercrest Blvd. .... LY. 3491
Miss W. L. Colbeck, 69 Humbercrest Blvd. .... LY. 3491
Mrs. W. J. Cryderman, 474 Glenlake Ave. .... LY. 1848
Mrs. G. W. Dettman, 45 Wychwood Park .... LA. 9515
Mrs. Jas. Dow, 188 St. John's Road .... LY. 3309
Mrs. M. E. Garner, 354 Clendenan Ave. .... JU. 2730
Mrs. A. J. Gillies, 24 Brumell Avenue .... LY. 3783
Mrs. F. S. Greenwood, 9 Highbourne Road .... HU. 9465
Mrs. P. E. Heeney, 29 Baby Point Road .... LY. 4386
Mrs. Charles Hudson, 298 Keele St. .... JU. 0510
Mrs. P. T. Jermyn, 213 Humberside Ave. .... JU. 5142
Mrs. F. J. Johnston, 107 High Park Ave. .... JU. 2006
Mrs. W. H. Kirkpatrick, 71 Humbercrest Blvd. .... LY. 8591
Mrs. H. E. Langford, 45 Poplar Plains Crescent .... KI. 4273
Mrs. D. D. MacDonald, 411 Annette St. .... LY. 2218
Mrs. M. J. McHenry, 58 Royal York Road North .... LY. 3804
Mrs. D. T. L. McKerroll, 19 Laws St. .... LY. 6407
Mrs. W J.. McNally, 394 Bloor E. (Ainger Apts.) .... RA. 5518
Mrs. J. R. Mutchmor, 86 High Park Avenue .... LY. 1074
Mrs. C. S. Patterson, 207 Glendonwynne Road .... JU. 3149
Mrs. George Rapsey, 11 Castle View Avenue .... KI. 8820
~~Mrs. A. B. Rice, 354 Clendenan Avenue~~ .... JU. 2730
Mrs. Gordon Rice, 32 Oakmount Road .... LY. 9950
Mrs. W. R. Sheppard, Simcoe.
Mrs. V. S. Stevens, 339 Annette St. .... JU. 6181
Mrs. W. E. Taylor, 135 Jameson Avenue .... LA. 3004
Mrs. Fred Thompson, 512 Brookdale Avenue .... ~~MA. 1537~~ OV. 5764
Miss Mary P. Watson, 511 Castlefield Avenue .... HY. 7504
Mrs. R. S. Wilson, 28 Ranleigh Avenue .... HU. 7240
Mrs. John Young, 70 DeLisle Avenue .... HY. 6491

HONORARY MEMBERS

Mrs. R. G. Agnew
Mrs. B. Bagshaw.
Mrs. J. B. McCuaig.
Mrs. A. H. Perfect.
Mrs. H. Reynolds
Mrs. W. A. Skeans.
Miss J. Watson.

Mrs Campbell.

Runnymede Travel Club

Organized 1909

POUR Y PARVENIR

"Mexico"

1947-48

Programme

October the Seventh

Evening Meeting. Hostess—Mrs. James Dow
Introduction to Mexico .... Miss Norah Belcher
My Mexican Trip .... Mrs. F. J. Johnston

October the Twenty-First

Afternoon Meeting. Hostess—Mrs. F. S. Greenwood
Indian Mexico .... Mrs. V. S. Stevens
*Legendary Tales .... Mrs. C. S. Patterson

November the Fourth

Evening Meeting. Hostess—Mrs. Fred Thompson
Spanish Mexico .... Miss W. Colbeck
*Maximillian and Carlota .... Miss G. Bog

November the Eighteenth

Afternoon Meeting. Hostess—Mrs. H. E. Langford
Modern Mexico .... Mrs. F. S. Greenwood
*Mexican Nation Builders .... Mrs. W. J. McNally

December the Second

Evening Meeting—Open.

December the Sixteenth

Afternoon Meeting. Hostess—Miss G. Bog
The Peacock Sheds his Tail—
Book Review .... Mrs. G. Rapsey
Everyday Life in Town and Country .... Mrs. Gordon Rice

January the Sixth

Evening Meeting. Hostess—Mrs. W. E. Taylor
Mexico City .... Mrs. W. H. Kirkpatrick
Climbing Popocatepetl with Richard Haliburton .... Mrs. Fred Thompson

January the Twentieth

Afternoon Meeting. Hostess—Mrs. John Young
Sight Seeing in Mexico City .... Mrs. P. E. Heeney
Side Trips—Xochimilco, Chapultepic Park, and Cuernavaca .... Miss D. Colbeck

February the Third

Evening Meeting. Hostess—Miss D. Colbeck
Arts and Crafts .... Mrs. R. S. Wilson
*Flora and Fauna .... Mrs. John Young

February the Seventeenth

Afternoon Meeting. Hostess—Mrs. A. Cherry
Guadalupe—
The Shrine of a Nation .... Mrs. S. Andrews
*Feasts and Festivals .... Mrs. J. L. Best

March th

Evening Meeting. Hoste
Mexican Ports ....
*Off the Beaten Path .....

2.30 **March the**

Afternoon Meeting.
A visit to the Museum.

March the

Evening Meeting. Hoste
Social Strata ....
Excerpts from Tortilla F

April the

Afternoon Meeting. H
The Treasure House of the World ....
*The Lure of Tehuantep

April the Tw

Evening Meeting Annual.
Mexico in 1948 ....

** Indicates twenty-minute*

At Home on Annette Street

by Gwen Morgan Couture

THE YEAR 1889 was very bleak indeed for Harriet Burford. The plans that she and Willie had made for their future were shattered. The telegram stated: "We regret to inform you that your husband William Burford died suddenly . . ." Inflamation of the bowel, she was told. Willie had been preaching across the US border, leaving her at home in Toronto with their four young children, born in quick succession since their marriage in 1880 — and she was again pregnant, due soon to give birth to her fifth child.

Harriet numbly endured the funeral ritual. The love and sympathy of family and friends helped, but could not solve her problems. How could she manage without him? When the young Welsh Evangelist came into her life, she fell in love and married him "for better or for worse . . . until death do us part". She was happy to be the mother of his children, but his children were now fatherless. It became her responsibility and hers alone to provide a home for them.

Where to live? She wanted the security of a home of her own. The papers gave generous space to news of Toronto's western neighbour known as The Junction. Numerous real estate agents were anxious to help her: Yes, good water was available, thanks to the newly constructed pumping station supplying water from Lake Ontario. . . . No, there were no sewers as yet. . . . Yes, gas was available for light . . . Yes, a new public school had recently opened on Annette Street.

Harriet liked what she saw and heard. With her meagre savings and Willie's life insurance money she could, with care, buy a lot and build a house. She chose property on Annette Street, directly across from the school. It was adjacent to that large piece of land at the corner of Laws Street purchased by Theodore Heintzman.

The Burford house and the Heintzman house were built about the same time, and both were of local orange brick, but there the similarity ended. The Burford place was simple and conservative, adequate for the family, but dwarfed by its grand neighbour. At last it was finished and 280 Annette Street became "home".

Now the staggering problem was how to support the family. For women the options were very limited, and there was no social assistance of any kind. Fortunately, Harriet was an excellent seamstress and she had a sewing machine. Furthermore, who could be more in demand in a small growing town than a capable needlewoman? The wife and children of every prosperous businessman needed dresses and petticoats, pantalets and pinafores. Soon Harriet had as many customers as she could han-

RIGHT
The Burford residence at 280 Annette Street ca. 1915. The Heintzman house is visible on the left. Newman Burford, age 2, stands with his mother May beside the front door.
Bill Burford

BELOW
The three older children of Harriet Burford (L-R) Ernest, Gertie on the table and Grace ca. 1890.
Courtesy of Gwen Couture

280 Annette St.

dle. She found satisfaction in her work and her home.

The two older children, Grace and Ernest, started attending school just across the road. In due course, Gertie and Minnie joined their siblings, and finally baby Bill was old enough to become a student.

But dirt, always dirt, and with five youngsters out playing in the dust, mud or snow, depending on the season, it was a constant struggle to keep clothes, bodies and house clean. Somehow Harriet managed, and come Sunday she would take her family off to church and Sunday school, clean and in "good" clothes, at the Annette Street Baptist Church.

So the last decade of the 19th century passed and babies became healthy teenagers. Remarkably, all five

survived, escaping the deadly diseases of the day.

The "280 house" never became an empty nest. Although Ernest left home in his teens, the others stayed as young adults. Grace graduated from Normal School and taught at Weston Road Public School for many years. She left home in 1911 to go west and marry. Gertie chose to work with her mother as a dressmaker. She married in 1912 and had a daughter. When her husband enlisted in World War I, she came home again and remained after her husband's death at Vimy Ridge.

Minnie lived at home until her mother's death. She left high school determined to earn money to buy a piano and study music — piano, organ and voice. Her first job was wrapping bars of Comfort Soap for Pugsley &

Dingman Co. in the Junction. Bill married young, lived in Brantford for a few years where he set up his own photography studio, but came home in 1913 with his wife and two boys. They rented rooms upstairs.

So Harriet had a full house during her final years: two daughters, a son and his wife, and three lively grandchildren. Due to long hours sitting and sewing for many years, she developed open ulcers on her legs. In early 1918 at about 65 years of age she died of pneumonia, at home with her family. The house was sold after her death. It still stands, more than a century later, although the front bay window is gone and the red brick is covered with white vinyl and paint.

In the summer of 1991, I (the daughter of Gertie) passed by the house, knocked at the door and was invited to go in. It was strange to go through the doors. I could almost feel myself as a child of three or four running along the hall, through the living and dining rooms. I could picture my mother as a shy little girl growing up there and being married in the parlour. I could look farther back and see my grandmother who did the impossible, raising a family by herself, within those walls.

Harriet Burford's name is not enshrined among the rich and famous of West Toronto Junction, but she is worthy of honour and respect. I, her granddaughter, offer this small tribute of love.

LEFT
The Burford residence at 280 Annette Street ca. 1915. Newman and his brother are on the upstairs balcony while Aunt Minnie Burford is sitting on the porch.
Bill Burford

BELOW
Back garden at 280 Annette St. in 1915
Bill Burford

Toronto Housing Company Buys a Big Property

Toronto Daily Star,
September 12, 1913

THE LATEST PURCHASE of the Toronto Housing Company is about two blocks north of St. Clair Avenue at the western end of the new civic car line in Ward 7. It comprises over 7,500 square feet, and is part of the old property known as the Silverthorn farm. The deal has just been completed for the price of a little less than $30 a foot.

The land is clear and level, entirely unbuilt upon, and has a frontage of 625 feet on Prescott, Rockwell, and Blackthorn Avenues. The company's architects are now working on the scheme and building is expected to commence early in the spring. There will probably be in the neighbourhood of thirty houses, all of them to be built differently from those that the company have erected before on Spruce and Bain Avenues [in east Toronto]. While the others had two families in a house, on the flat style, these will be known as the 'self-containing family house'. Each family will live alone in one building.

The property is ideally situated for the labouring classes, being in close proximity to several large industries. Among these are three abattoirs, a motor works, brick yard, the Canada Foundry, lace and braid works, Nordheimer piano works and the CPR shops.

While at present there is a rather indifferent style of buildings going up in that vicinity, it is intended to reform the neighbourhood with clean and neat buildings. Even going so far as to do away with unhealthy backyards, the company had designed a large courtyard at the rear of the houses which will have 100 feet by 260 feet dimensions. As the block from street to street at that width is 225 feet, there is ample room for the houses with the courtyard. Bowling greens and other forms of recreation grounds will be built, and every effort will be made to keep them clean and sanitary. They will serve the purpose of keeping the children off the street.

All the streets coming in touch with the property already have cement sidewalks. They are also included in the Ward 7 sewerage scheme recently passed by the City Council and shortly to come into being. This will mean paved streets on its completion. The houses will be touched by two car lines, at a distance of about three blocks. The civic car line on St. Clair Avenue and the Suburban railway on Davenport Road are of equal handiness.

1814 St. Clair Ave. W., north side near [Old] Weston Road. The photo was taken August 30, 1911, to document conditions before the street was widened in preparation for streetcar tracks and sewers.
City of Toronto Archives

Picturesque Rural Scene Presented at Runnymede

by Diana Fancher

MISS JENNIE BROWN was looking after a herd of 14 cattle, living on the remaining 30 acres of the former Kennedy Estate in an ancient cottage at Kennedy Road and Bloor Street when a *Globe* photographer took her picture on July 27, 1923. The headline is from the *Globe* story published the following day.

Miss Brown was accompanied by several lads and lasses of the neighbourhood, earning vacation money by keeping track of Georgie, Betty, Spot, and other cows and calves which also apparently served as the local petting zoo.

Miss Brown, who had been a tenant of the farm for 25 years or so, must have left the area soon after, although perhaps she left the cows behind. A *West Toronto Weekly* article the following summer refers to "mysterious tenants"and "many petitions" delivered to City Hall, "to stop the grazing of cattle on this estate." At one time the cattle made their way across Ardagh and Colbeck Streets to graze along the Humber River as well.

However the "beautiful lawns, well-paved streets and nice homes" were soon to be free of the nuisance when the owners registered a new plan of subdivision and actively promoted the sale of building lots, bringing "great joy" to the neighbourhood and more assessment income to the city, according to *West Toronto Weekly*.

TOP
Miss Jennie Brown at Glendonwynne Road and Evelyn Crescent in 1923
The Globe & Mail Collection, City of Toronto Archives

BOTTOM
Those pesky cows munch contentedly under the oak trees on Evelyn Crescent in 1923.
The Globe & Mail Collection, City of Toronto Archives

138

Can you spot Jenny Brown's cows? Chances are they are a landscape feature in this aerial view in the National Air Photo Library from 1921. Bloor Street is at the bottom left corner, and High Park Avenue is at right. Sand pits are evident, separating the cows from a lush corner at Glendonwynne and Kennedy Park Roads — the future site of Western Technical and Commercial School. *Courtesy of John Dyk*

H21-60-1921 (DUPLICATE)

Pictures and Time

THE GREAT VARIETY of pictures on these pages mean to accompany and support the specific articles and stories, rather than the other way around. But the illustrations here are often much more than simply supporting players, and many deserve close study. Never mind the nostrum, "there is more than meets the eye" — in these pictures there is more *that does* meet the eye.

While some of the more interesting pictures are page-size or bigger, there are visual treasures in the small corners, too. The clearer and more detailed the original, the more the picture may be able to reveal about the time and place it was made than the adjoining text might be letting on.

For example . . .

The photograph on page 138 appears to show an empty rough-cast dwelling and a couple of rather ramshackle frame workshops, with what observers of the time would have called a "street urchin" posed in front. As a suburb of the city of Toronto, the Junction of 1911 is supposedly well outside the areas of poor housing and poor people that preoccupied the urban reformers of the early 20th century. Yet this "official" photograph is no different in both style and content from period pictures of the Ward, or Cabbagetown, or any inner-city precinct: filled with the impoverished, in tightly spaced factories and houses, and without decent sanitation, or for that matter any other public service.

These were places to be reformed, through the "creative destruction" of new roads, or new hospitals and schools. Just like this house on St. Clair. Whether photographed for the city engineer or for the board of health, or for the police, such pictures ought to be understood as exceptionally eloquent images of their time — not just for the evident skill of the photographer in composing viewpoint, light and time, but for what is going on behind the camera and for who commissioned the picture. Compare this with the viewpoint and content of the aerial view of the Stock Yards a decade later, pages 62–63.

These pages include as well a number of street views photographed for the Toronto Transit Commission. For the most part these are views of construction or repairs in progress, another series of official or technical documents. A magnifying glass taken to the corners of the TTC photographs can reveal a great deal about the earlier and more pleasing state of some of the more venerable streetscapes that might no longer be so attractive. But while the usual attention goes to the architectural style of individual buildings and the varied personalities of storefront or front yard, the overall appearance and character of the street sometimes escapes our attention.

The spaces between, around, above and below the buildings are right in front of us and we don't see or remember them. Think about the many overhead wires that have been removed incrementally over the past decade — it's now hard to recall just how much the sky of every arterial route was once absolutely defined by its ceiling of wires. Look at pages 16–17, or 88–89, or 93, or 116–117. An artist's depiction of the spider's web of trolley wires that once provided a ceiling over the intersection of Keele and Annette crystallizes the unique character of the place — buildings are simply a backdrop. These are not the inadvertent lines of a photograph, but the deliberate strokes of a skilled and attentive visual artist. They celebrate something conventionally "ugly." What becomes conspicuous when the wires are gone may — or may not — be an aesthetic improvement.

There are regrettably few pictures here that show an event in progress. The funeral cortège on pages 78–79 is such an occasion, though hardly a happy one. Yet the photgraph offers a quintessential image for what a geographer or historian would call the "personality" of a place. Here, Keele Street becomes a theatre, with stage set and attentive audience illuminated by the late-afternoon sun. It is a compelling picture of an urban landscape, populated by its urban citizens. Look carefully and you can make out what is still there after almost a century, and what has gone. It is the sort of scene that many might try to rephotograph from the same viewpoint and perspective. But here it might better to resist that temptation. The event itself is not reproducible.

The Oxford English Dictionary defines the word "timeless" this way: "2. a. Not subject to time; not affected by the lapse of time; existing or operating without reference to duration; eternal. Chiefly poet. and rhet., esp. in phr. *timeless moment.*"

In this sense, perhaps the most timeless picture appears along the bottom of pages 122-123. It is a more precise moment than the funeral procession, though by no means an "event". It is a place and a moment extremely, richly and quietly mundane. It's a technically imperfect photograph: sharp and clear but somehow stained in the taking or the developing so that it has a sort of internal frame or filter, like looking through windowglass both dirty and warped. It is a winter's day with a sky darker than the ground; light comes from everywhere, and nowhere. It isn't so cold, but the dampness must be bone-chilling. Barely visible in the distance at the right are some women walking up and down the sidewalk on the bridge. The hulking bundle of a cartman urges his horses along through the slush. An unoccupied convertible roadster (top down!) sits in front of the Standard Fuel Company's office building, smaller than any two-car garage. And in the tower at the upper left is the railway signalman, watching, his job to wait for long minutes, flip a lever, wait more long minutes, flip another lever, and so on, for a twelve-hour shift.

Arguably, there is more time in this picture than most of the rest put together, and that makes it timeless.

Get out your magnifying glass and look at the pictures again.

Mark Fram

Isabel (Rowe) Cleland, *Homage to Meryon,* 1976. Dry-point etching, h 27.2 x w 34.2 cm. *Collection of the Corporation of the City of Toronto*

The West Toronto Junction Historical Society is a non-profit, charitable, volunteer-run organization which welcomes new members. *The Leader & Recorder* is our quarterly newsletter.

We eagerly accept donations of photos, memorabilia, artifacts and information about the Junction. Cash donations are also appreciated.

West Toronto Junction Historical Society
145 Annette Street
Toronto, Ontario M6P 1P3
(416) 763-3161
www.junctionhistory.ca